T0399810

Ideologies and the European Union

This volume examines what the concept of ideology can add to our understanding of the European Union, and the way in which the process of European integration has inflected the ideological battles that define contemporary European politics, both nationally and transnationally.

Contemporary debates on the nature and value of the European Union often touch on the notion of ideology. The EU's critics routinely describe it as an ideologically motivated project, associating it from the left with a form of 'neoliberal capitalism' or from the right with 'liberal multiculturalism'. Its defenders often praise it in explicitly post- or anti-ideological terms, as a regulatory body focused on the production of output legitimacy, or as a bulwark against dangerous ideological revivals in the form of nationalism and populism. Yet the existing academic literature linking the study of the EU with that of ideologies is surprisingly thin. This volume brings together a number of original contributions by leading international scholars and takes an approach that is both historical and conceptual, probing the EU's ideological roots, while also laying the grounds for a reappraisal of its contemporary ideological make-up.

The chapters in this book were originally published as a special issue of the *Journal of European Public Policy*.

Carlo Invernizzi Accetti is Associate Professor of Political Science at the City University of New York – City College, USA, and Associate Researcher at the Center for European Studies of the Institut d'Etudes Politiques de Paris – Sciences Po, France. He is the author of *What is Christian Democracy? Politics, Religion and Ideology* (Cambridge UP, 2019) and *Technopopulism. The New Logic of Democratic Politics* (co-authored with Christopher Bickerton, Oxford UP, forthcoming).

Jonathan White is Professor of Politics at the London School of Economics, UK. His most recent book is *Politics of Last Resort: Governing by Emergency in the European Union* (Oxford University Press, 2019); previous titles include *The Meaning of Partisanship* (with Lea Ypi, Oxford University Press, 2016), and *Political Allegiance after European Integration* (Palgrave Macmillan, 2011).

Journal of European Public Policy Series

Series Editors

Jeremy Richardson *is Emeritus Fellow at Nuffield College, Oxford University, UK, and an Adjunct Professor in the National Centre for Research on Europe, University of Canterbury, New Zealand.*

Berthold Rittberger *is Professor and Chair of International Relations at the Geschwister-Scholl-Institute of Political Science at the University of Munich, Germany.*

This series seeks to bring together some of the finest edited works on European Public Policy. Reprinting from Special Issues of the *Journal of European Public Policy*, the focus is on using a wide range of social sciences approaches, both qualitative and quantitative, to gain a comprehensive and definitive understanding of Public Policy in Europe

EU Socio-Economic Governance since the Crisis
The European Semester in Theory and Practice
Edited by Jonathan Zeitlin and Amy Verdun

The Future of the Social Investment State
Policies, Outcomes and Politics
Edited by Marius R. Busemeyer, Caroline de la Porte, Julian L. Garritzmann and Emmanuele Pavolini

The Politics and Economics of Brexit
Edited by Simon Bulmer and Lucia Quaglia

Free Movement and Non-discrimination in an Unequal Union
Edited by Susanne K. Schmidt, Michael Blauberger and Dorte Sindbjerg Martinsen

The Political Economy of Pension Financialisation
Edited by Anke Hassel and Tobias Wiß

The European Union Beyond the Polycrisis?
Integration and Politicization in an Age of Shifting Cleavages
Edited by Jonathan Zeitlin and Francesco Nicoli

Ideologies and the European Union
Edited by Carlo Invernizzi Accetti and Jonathan White

For more information about this series, please visit: https://www.routledge.com/Journal-of-European-Public-Policy-Special-Issues-as-Books/book-series/JEPPSPIBS

Ideologies and the European Union

Edited by
**Carlo Invernizzi Accetti
and Jonathan White**

Routledge
Taylor & Francis Group

LONDON AND NEW YORK

First published 2021
by Routledge
2 Park Square, Milton Park, Abingdon, Oxon, OX14 4RN

and by Routledge
605 Third Avenue, New York, NY 10017

Routledge is an imprint of the Taylor & Francis Group, an informa business

© 2021 Taylor & Francis

British Library Cataloguing-in-Publication Data
A catalogue record for this book is available from the British Library

ISBN 13: 978-0-367-68983-4 (hbk)

Typeset in Myriad Pro
by codeMantra

Publisher's Note
The publisher accepts responsibility for any inconsistencies that may have arisen during the conversion of this book from journal articles to book chapters, namely the inclusion of journal terminology.

Disclaimer
Every effort has been made to contact copyright holders for their permission to reprint material in this book. The publishers would be grateful to hear from any copyright holder who is not here acknowledged and will undertake to rectify any errors or omissions in future editions of this book.

Contents

Citation Information

The chapters in this book were originally published in the *Journal of European Public Policy*, volume 27, issue 9 (August 2020). When citing this material, please use the original page numbering for each article, as follows:

Chapter 1
Europeanizing ideologies
Jonathan White
Journal of European Public Policy, volume 27, issue 9 (August 2020)
pp. 1287–1306

Chapter 2
Kant's mantle: cosmopolitanism, federalism and constitutionalism as European ideologies
Kalypso Nicolaidis
Journal of European Public Policy, volume 27, issue 9 (August 2020)
pp. 1307–1328

Chapter 3
The European Union as a Christian democracy: a heuristic approach
Carlo Invernizzi Accetti
Journal of European Public Policy, volume 27, issue 9 (August 2020)
pp. 1329–1348

Chapter 4
The social democratic case against the EU
Fabio Wolkenstein
Journal of European Public Policy, volume 27, issue 9 (August 2020)
pp. 1349–1367

Chapter 5
European integration and the reconstitution of socioeconomic ideologies: Protestant ordoliberalism vs social Catholicism
Josef Hien
Journal of European Public Policy, volume 27, issue 9 (August 2020)
pp. 1368–1387

For any permission-related enquiries please visit:
http://www.tandfonline.com/page/help/permissions

Contributors

Carlo Invernizzi Accetti is Associate Professor of Political Science at the City University of New York (City College), USA, and Associate Researcher at the Centre d'Etudes Européennes of the Institut d'Etudes Politiques de Paris (Sciences Po).

Hauke Brunkhorst is Senior Professor of Sociology at the European University Flensburg, Germany.

Josef Hien is Senior Lecturer at Mid Sweden University and Researcher at the Institute for Future Studies, Stockholm, Sweden.

Marta Lorimer is Postdoctoral Research Associate at the University of Exeter, UK.

Glyn Morgan is Co-Director of the Moynihan Center for European Studies, The Maxwell School, Syracuse University, USA.

Kalypso Nicolaidis is Professor at the EUI School of Transnational Governance in Florence, Italy, and Professor of International Relations at the University of Oxford.

Jonathan White is Professor of Politics at the LSE.

Fabio Wolkenstein is Associate Professor of Political Science at Aarhus University, Denmark, and Researcher in Political Theory at the University of Amsterdam, the Netherlands.

Acknowledgements

We would like to thank the following individuals for valuable input during the preparation of these papers: Duncan Bell, Chris Bickerton, Michael Freeden, Florence Haegel, Markus Jachtenfuchs, Joseph Lacey, Tom Theuns, and Lea Ypi. We are especially grateful to the editors of the *Journal of European Public Policy*, Berthold Rittberger and Jeremy Richardson, for their consistent support in seeing the collection through to completion.

This volume builds on a workshop on 'Ideologies and the EU' organised by the editors at the Nicosia ECPR Joint Sessions in April 2018, and a workshop on 'Ideologies and EU Design' held at the Wissenschaftskolleg zu Berlin in May 2015. For supporting these initiatives, we would like to thank Peter Niesen, Carmen Pavel, Vera Kempa and Thorsten Wilhelmy, the EURIAS Fellowship Programme, and the Otto and Martha Fischbeck Foundation. Additionally, Jonathan White acknowledges the support of the Alexander von Humboldt Stiftung, for a fellowship at the Hertie School of Berlin during which this project was completed.

Carlo Invernizzi Accetti and Jonathan White

Europeanizing ideologies

Jonathan White

ABSTRACT

This article explores the relationship between ideology, the state and the transnational as it bears on European integration. Though typically studied in national contexts, ideologies and their clash have been Europe-wide since their emergence. As I argue, the European Union (EU) can be understood both as the continuation of these long-standing cross-border dynamics, and as the attempt to supersede them. Contemporary developments renew this dialectic. By exploring how ideology and European integration entwine, the paper underlines the value of a research agenda of heightened importance as the ideological hegemony of recent decades breaks down.[1]

The emergence of political ideologies tracked the emergence of the modern state. Accepting the ambiguities of definition and causality, a temporal overlap seems clear. Isms of diagnosis and prescription tied to groups of various kinds developed with the reorganization of authority that brought the feudal period to a close. Whether in the guise of doctrines intended to legitimise new institutions, contest them in the name of self-determination, or restore the world that preceded them, ideologies came to the fore with the emerging state. Yet equally, ideologies were never likely to be constrained by state boundaries. Already in the late-eighteenth century, isms developed wider horizons, being extended to conflicts international in scope and deployed for cross-border constituencies. From the conflicts of the French Revolution to defences of empire, ideologies became transnational phenomena.

It is the extension of ideologies outwards from the state that this article examines, with an eye in particular to European integration. Scholars typically approach ideology as a phenomenon of national settings, or else leave its sphere undefined (Bell, 2002, p. 224). Studies that set the likes of liberalism, socialism and conservatism in transnational context are rarer, like those of ideologies linked to transnational institutions (Martill, 2017). Where scholars look beyond the state, it is often to the global level. Steger's work on ideologies and globalization is one example (Steger, 2009); studies of the ideologies of nineteenth-century empires (Bell, 2013), of white racism (Lake & Reynolds, 2008), global Islamism (Aydin, 2017) or the United Nations (Thérien, 2015) are others. Largely overlooked has been the space between the state and the global – ideologies in and of the *regional*. As one of the major experiments of the post-war era, the EU is a rich place to study ideologies transnational but less than global in extension. Their analysis remains under-developed in EU studies, something only now changing in the context of recent upheavals.

Studying ideologies cross-nationally presents distinct problems given the opacity of the research object. To speak confidently of the existence and influence of an 'ism' is never easy, and the challenges look greater beyond the state, not just because ideologies have often been denied, but because of their frequent detachment from visible organizations, and the semantic ambiguities born of language diversity. But still they demand closer reflection. Such currents of thought tend to be amongst the most deeply-held, widespread and lasting, and also those closest to power. These are ideas oriented to action and underpinned by collectives (Freeden, 1996, p. 105), with the influence and durability this can bring. How the social world is signified, the opinions formed, the interests appraised, and their connection to institutions, are all matters in which ideologies are implicated. Even things treated as cultural givens, including (supra-)national identities, can be the legacy of ideological projects. Given the state of flux in Europe today, the significance of the form only increases.

As this paper argues, the EU has been built on ideology, and also against it. The Union is the expression of two countervailing tendencies. On the one hand, it is a continuation of the long-standing projection of ideologies across borders that has characterized Europe since the French Revolution. As the first section examines, the ideological conflicts of modern Europe typically unfolded on a regional stage, reflecting and consolidating a frame of reference (or 'imaginary') that was Europe-wide. European integration would mark the institutionalization of those ideologies pre-eminent in these contests in a given period. On the other hand, and as the second section examines, the ideologies shaping the EU were defined exactly by their hostility to this wider pattern. They were efforts to *transcend* ideological conflict and its cross-border reverberations, informed by an idea of the supranational as a realm beyond ideological division. Initiated in an era of heightened anxiety about political isms, European integration was defined in contradistinction as an anti-ideological project, its institutions intended to escape such clashes.

The present period sees the former tendency renewed and the latter challenged. As the third section examines, whereas for decades the EU could be dissociated from isms and these ascribed to its critics, with increasingly regularity it meets the charge of being an ideological project itself. This is a form of politicization where ideology and its attribution plays a central role. The section considers the specificity of critique on ideological grounds and its wider implications for the EU. In periods of 'interregnum' between one ideological settlement and another (Gramsci, 1947/1971, p. 276), future trajectories may be more open. Whereas this threatens to break up an order designed to exclude rather than accommodate ideological conflict, it also points to a distinct rationale for supranational institutions: as an arena in which to regulate these cross-border conflicts. Such a role depends on institutions being separable from ideologies, and how far such a decoupling is possible remains one of the central questions in contemporary EU politics.

Ideology and the modern European state

The first modern 'isms' were coined to describe heresies. Emerging in Reformation Europe, they were descriptions of religious doctrines advanced by their critics in the Catholic Church. Lutheranism, Calvinism, Puritanism and Anabaptism were amongst the first examples (Höpfl, 1983, pp. 1–2). For the pioneers of this pejorative rhetoric, isms denoted patterns of deviant thought and the ways of life said to attach to them. They evoked social groups, the '-ists' amongst whom these ideas were at home. While the attribution of shared belief was characteristic, its content could be a matter of debate, also indifference (Höpfl, 1983, p. 5). One of the functions of the idiom was to position the speaker as orthodox and rightful, and by highlighting distorted views, to reaffirm more generally the core tenets of the Catholic faith. The identification of heresy served the identification and protection of orthodoxy (Kurtz, 1983).

The isms of early-modern Europe were used sporadically though, rarely being adopted by those they were said to describe. They were not ideology as we would come to know it, with its self-aware groups and political focus. To the extent they corresponded to real-world collectives, these were dispersed and weakly integrated, and their concerns mainly religious. Only in the *eighteenth* century did isms take on the characteristics we associate with ideology. In the years after the French Revolution especially, they became terms of *self*-description for those claiming like-minded views (Höpfl, 1983, p. 7), denoting idea-clusters centred on political interpretation and prescription. Spurred in part by the experience of revolution, with its suggestion of altered and alterable futures, collectives emerged defined by their transformative agenda. A new vocabulary developed centred on 'concepts of movement' (Koselleck, 2004, p. 273ff.), as words like republic, liberty, and society came to define future-oriented projects of change.

Ideology as we shall understand it has its origins in this period (Freeden, 1996, pp. 141–142).[2] It can be defined as patterned sets of ideas about the world as it is and as it should be, embraced by groups (often consciously *as* groups), and the basis on which they pursue some form of power (Freeden, 1996, pp. 22–23, p. 105; Leader Maynard & Mildenberger, 2018). Such ideas find their most coherent expression in canonical texts and statements, but appear also in tacit and everyday contexts. While the pejorative connotations of early-modern isms have never been shed, accounts of ideology today tend not to define it in terms of deception and domination, close at hand though such effects may be. Emphasis is retained on its collective basis, whether in movements, parties or less visible groupings, and its practical orientation. We are dealing with ideas intended to shape the exercise of power, whether by direct application to decision-making institutions or by wider processes of (de-)contestation (Freeden, 1996, p. 77).

Analyses of the historical origins of ideology tend to emphasize processes of nation-state-formation. Steger connects ideology's appearance to the emergence of what he terms the 'national imaginary' – 'the taken-for-granted understanding in which the nation – plus its affiliated or to-be-affiliated state – serves as the communal frame of the political' (Steger, 2009, p. 9). This shared cultural space supplied the background ideas, symbols and reference-points on which ideologists drew. Liberalism, conservatism, socialism and their successors were built on this foundation, he suggests, and in turn replenished it as they were deployed in the nation's name. Steger's terminology is intended to highlight the novelty of more recent developments – the emergence of a *global* imaginary and its distinctive ideologies – but the primary suggestion is historical: that ideology in its formative period was inextricably linked to the national.

One needs to move carefully here, since speaking of national imaginaries risks positing the cultural unity that nationalists themselves tend to proclaim. One can slip from observing the centrality of nation-talk to accepting the reality of the community described. Surely correct though is that emerging discourses of nationhood provided a central object for contestation. Precisely because the nature, boundaries and interests of the nation were unclear, such concepts opened a space for competing interpretations. This revolutionary, secular language evoked a social world separable from political structures and with its own constituting power, contra divine-right theories and the unchanging communities supposed by traditional religion. Only then did it become possible to conceive doctrines of transformation and restoration, ones that would spark conflicts not least because the identity of that to be transformed was unclear.

To these symbolic shifts one may add the socio-economic upheavals of the period. As 'dislocation' theorists of nationalism have argued, the advance of the class structures of modern capitalism, accentuated by urbanization and industrialization, exposed people to new schemes of understanding (Gellner, 1983). Ideas of nationhood were just some: 'it is here that the coining of numerous 'isms' belongs, serving as collective and motivating concepts capable of reordering and mobilizing anew the masses robbed of their place in the old order of estates' (Koselleck, 2004). As communication and education structures developed, the constituency for such ideas expanded (Freeden, 1999; Koselleck, 2004, p. 251). Again, these transformations tracked processes of state-formation, as state representatives sought to steer, reinforce and take advantage of them. State institutions, increasingly defined and differentiated, enabled ideologies to take organized form (Freeden, 1999). In political parties, ideologies found their clearest expression.

The emergence of ideologies is inseparable then from the emergence of the modern state. Yet ideologies were never an intra-state phenomenon, even in the nation-state's heyday. Ideological politics has been cross-border in scope since its emergence, a source of enthusiasm and anxiety in part for this reason.[3] Such tendencies were visible already in the heresies of the sixteenth century, often explicitly transcontinental in outlook (Baskerville, 1994), given broad distribution by the papacy and the wider Catholic Church, and producing the first doctrinal wars by the seventeenth century (Pagden, 2002, p. 1). They are unmistakeable in the isms of the late-eighteenth century. The French Revolution, their catalyst, was recognized by contemporaries as of transnational status, like the conflicts it spawned.

Taking shape from the 1750s, the ideals of the French Revolution can be regarded, with all due caution about retroactive definition, as a brand of classical liberalism. As interrelated views about present conditions and their transformation, advanced by groups keen to imprint them on the exercise of power, they fit the definition of ideology well, albeit as an evolving combination of diverse intellectual strands, loosely centred on concepts of justice, reason and will (Baker, 1990, Ch. 1; Hobsbawm, 1997, pp. 58–59; Rosenblatt, 2018, p. 41ff.; Sewell, 1985, p. 74ff.). Early revolutionaries sought constitutional monarchy on the British model – liberalism as anti-feudalism and anti-despotism, combined with an insistence on law and individual freedoms. From 1791, under the Girondins and Montagnards, the goals turned to abolition – liberalism as republicanism, combined with democratic ideas of equality (Cassells, 2002, p. 39; Cattaneo, 1964; Haas, 2005, p. 46ff.). A constant throughout was that these were doctrines intended to travel (Hobsbawm, 1997, p. 54). Though proclaimed in the nation's name, the Declaration of the Rights of Man was phrased in abstract terms, evoking something more expansive than could be denoted by cultural criteria (Fontana in Hobsbawm, 1997, p. 65; Pagden, 2002, p. 121). Under the Girondins especially, spreading these ideals was an intrinsic goal; under the Montagnards, it seemed the best way to protect them at home (Cassells, 2002, p. 29).

As transnational as the revolutionaries' goals was the concern their actions sparked. Confronted with movements seeking rupture with the past, the makings of a conservative ideology took shape across Europe's centres of power. The Pillnitz Declaration of 27 August 1791, authored by Prussia and the Holy Roman Empire, announced the condition of the French monarchy to be 'a matter of common interest to all the sovereigns of Europe', and committed them to aiding the French king in restoring 'the foundations of a monarchical form of government'.[4] Although reluctant to go to war, their position consolidated the beginnings of a cross-national ideological divide, one the Girondins were also keen to talk up with their own statements of principle to the international world.[5]

A central theme of nineteenth-century Europe was the periodic re-emergence of these ideological conflicts. Despite the variety of ideas across time and space, and internal disputes amongst friends of the Revolution concerning the militarism of the Napoleonic period, international affairs in the following decades can be grasped in terms of a liberal / conservative divide (Cassells, 2002; Hobsbawm, 1997, p. 53; Rosenblatt, 2018, p. 67ff.). As franchises were extended and parties consolidated, isms became habitual forms of self-definition, and the recurrence of the same labels across Europe added to the sense of equivalence between the conflicts described. Given its ease of translation and capacity to abstract from local groups and demands (Kurunmäki & Marjanen, 2018, p. 247), ideologists aligning with an ism found themselves in possession of a vocabulary that could travel, one easily deployed to name a wider movement.[6] Socialists especially took advantage, while liberals and conservatives sought to consolidate themselves cross-nationally against the Second International. As an historian observes, only 'the Franco-Russian alliance [of 1894] put to an end the right-left divide in international politics dating from 1791' (Cassells, 2002, p. 116) – and it did so only temporarily.

What these brief remarks suggest is the existence of a *European* imaginary, additional to the national frame. Ideologists of different persuasion pursued their ends with an eye to the wider European context. The ideologies they imputed to their adversaries, like principles they claimed for themselves, unfolded in an arena European in scale. For reasons of ideology, domestic politics was transnational and often the object of interference, sovereignty claims notwithstanding. This was why ideologies could be developed for export, and why certain European states, France most obviously, could come to be viewed as a *crucible* – a place where doctrinal conflicts of general significance unfolded, in the outcome of which outsiders felt implicated. For reasons both offensive and defensive, the outlook was decidedly transnational.

Different explanations are possible, one of them materialist. The French Revolution has been called a bourgeois revolution, given its leading concerns – with individual liberty, the rights of property holders, and the moral qualities of commerce – were those of an ascendant bourgeoisie (Abercrombie & Turner, 1978, p. 156; Hobsbawm, 1997, pp. 58–59, p. 234ff.). It was a challenge to the feudal order raised by an emerging class of traders, opposed by the conservative aristocracy of the *ancien regime*. Given this commercial class was anything but nationally-bound, and a divide between bourgeoisie and aristocracy recurred across Europe, one could expect the same of liberal / conservative conflicts. Countries where the bourgeoisie was strongest, including Britain, France and the Low Countries, saw middle-class liberalism triumph by the 1830s, and spread beyond Europe as the same class projected itself outwards with empires (Herzfeld in Pagden, 2002).[7] If, as the materialist view holds, ideology is produced when changing socio-economic structures need legitimation, the transnational processes of capitalist development unfolding across Europe invited this wider extension.[8]

But equally one may note factors more political. Expanding the 'scope of conflict' (Schattschneider, 1975) so as to organize transnationally was often about overcoming domestic weakness. The internationalism of nineteenth-century socialists was inspired by the hegemony of liberals and conservatives in the major European states – in Mannheim's terms, it was not the ideology of established agents but the creative and destabilizing 'utopia' of subaltern groups (Mannheim, 1991). Projecting ideas across borders was a way to pursue transformations otherwise obstructed. To follow the fortunes of the like-minded abroad was also to track the progress of ideas that had become the basis of self-definition, and to seek confirmation that history would favour them. The transnational arena could have intrinsic significance, associated with universalist ambitions or structures like the Church and Carolingian empire. Such considerations might mix with defensive ones too. By forestalling the advance of opposing ideologies abroad, agents might aim to interrupt a momentum that, should it spread, would jeopardise their own de-contestations (Haas, 2005, p. 7). And to all these agentic considerations one may add the circulation of ideas unintentionally, without political aim, as concepts were deployed in new contexts, brought associations with them, and evolved in their encounter with new surroundings.

To speak of a *European imaginary* is not to deny the centrality of the national. All ideologies of the nineteenth century were interlaced with it in some way, either as could be traced to revolutionary ideals of liberty and self-determination, or as part of the counter-revolutionary tradition. But even those oriented to the good of one nation found reason to be concerned with tendencies further afield, and nationalism itself became something of a transnational ideology, a common frame given local content. Europe was not necessarily a strong leitmotif: it could be part of the assumed context without being a theme. Nor was the arena clearly bounded: its contours were expansive and contested, from the American Revolution to the Haitian Revolution, and the imperialist outlook that coloured nineteenth-century thought took the borders of 'Europe' far beyond the continent (Armitage, 1996; Bell, 2013; Rosenblatt, 2018). Key to observe is an assumed frame of reference wider than the national yet short of the global – a template that in time would be adopted by Europe's critics too (Younis, 2017). Ideology emerged in a regional frame.

The post-national and the pursuit of the post-ideological

One reason this matters is because the making of the EU, as the effort to institutionalize certain ideologies of transnational ambition, can be seen as the extension of this pattern. The EU emerged from a hinterland of pan-European ideological politics that long predated it and of which it was a continuation. But this context matters also because these same transnational tendencies were a persistent source of dissatisfaction, encouraging the countervailing impulse to transcend them. Precisely because ideological politics had an explosive, cross-border character, interest was spurred in conceiving a world 'beyond' this. From a diversity of perspectives, the supranational sphere was cast as a realm detachable not just from nationalism but isms more generally. One of the motivations for European integration in the 1950s would be the desire to supersede ideological conflicts and the unstable system they generated. The EU was to be built in their counter-image.

Ideology entails a preoccupation with worlds preferable to the here and now,[9] and transnational politics has always offered something to this sentiment. However much ideology- and state-formation went hand in hand, the world beyond the state has held fascination as a place of contrast. One sees this anticipated in the history of utopian thought, where places overseas traditionally functioned as the objects of imaginative projection. Before utopias were located in the future, they were located in faraway lands: the genre depended on the ultra-liminal for its imaginative horizon (Levitas, 2011, pp. 220–221). In the age of ideology the horizon was temporalized: the question became how the future could be different from the present. But the world beyond borders retained its importance, often signifying exactly the possibility of new beginnings. Pursuing ideological projects beyond the state became a way to cut loose from the inheritance of the recent past.

With the advent of the state, democracy and ideology, the world beyond the state could be conceptualized as a counter-realm to precisely these things. The transnational sphere, specifically the supranational, could be identified as a way to pursue projects defined in contradistinction to the state setting, detached from its associations, legacies and constraints. In strands of left-wing cosmopolitanism, notably expressed in the *Ventotene Manifesto*, this would mean departing from statist pathologies like fascism and chauvinist nationalism. For others, including thinkers of benevolent dictatorship and technocracy (Wells, 1933/2011), it could mean escaping democratic and parliamentary processes. For others still, it could mean breaking with ideology itself, seeking a form of administration insulated from it. Two twentieth-century bodies of thought in which such currents emerged, significantly for the later course of European integration, are Christian Democracy and economic liberalism. While both very much ideological formations themselves, descended from the conflicts of nineteenth-century Europe, they developed influential conceptions of the supranational shaped by aversion to ideology.

In strands of German Catholic thought adopted and adapted by Christian Democrats, the concept of the *Abendland* described a supranational space of shared values and faith that transcended the ideological divisions born of the French Revolution. Explicitly regional in focus,[10] it was described in contradistinction to various ideologies and sub-themes subsumed under 'materialism', including liberalism, individualism, nationalism, fascism, socialism and communism (Forlenza, 2017, esp. p. 278; Mitchell, 1995, p. 283ff.). The Abendland evoked the presumed oneness of Christian Europe prior to its fragmentation by ideology. The political task, as later construed by Christian Democrats, was to recreate the unity of this space, countering the isms dividing it from within (and sovereignty-system felt to support them) and those threatening it from without (notably from the East) (Cellini, 2018, p. 81; Forlenza, 2017, p. 268ff.; Müller, 2011, p. 132ff.). Part of a long-standing counter-Revolutionary tradition, this body of thought was on the one hand a position within transnational ideological conflicts, on the other an effort to overcome them.

Liberal-economic thought in 1930s/40s Europe did not display the same religious commitments,[11] but shared a conception of the supranational as a way to exit the destructiveness of ideological politics. From its inception, German Ordoliberalism had, in addition to its economic critique of monopoly-capitalism, a political critique of party democracy and the currents of mass opinion it expressed (Manow, 2001, p. 181ff.). 'Demagogues spreading ideologies' (Biebricher, 2017, p. 107) were what these unfortunate arrangements were said to support.[12] The alternative was to seek reinforced institutions of expertise where fact-based men of science could reign (Böhm et al., 1936/2017, p. 27ff.), undisturbed by 'ideologists of the planned economy' (Eucken, 1932/2017, p. 70). Market-enabling policies would be built into an 'economic constitution' protected from political pluralism and its attendant instability (Bonefeld, 2017; Gerber, 1994). While for some this demanded nothing less than a global approach, others saw the merit of a regional approach based on European law (Slobodian, 2018, p. 183ff.). In a related but distinct tradition, Austrian liberals such as Hayek also took interest in supra-state solutions, partly for the very reason that they would be detached from the communitarian and egalitarian ideologies that shaped nation-state politics (Hayek, 1939/1948).

By the mid-twentieth century one thus saw ideologies prescribing efforts to build a realm that would minimize ideological conflict. Hostility to totalitarian ideologies especially was pronounced – Christian Democracy and economic liberalism were movements of anti-socialism, anti-communism and anti-fascism first and foremost. But they also displayed a pronounced scepticism towards ideology as such, tied to an embrace of religious faith and spiritual values, or claims to be going beyond left and right. If often they recoiled from democratic institutions, it was because they considered mass politics inseparable from ideological tendencies. Nationalism was a central concern, but it was isms more generally they sought to transcend. While these sentiments would be shared by many in the 1950s, also in the US (Bell, 1962), in Europe they acquired a spatial connotation that mapped onto the supranational sphere.

In an analysis of ideologies of the international, Bell distinguishes 'vertical' ideologies, focused on relations *within* a state, from 'horizontal' ideologies that address questions of the relations *between and across* them (Bell, 2002, p. 223ff.). By the 1940s, economic liberalism and Christian Democracy had become horizontal in this sense, though they addressed something beyond the national *and* international. Defined against the state and its characteristic forms, theirs was a vision of the *supra*national. Consistent with the European imaginary inherited from previous generations, continental Europe was considered the place to initiate it. Whether to restore an earlier unity centred on Christendom and empire (Carolingian, Holy Roman, Habsburg) or consciously to break new ground, Europe was the assumed frame of reference.

The making of the EU can be seen as the institutionalization, amongst other influences, of Christian Democracy and economic liberalism (Bonefeld, 2017; Kaiser, 2007).[13] Many of the preoccupations of these ideologies, including their anti-ideological concerns, found expression in Europe's integration process and the views of those involved. Rarely perhaps are ideologies sufficient reasons for action, and motives often entwine. But the desire to maintain consistency with professed goals may encourage certain choices over others, and shape the meanings ascribed both by onlookers and actors (Skinner, 2002). Figures such as Schuman, Adenauer, de Gasperi, Erhard, Müller-Armack, Hallstein, von der Groeben and Mestmäcker found in these traditions a repository of cultural and political-economic ideas about the supranational that could help rationalize practical steps of coordination.[14]

Their hostility to ideological politics as they saw it meant those inspired by Christian Democracy and economic liberalism would often be drawn to organizational methods different to those found in the state. Rather than announce themselves in public forums as partisans under the banner of an ism, they would often seek less visible modes of association, particularly when coordinating transnationally. Informal circles of the like-minded formed in closed institutions, often aiming for executive and judicial rather than legislative power (Forlenza, 2017, p. 278; Kaiser, 2007; Slobodian, 2018). The diffuse structure of the EU realm, in part a reflection of the influence of these ideologies

(Invernizzi Accetti, 2019, ch. 4; White, 2019, ch. 2), contributed further to masking the agency of those involved. Ideology is the basis on which groups pursue power, but whereas in the state this has tended to map onto centralized institutions that highlight actor-responsibility, the absence of formal hierarchy in the transnational sphere meant ideology would be dispersed across multiple structures and its agents harder to identify.

A striking feature of the EU's subsequent development would be the intermingling of ideologies and scholarship (White, 2003). The organizational carriers of ideology in the nation-state have tended to be parties and related associations, but in the EU context this role would typically be played by intersecting circles of academia and bureaucracy, consolidating ideology's low visibility. Parties, conventionally, present their ideologies as such – as systematic diagnoses and prescriptions intended to influence power's exercise. Academics, scientists and bureaucrats tend not to. EU studies is not without isms – neofunctionalism, intergovernmentalism, federalism, constitutionalism and others mark traditions of both analysis and advocacy – but these have rarely been intended for mass consumption. They are of interest as the constructs of an intellectual elite, conceivably an avant-garde, but hardly as landmarks of public debate. By detaching themselves from the organizational structures that have tended to advertise ideology, the architects of the EU could better distance themselves from the ideological mode of politics they sought to avoid.

Contesting the EU settlement

For much of the last century, Europe was the site of ambitious ideological projects centred on the design of shared institutions. The descendants of nineteenth-century ideologists saw opportunities in European integration to advance their visions and challenge foes. Either as a bridgehead to a global order, or as a distinctly regional entity, they sought a supra-national framework of some kind. If institutions can be seen as 'solidified political thought' (Müller, 2011, p. 243), the EU's basic framework reflects the influence of its makers. And yet, as we have seen, though ideological themselves, these projects were typically efforts at transcending ideology. The EU marks the intersection of two countervailing impulses.

Rather than the rendition of a single ideology, the post-War European order was the amalgam of several. The concepts on which it was built – freedom, growth, a 'market economy' that is also 'social' – were shared by more than one tradition. Indeed, the art of building transnational institutions has arguably required finding a language that those of different persuasion (Christian Democrats, economic liberals and others) might claim as their own. Partly because of this intermixing, but especially because of the background scepticism towards ideology, the currents in question have rarely been announced as such. There has been little desire to identify them publicly as *isms* and cultivate their wider recognition – rarely has the EU been sold to mass publics *as* a Christian-Democratic or liberal-economic project. Whether these ideologies ever percolated into general consciousness may be doubted: their societal reach has been more limited. These have been ideologies for elites rather than masses.

Legitimation of the EU to mass publics has generally emphasized material benefits. The common-market programme has been explained as a route to peace and prosperity – classically liberal concerns, but here cast as pragmatism and necessity (Schrag Sternberg, 2013, ch. 1). EU representatives have cultivated notions of a common European interest, but one identifiable technocratically by 'independent' institutions (Vauchez, 2016). Where the views of a European people have been evoked (Schrag Sternberg, 2013, ch. 3), it has been as an aggregate of preferences to be identified by polling (e.g., Eurobarometer) rather than as integrated normative viewpoints. Much of the ideological production of the EU-sphere, particularly where it reflects the influence of coherent, self-standing traditions, has been inward-facing – a basis for like-minded elites to coordinate rather than to connect with a wider public.

One expression of the EU's casting as a post-ideological space lies in how popular disaffection has been classified and contained. The first modern isms were the names given to heresies by the Church, and it would not be far-fetched to draw a parallel. Controlling the meaning of dissent, even making it useful, has been an important goal for EU officials – a form of *pre-emptive* ideological politics. The concept of nationalism and the spectre of its 'return' has been a resource for supranationalists since the time of Coudenhove-Kalergi (Kettunen, 2018, p. 350, 360). Schuman himself used the term 'heresy' to describe nationalism in Europe (Forlenza, 2017, p. 273). More recently, the concept of euroscepticism – one that, like so many, migrates freely across scholarship and practice – has been used to denote deviations from EU support. Here as so often, an ism has been announced by its critics. Partly a scientific concept, euroscepticism is deeply political too, shaping the meaning of what it describes (Flood, 2002). Defining things in terms of deviance from a reference standard will generally conflate different phenomena. Euroscepticism merges wholesale opposition to a European polity with opposition to the EU's structure and policies; left-wing with right-wing opposition; political critique with socio-cultural aversion; reasoned dislike with an emotional response. It conflates things whose unity lies mainly in the eye of defenders of the status quo, and equates transnational sympathy and solidarity with support for the EU in existing form. Such 'de-contestations' are ideological, but entail not so much endorsing a world-view as attributing one to others.

The making of the EU has been characterized then by the projection of ideologies across borders, coupled with open hostility to ideological politics. How, one might wonder, could it be otherwise? How could the EU not reflect the orientations of its makers, people of common beliefs building institutions largely from scratch; equally, how could its representatives not distance themselves from this fact, given the supranational sphere was meant to be an escape from politics as usual, and given the strategic risks of too partisan a project? Here is not the place to explore the problems connected: the blurring of value choices, rigidity before changing socio-economic circumstances, and the obscuring of agency. The difficulty of articulating larger visions of what the EU is for, and the need to supplement arguments from material benefit with those from emergency, are arguably effects of avoiding an ideological register. Deprived of the chance to draw on the prestige of political traditions, EU representatives have had to base their arguments on an aggregate of particularities, with the problems of narrativization that follow (White, 2011, 2019). What can be highlighted here is the significance of contemporary rejoinders – the critiques to which the EU has increasingly become prone, and in which ideology and the suspicion of it is central.

Just as ideologies have been pivotal to transnational institutions yet generally hidden from view, they have become pivotal to their condemnation. Much has been written on the EU's politicization and the social cleavages that invite it, but ideology's significance is generally underplayed (De Wilde, 2019). By those seeking to undo those institutions or reorient them, as well as by those wanting to add colour to a wider worldview, the EU has been denounced as an ideological project. Socialists, Greens, far-Right figures and others have condemned its institutions and policies not just as deficient but *ideological* – as instantiations of neoliberalism, cosmopolitanism, Catholicism, federalism and other isms. The 2005 French and Dutch referenda on an EU constitution brought such claims to the fore. Whereas the EU had long been criticized – as undemocratic or 'sclerotic' (Schrag Sternberg, 2013, p. 156ff) – with these attributions of ideology it could now be cast as *symptomatic* of wider problems.

Insurgent formations thereby take aim not just at particularities but the patterns these are said to embody. The EU has often been viewed as *sui generis* (one effect of the refusal to connect it with ideologies); to re-associate it with isms is to re-insert it into a larger history. It is to treat it as epiphenomenal of tendencies played out elsewhere. Indeed – to re-join Steger (2009) – critiques of this kind increasingly set the regional in a *global* space, with the EU cast as one more front in a clash with neoliberalism, globalism and the like. The EU becomes an expression of politics as elsewhere. Imputations of ideology thereby allow a more far-reaching politicization of the EU than is achieved by targeting its specifics, and are the basis on which politicization dynamics ripple across domestic, global and European settings (Zürn, 2019, p. 988).

By criticizing the EU as the expression of an ism, such critics also suggest the influence of '-ists'. They present the EU as the outcome of someone's agency – as having been initiated by, or fallen under the sway of, certain groups and all they represent. Such claims challenge those who, casting the Union as a space beyond ideology, have tended to suggest an anonymous process responding to functional imperatives. (The reticence of EU officials in self-identifying with ideological labels allows their critics more freedom to attribute isms as they please.) It is important to acknowledge both the kernel of truth such critiques contain, and the extent to which they typically overshoot, presenting the EU as the offspring of a single ideology rather than a hybrid. By simplifying a complex reality, they invite counter-claims that perpetuate a cycle of contestation.

As critics denounce the EU as an ideological project, they sharpen lines of division and refashion the EU as the site of contending ideologies rather than the solidification of some. The end of the 'permissive consensus' reflects not just changes in the EU itself, increased non-majoritarian powers spelling increased contestation (Zürn, 2019, p. 989), but the re-contestation of the ideological settlement expressed in it. Perhaps one should not be too quick to identify the challengers as representing fully-fledged ideologies them-selves, but – characteristically of such transition periods – their critiques restore the visibility of ideology and the expectation of it. They renew an idea of Europe as a conflictual arena, and of politics as the stuff of ideals and collectives, things the EU was conceived to depart from. Such moves may encourage established authorities to develop ideologies of self-justifica-tion, as advocates of 'liberal Europe' are beginning to.

We saw in the first section, discussing revolutionary France, the original form in which ideologies transnationalise, whereby a particular setting becomes a crucible of wider interest. A sense of shared predicament amongst the like-minded emerges, expressed in cross-border coordination, forms of intervention and imitation, and the migration of labels, concepts and narratives. Just as numerous episodes have extended this template, from the Spanish Civil War to the Cold War, one sees traces of it again in recent European politics. Cross-border interest in the standoff between the Greek government and the Eurozone Troika in spring 2015, and its interpret-ation as a conflict between Left and Right, or 'populists' and 'technocrats', is one example of the willingness to see particular sites as crucibles of some-thing larger.

Whereas the 1990s and 2000s saw renewed declarations of the end of ideologies (Brick, 2013), more recently these seem hard to sustain. Ideological alternatives to the status quo remain ill-developed, but public consent seems more fragile. Institutions and policy regimes endure, but their intellectual underpinnings look weaker, challenged by both left-wing and nationalist internationalism (Stahl, 2019). Evolving in the shadow of European integration, these latter have in turn been shaped by it: ideologies have been Europeanized, just as they have been mechanisms of Europeanization. Is self-identification with ideological politics returning too? This is less clear, yet plausible. In contemporary critiques of technocracy, conspiracy, compromise and lost sovereignty, one detects the desire for clarity, purpose and commitment. Such are the qualities traditionally sought in isms, and many far-Right groups, Greens and Leftists seem inclined to capitalize by casting themselves as ideas-based traditions transnational in scope. In the global dislocations initiated by Covid-19, new opportunities await them. Once the refuge of those seeking to escape ideology, the transnational sphere begins to look like the heart of it once more.

On an optimistic reading, out of the dual tendencies to project ideologies across borders and to build transnational institutions against this, a valuable synthesis is possible. A logical reason for supranational institutions to exist is to give platform to the transnational ideological divides that predate and evolve with them. One might look to the EU precisely to institutionalize the 'imagined' European arena of conflict that has existed for more than two centuries. Quite contrary to the reasons for which it was initiated, one might rationalize the Union as a way to allow the orderly expression and adjudication of long-standing cross-border ideological conflicts, and seek to reshape its institutions accordingly. Arguments for a stronger European Parliament, as the place where transnational parties can take root, build on such reasoning. But these readings depend on EU structures being more than the instantiation of ideologies themselves: whether such a decoupling is truly possible remains one of the central questions in EU politics.

Conclusion

Ideological politics was European in scale from the moment the French Revolution became a wider example. These events gave expression to a European imaginary – a Europe-wide frame of reference for principled struggles – that encouraged cross-border mobilisations and interventions. The EU is a legacy of these long-standing dynamics, whilst also inspired by dissatisfaction with them. It has opened up new fronts of ideological politics – as a conduit for their influence on supranational institutions and policies; as the source of new labels advanced to control the meaning of dissent; and as an object of critique on ideological grounds. Ideology, and the suspicion of it, has been central to how the EU has developed.

The border-leaping tendencies of ideological politics are one reason it has often been feared. In addition to the usual concerns about rigidity of thought, here it threatens to mobilize at the expense of the institutions and ties of the nation-state. The ambitions get grander, the need for compromise perhaps weaker. And when ideologies are inserted into supranational structures, and in the name of taking distance from ideological conflicts, they may be consequential yet hard to discern. Rather than associated with public-facing entities such as parties and legislatures, they have tended to be buried in law, interlocking bureaucratic and academic circles, and executive institutions. The groups underpinning ideology have often been informal, and keen to cast supranational administration as a space beyond ideology. At least for a period, their claims may be decontested more thoroughly.

But as more recent events indicate, such a settlement is precarious. The institutionalization of ideologies can be doubled-edge. Though in some ways the apogee of an ideological project, hegemony can be a source of weakness, as diagnoses and prescriptions become taken for granted and under-theorised in the absence of challengers. The very capacity to detach ideological projects from mechanisms of mass participation leaves them vulnerable as circumstances change and consent to new arrangements is sought. As the EU and its ideological underpinnings are contested, they become more visible. One possible outcome is that Europe becomes an arena of ideological conflict once more, with the EU's institutions formalizing the 'imagined' European arena that has existed since the late eighteenth century.

The pursuit of ideological projects on a transnational scale seems unlikely to disappear, and the Union's demise would surely not terminate it. Something like a European imaginary, and increasingly something more expansive still, would presumably persist, just as it long preceded the EU. Ideals of national sovereignty promise non-interference, and for those dissatisfied with the contemporary EU, the nation-state seems to promise an escape of sorts. Reversing the relation characteristic of the twentieth century, the nation-state has become the site of utopian projection, a place of extrication from the ills and constraints of the transnational. But for as long as ideological conflict can still be observed or imputed across borders, non-interference seems fanciful. The politics of the nation-state was never national in extension, and is unlikely to be so in future. What remains to be determined is how the cross-border tendencies of ideology will unfold, and to the benefit of which kinds of project.

Notes

1. For comments I thank Štefan Auer, Duncan Bell, Carlo Invernizzi Accetti, Fabio Wolkenstein, Lea Ypi, and three referees. The article was completed while on a Humboldt Stiftung fellowship at the Hertie School, Berlin.
2. The late-eighteenth century also saw the emergence of the *concept* of ideology (Stråth, 2013). Note too historiographical debates about how to conceive the preceding period, notably whether seventeenth-century thinkers like Locke were forerunners of liberalism (Bell, 2014), and what debt was owed by republicanism to a longer tradition of republican thought (Koselleck, 2004).

3. As will transpire, the transnational currents in ideology can take different forms: the cross-border spread of ideas and terminology (including ism labels), the widening of the constituency at whom they are aimed, the expansion of the movements they successfully inspire, their attachment to transnational institutional projects, or the conscious thematization of matters international in their content.
4. https://en.wikisource.org/wiki/The_Constitutions_and_Other_Select_Documents_Illustrative_of_the_History_of_France,_1789–1907/14.
5. See the 'Propagandist Decrees' of November / December 1792, offering 'fraternity and aid to all peoples who wish to recover their liberty': Haas (2005, p. 51).
6. That labels may be more mobile than the ideologies they denote makes cross-border unity always fragile.
7. Cf. Marx and Engels (1974, p. 64): the ideas of 'the ruling class are in every epoch the ruling ideas, i.e., the class which is the ruling *material* force of society, is at the same time its ruling *intellectual* force'.
8. As pioneers of 'cleavage theory' would later observe, divisions of class were not the only kind to which ideologies might adhere (Lipset & Rokkan, 1967).
9. Even conservatism, one may generalize, tends to go beyond status-quo maintenance to seek the restoration of an idealized past.
10. The region corresponded broadly to the pre-Reformation Church; whether it extended to North America was a point of disagreement: Forlenza (2017, p. 264, p. 283).
11. The religious inspiration, if any, was generally Protestant (Manow, 2001).
12. For Walter Eucken, this was a macro-historical story, traceable to how the democratic ideals of the French Revolution undermined the values they were meant to advance: 'For these ideologies there is a curious explanation. *They affirm and promote movements that achieve exactly the opposite of that which ideologists hope from them.* The democratization of the world and the consequent unleashing of the demonic powers of peoples eliminated the old international politics of equilibrium, destroyed the political order of Europe and the world, sidelined the principle of peace, and created general insecurity' (Eucken, 1932/2017, p. 69).
13. The EU is not the only example of the institutionalization of ideology: the League of Nations was in many ways the expression of Wilsonian liberalism, pursued to restrain another internationalism (Leninism).
14. See e.g., Germany's Chancellor (Adenauer, 1956) on the dangerous, French-Revolutionary doctrine of nationalism (p. 8), the rise of the 'materialistic attitude' and 'mass-mindedness' (pp. 12–13), and the deeper rationale behind the Coal and Steel Community (pp. 12–14): 'The world cannot exist without a Christian and Occidental Europe. ... We want to save this Europe of ours. For Europe is in truth the mother of the world, and we are her children. ... The salvation of the Occident, the salvation of Christian culture, will be made possible only by an alliance among those political forces whose basis is Christianity. If the Christian parties of Belgium, Germany, Holland, Italy, Luxemburg, Austria and Switzerland would establish a firmer alliance, with mutual exchange of information and mutual support, what a telling effect it would have upon events in Europe ... '

Disclosure statement

No potential conflict of interest was reported by the author(s).

References

Abercrombie, N., & Turner, B. (1978). The dominant ideology thesis. *The British Journal of Sociology*, *29*(2), 149–170. https://doi.org/10.2307/589886

Adenauer, K. (1956). *World indivisible: With liberty and justice for all* (Richard and C. Winston, Trans.). Allen & Unwin.

Armitage, D. (1996). *The ideological origins of the British Empire*. CUP.

Aydin, C. (2017). *The idea of the Muslim world: A global intellectual history*. Harvard UP.

Baker, K. (1990). *Inventing the French Revolution: Essays on French political culture in the eighteenth century*. CUP.

Baskerville, S. (1994). Protestantism as a transnational ideology. *History of European Ideas*, *18*(6), 901–911. https://doi.org/10.1016/0191-6599(94)90343-3

Bell, D. (1962). *The end of ideology: On the exhaustion of political ideas in the fifties*. Harvard UP.

Bell, D. (2002). Anarchy, power and death: Contemporary political realism as ideology. *Journal of Political Ideologies*, *7*(2), 221–239. https://doi.org/10.1080/13569310220137557

Bell, D. (2013). Ideologies of empire. In M. Freeden, L. Sargent, & M. Stears (Eds.), *Oxford handbook of political ideologies* (pp. 536–561). OUP.

Bell, D. (2014). What is liberalism? *Political Theory*, *42*(6), 682–715. https://doi.org/10.1177/0090591714535103

Biebricher, T. (2017). Ordoliberalism as a variety of neoliberalism. In J. Hien & C. Joerges (Eds.), *Ordoliberalism, law and the rule of economics* (pp. 103–113). Bloomsbury.

Böhm, F., Eucken, W., & Grossmann-Doerth, H. (1936/2017). The Ordo Manifesto of 1936. In T. Biebricher & F. Vogelmann (Eds.), *The Birth of austerity: German ordoliberalism and contemporary neoliberalism* (pp. 27–39). Rowman & Littlefield.

Bonefeld, W. (2017). *The strong state and the free economy*. Rowman & Littlefield.

Brick, H. (2013). The end of ideology Thesis. In M. Freeden, L. T. Sargent, & M. Stears (Eds.), *Oxford handbook of political ideologies* (pp. 90–113). OUP.

Cassells, A. (2002). *Ideology and international relations in the modern world*. Routledge.

Cattaneo, M. (1964). *Il partito politico nel pensiero dell'illuminismo e della rivoluzione francese*. Giuffrè.

Cellini, J. (2018). The idea of Europe at the origins of the European people's party. *Journal of European Integration History*, *24*(1), 79–94. https://doi.org/10.5771/0947-9511-2018-1-79

De Wilde, P. (2019). The making of four ideologies of globalization. *European Political Science Review*, *11*(1), 1–18. https://doi.org/10.1017/S1755773918000164

Eucken, W. (1932/2017). Structural transformations of the state and the crisis of capitalism. In T. Biebricher & F. Vogelmann (Eds.), *The birth of austerity* (pp. 51–72). Rowman & Littlefield.

Flood, C. (2002). *Euroscepticism: A problematic concept* [Paper presented] UACES 32nd Annual Conference, Belfast, 2–4 September.

Forlenza, R. (2017). The politics of the *Abendland*: Christian Democracy and the idea of Europe after the Second World War. *Contemporary European History*, *26*(2), 261–286. https://doi.org/10.1017/S0960777317000091

Freeden, M. (1996). *Ideologies and political theory*. OUP.

Freeden, M. (1999). The "beginning of ideology" thesis. *Journal of Political Ideologies*, *4* (1), 5–11. https://doi.org/10.1080/13569319908420786

Gellner, E. (1983). *Nations and nationalism*. Blackwell.

Gerber, D. (1994). Constitutionalizing the economy: German neo-liberalism, competition law and the "new" Europe. *The American Journal of Comparative Law*, *42*(1), 25–84. https://doi.org/10.2307/840727

Gramsci, A. (1947/1971). *Selections from the prison notebooks* (Q. Hoare & G. Nowell Smith, Trans.). Lawrence and Wishart.

Haas, M. (2005). *The ideological origins of great power politics, 1789–1989*. Cornell UP.

Hayek, F. (1939/1948). The economic conditions of interstate federalism. In F. Hayek (Ed.), *Individualism and economic order* (pp. 255–272). Routledge.

Hobsbawm, E. (1997). *The age of revolution: 1789–1848*. Weidenfeld & Nicolson.

Höpfl, H. M. (1983). Isms. *British Journal of Political Science*, *13*(1), 1–17. https://doi.org/10.1017/S0007123400003112

Invernizzi Accetti, C. (2019). *What is Christian democracy? Politics, religion and ideology*. CUP.

Kaiser, W. (2007). *Christian democracy and the origins of European Union*. CUP.

Kettunen, P. (2018). The concept of nationalism in discussions on a European society. *Journal of Political Ideologies*, *23*(3), 342–369. https://doi.org/10.1080/13569317.2018.1502943

Koselleck, R. (2004). *Futures past: On the semantics of historical time*. Columbia.

Kurtz, L. (1983). The politics of heresy. *American Journal of Sociology*, *88*(6), 1085–1115. https://doi.org/10.1086/227796

Kurunmäki, J., & Marjanen, J. (2018). Isms, ideologies and setting the agenda for public debate. *Journal of Political Ideologies*, *23*(3), 256–282. https://doi.org/10.1080/13569317.2018.1502941

Lake, M., & Reynolds, H. (2008). *Drawing the global colour line: White men's countries and the international challenge of racial equality*. CUP.

Leader Maynard, J., & Mildenberger, M. (2018). Convergence and divergence in the study of ideology: A critical review. *British Journal of Political Science*, *48*(2), 563–589. https://doi.org/10.1017/S0007123415000654

Levitas, R. (2011). *The concept of Utopia*. Peter Lang.

Lipset, S., & Rokkan, S. (1967). Cleavage structures, party systems, and voter alignments: An introduction. In S. Lipset, & S. Rokkan (Eds.), *Party systems and voter alignments: Cross-national perspectives* (pp. 1–64). Free.

Mannheim, K. (1991). *Ideology and Utopia*. Routledge.

Manow, P. (2001). Ordoliberalismus als ökonomische Ordnungstheologie. *Leviathan*, *29*(2), 179–198. https://doi.org/10.1007/s11578-001-0012-z

Martill, B. (2017). International ideologies: Paradigms of ideological analysis and world politics. *Journal of Political Ideologies*, *22*(3), 236–255. https://doi.org/10.1080/13569317.2017.1345139

Marx, K., & Engels, F. (1974). *The German ideology* (2nd ed., C. J. Arthur, Ed.). Lawrence and Wishart.

Mitchell, M. (1995). Materialism and secularism: CDU politicians and national socialism, 1945–1949. *The Journal of Modern History*, *67*(2), 278–308. https://doi.org/10.1086/245092

Müller, J.-W. (2011). *Contesting democracy: Political ideas in twentieth-century Europe.* Yale UP.

Pagden, A. (Ed.). (2002). *The idea of Europe: From antiquity to the European Union.* CUP.

Rosenblatt, H. (2018). *The lost history of liberalism: From Ancient Rome to the twenty-first century.* PUP.

Schattschneider, E. E. (1975). *The semisovereign people: A realistic view of democracy in America.* Dryden P.

Schrag Sternberg, C. (2013). *The struggle for EU legitimacy, 1950–2005.* Palgrave MacMillan.

Sewell, W. (1985). Ideologies and social revolutions: Reflections on the French case. *The Journal of Modern History*, *57*(1), 57–85. https://doi.org/10.1086/242777

Skinner, Q. (2002). *Visions of politics, Vol. 1: Regarding method.* CUP.

Slobodian, Q. (2018). *Globalists: The end of empire and the birth of neoliberalism.* Harvard UP.

Stahl, R. M. (2019). Ruling the interregnum: Politics and ideology in nonhegemonic times. *Politics and Society*, *47*(3), 333–360. https://doi.org/10.1177/0032329219851896

Steger, M. (2009). *The rise of the global imaginary: Political ideologies from the French revolution to the global war on terror.* OUP.

Stråth, B. (2013). Ideology and conceptual history. In M. Freeden, L. T. Sargent, & M. Stears (Ed.), *Oxford handbook of political ideologies* (pp. 3–19). OUP.

Thérien, J.-P. (2015). The United Nations ideology: From ideas to global politics. *Journal of Political Ideologies*, *20*(3), 221–243. https://doi.org/10.1080/13569317.2015.1075262

Vauchez, A. (2016). *Democratizing Europe.* Palgrave Macmillan.

Wells, H. G. (1933/2011). *The shape of things to come.* Gollancz.

White, J. (2003). Theory guiding practice: The neofunctionalists and the Hallstein EEC commission. *Journal of European Integration History*, *9*(1), 111–131.

White, J. (2011). *Political allegiance after European integration.* Palgrave Macmillan.

White, J. (2019). *Politics of last resort: Governing by emergency in the European Union.* OUP.

Younis, M. (2017). 'United by blood': Race and transnationalism during the Belle Époque. *Nations and Nationalism*, *23*(3), 484–504. https://doi.org/10.1111/nana.12265

Zürn, M. (2019). Politicization compared: At national, European, and global levels. *Journal of European Public Policy*, *26*(7), 977–995. https://doi.org/10.1080/13501763.2019.1619188

Kant's mantle: cosmopolitanism, federalism and constitutionalism as European ideologies

Kalypso Nicolaidis

ABSTRACT

This article explores the ways cosmopolitanism, federalism and constitutionalism have evolved in Europe from core philosophical concepts to political programmes, and ultimately 'ideological benchmarks' with highly contested meanings. I identify three alternative intellectual strategies for their appropriation, and through them the appropriation of 'Kant's mantle', which both reflect and affect the EU public sphere. In the process, I ask how they can serve as resources conceptually to ground a third way for Europe. First, essentialist strategies appeal to affinities with the essence of these traditions, an essence anterior to or distinct from the particular variant of the 'state writ large' with which they might be identified in the public and scholarly imagination. Second, composite strategies employ various modifiers to deflect criticism. Thirdly, pollination strategies retain the flavor and questions raised by the three isms without necessarily coopting their labels.

'Mal nommer un objet, c'est ajouter au malheur du monde' Albert Camus, 1944

An early *indignados,* Albert Camus revolted against the many ways in which citizens were manipulated by politicians lying over the objects of their shared collective worlds, of their struggles or desires. For him, a politics unconcerned by the search for truth is simply a crime, a well disguised and subtle crime perhaps, but one which in the end will engender either the apathy or the wrath of the people, hence, the misery of the world.

To be sure, Camus was concerned with the fateful isms of his time – nazism, fascism, totalitarianism, nationalism, colonialism, communism – that had congealed one way or another to subjugate their respective victims. We now live in a Europe built to ward off these particular isms, through a Union which stands at its best as a form of collective atonement for the havoc they created. And yet, we may ask, what of the isms which EU founders, thinkers and activists have themselves marshalled in order to bolster its legitimacy.

It is striking how many of the terms used to understand European integration are framed as 'isms', including its three core referents, namely, cosmopolitanism, federalism and constitutionalism. These may be placeholders for long and respected traditions in political philosophy, idealistic and benevolent isms we may say, appealing to the better angels of our political nature. But struggling for their continued relevance, these isms have long operated as shape-shifters, evolved from their roles as conceptual repositories to labels for actual political programmes, and more broadly become core contenders in framing an over-arching ideology which can be referred to in short-hand as Europeanism.

As discussed by Jonathan White in this special issue, this evolution is not a straightforward one. After all, the post-war European project was imagined as a way to cut loose from the grip of state-bound ideological pathologies and create a post-ideological technocratic engine devoted to the well-being of citizens, what some of us have referred to as the eurocrat's dream (Chalmers et al., 2016; White, 2019). Heed the irony of a settlement between Christian, social and liberal democrats precisely to articulate supranational mechanisms to transcend (mass) democratic politics. In this a-ideological universe, Europeanism merely stood as a transnational sociology, to mean that Europeans of different nationalities share a set of values, like secularism, multiculturalism, or welfarism (McCormick, 2010).

Such a conceit, however, has long ceased to serve the cause of European politics, at least of the 'honest' kind envisaged by Camus. Today, European cosmopolitanism, federalism and constitutionalism must be understood as part of an ideology, a system of political thinking 'loose or rigid, deliberate or unintended, through which individuals and groups construct an understanding of the political world they, or those who preoccupy their thoughts, inhabit, and then act on that understanding' (Freeden, 1996). Indeed, our European public space is being fractured symbolically as well as ideologically, as political sides mobilize around discourses of enmity borrowing from the power of these words used as codes of belonging: cosmopolitans against nationalists, federalists against sovereignists, (euro)constitutionalists against statists. In this collective affliction of polarization, cosmopolitans, federalists, constitutionalists become either my friends or my foes, falling univocally on one side of binary equations in the public imagination, praised or derided against their supposed opposites.

But isn't this simplistic highjacking of our 'isms' on the side of 'unity' against 'fragmentation', or 'openness' against 'closeness', an instance of Camus' misnaming curse? For in fact, like other 'isms' originating in political theory, they each reflect a combination of distinct and often conflicting doctrines and it is precisely their polymorphic and obscuring character that makes them a nexus of ideological struggles in Europe (Kurunmäki & Marjanen, 2018). Their fluid role as 'benchmark ideologies' testifies not only to their own multi-facetted meanings but to the EU's highly contested nature. If this is the case, I will argue, we may want to take Camus' challenge head on and ask what we can learn from analysing as ideological struggles the various strategies behind the deployment of these concepts in Europe's public sphere.

Why refer to Kant's mantle to tell this story? Certainly, the three longstanding concepts of cosmopolitanism, federalism and constitutionalism all hail from much earlier than the eighteenth century enlightenment philosopher, each having its own scholarly and political trajectory. But it is with Immanuel Kant that they were weaved together under a single umbrella to serve as the foundation for his vision of a new legal order promising perpetual peace among nations. Kant employed all three concepts in interrelated ways to describe his political project – the creation of a federation of free Republics committed to cosmopolitan law – and in doing so imbued them with a particular shared programmatic connotation, each shading off into one another (Kant, 1991[1795], 1996[1797], 1997[1785]).

My aim here is not to enter the fray of Kantian exegesis in international relations (*inter alia,* Bohman & Lutz-Bachmann, 1997; Cavallar, 1994; Hurrell, 1990; Kleingeld, 2009). Instead, as Hoffe (1994) argues in response to critics of lax readings and misappropriation of Kant to suit contemporary debates, 'one can still make use of Kant in order to go beyond Kant'. For Europeans who fight over Kant's mantle to dress up the EU do not always do so explicitly, or accurately (since his outlook was universal), and they do so in circumstances he could hardly have imagined.

Nevertheless, Kant's vision has served as the scholar's core referent for the most advanced horizon for inter-state cooperation, the third of three stages of anarchy for the English school and constructivists alike. And more often than not, at least until the last 'crisis decade', the EU was presented as the incarnation, or at least the promise, of such a Kantian frontier (Linklater, 1998). But if we were to stop at that we would neither do justice to the EU nor to the ambivalence of Kant's worldview. Indeed, we cannot but take note of how Kant's thinking evolved over his lifetime regarding the proper balance between statist and cosmopolitan attributes of a desirable world order, as he moved from espousing the virtues of a possible 'world republic' in his pre-1793 writings such as *The Idea of a Universal History,* to praising *foedus pacificum* (akin to a more loosely organized 'congress' or 'league' of states) against the danger of a despotic universal monarchy in *Perpetual Peace* (1795) and *The Metaphysics of Morals* (1797). Throughout, Kant's writings always seem tentative, displaying a keen awareness that all solutions involve trade-offs and costs (Hurrell, 2013). No wonder that even the prime realist Kenneth Waltz managed to praise Kant for recognizing the anarchical character of international relations while believing that states may 'learn enough from the suffering and devastation of war to make possible a rule of law among them that is not backed by power but is voluntarily observed' (Lechner, 2017).

If, more than two hundred years after his death, our debates continue to take place under Kant's long shadow, we tend to do so each from our norma-tive vantage-points. My own lies alongside those who, roughly speaking, embrace a third way for Europe, thus rejecting the dogmatic dichotomy between calling for transcending or upholding the European state system. Instead, this third way sees the EU as a way of transforming the system, drawing from both descriptive and critical accounts. Among many scholarly variants, demoicratic theory is most explicitly normative, advocating as it does the imperative of remaining on the Rubicon where democracy in the EU is not equated with a single people, be it national or European (Ferry, 2005, Nicolaidis, 2004, 2013, 2018; Cheneval, 2005; Cheneval & Schimmelfen-nig, 2013, Bellamy, 2019). Accordingly, as 'a union of peoples who govern together but not as one', the EU should aspire to retain the plurality of its inter-linked peoples as popular sovereigns as opposed to their incorporation into a single demos or their closure as separate demoi.

In this spirit, I ask here how the meaning of our 'isms' can be mobilized to support an understanding of the EU as a third way by translating the Kantian commitment to the horizontal sharing of sovereignty into a XXIst century democratic vernacular. In doing so, I explore alternative strategies for how 'federal' 'cosmopolitan' or 'constitutional', when used as ideological bench-marks, may escape the dogmatic binaries which impoverish our democratic conversation. These strategies are deployed in two overlapping spheres of dis-course, the academic and the political. How public intellectuals translate and are in turn translated into political blueprints in the incipient European public sphere is a complex story which can only receive a cursory treatment here (Lacroix & Nicolaidis, 2010; Risse, 2015). Suffice to say that philosophical con-cepts become ideologies when appropriated in the context of political and legitimation struggles, thus migrating from elite consumption to selective appropriation by a wider public, whereby citizens pick and choose what they will amplify or forget, reward or punish at the polls, or exhibit on dem-onstration placards (Díez Medrano, 2010). In the process, these concepts are both enriched and impoverished as they fall from their philosophical ped-estals to reflect socio-political interests over and above mere logical con-structs (Freeden, 1996). But while participants in the social world – citizens, firms, politicians, bureaucrats – are the ultimate object of my concern, the bulk of enquiry is focused on those who articulate concepts and thus create the mood music for Europe's incipient public sphere, short of assuming a causal link between thought-worlds and policy-worlds.

I speak of a 'nexus' of ideological struggles to convey the idea that defend-ing or deriding the isms in question and their Kantian genealogy can serve as a proxy for at least three intersecting debates related to the locus of EU power.

First, over the nature of the polity, the (federal) bond between states and the desirable balance between the one and the many. Second, over the nature of economic governance, supranational rights enforcement, and the desirable balance between public and private preponderance in managing exchanges. Third, over the nature of Europe's role in the world, and attitudes regarding Europe as a vanguard Kantian project.

In this spirit, I identify three types of strategy. First *essentialist* strategies appeal to affinities with the 'essence' of these traditions, an essence anterior to or distinct from the particular variant of the 'state writ large' which dominate the public and scholarly imagination. Second, and alternatively, to make up for the capture by statist or market-centric lenses of each of these 'isms', *composite* strategies employ qualified notions. Thirdly, *pollinization* strategies retain the flavor and questions raise by our isms without coopting their labels. Within each of these alternative strategies, I observe the boundaries and relative emphasis between our 'isms', and the relationships they imply between the EU and the state, markets and citizens as well as the rest of the world.

Essentialist Strategies

In the political world out there, some words' reputation betrays them. 'Cosmopolitanism', 'federalism' and 'constitutionalism' were long enlisted to serve a distinctly 'unitary' interpretation of supranationalism, if not the dreaded 'superstate', at least a construct whereby 'ever closer union' was to take precedence over the continued plurality of 'the peoples of Europe'. By the 1990s and the turn of the millennium however, as post-cold-war constitutional debates gathered pace, the question emerged: could Europeanism be saved from the Christian yearning for oneness and its connotation as an anti-national project, by appealing to the 'essence' of these traditions, anterior to or distinct from the particular variants which might have tainted them in the public and scholarly imagination?

Federalism remained for a long time the primary *telos* of European integration, as early as Aristide Briand's call for a Federal union of European Union in 1929. Many of the founding thinkers of both the inter-war and post-war era, including Altiero Spinelli and Ernesto Rossi in their 1941 *Ventotene Manifesto*, found it obvious to anchor the European project in the idea of a Federal pact against statist pathologies (Glencross & Trechsel, 2010). Whether through Monnet's incremental functional spillover or Spinelli's insistence on popular anointment, the project would culminate in over-arching federal constraints on state autonomy, as ultimate rampart against the rebirth of nationalism (Schrag Sternberg, 2013). But the motto of 'United States of Europe' came to be eclipsed by the ups and downs of the integration project, only to be revived during the Constitutional Convention of 2001–2003 where federalists spoke of the failure of EU leaders to pursue integration to its 'logical conclusion', its 'federal destination' (Fabbrini, 2010; Benz & Broschek, 2013).

Against this historical backdrop, the appeal to the 'essence' of federalism during the Convention took various forms. At a minimum, it meant stressing the decentralizing and power-limiting features of federalism dear to mainstream German interpretation, as wll as the import of 'cycles of federalism' familiar to other federal constructs which require a reverse gear to bring competences back down, legislative sunset clauses and ring-fencing exclusive national powers. More radically, some of us argued at the time, we should not rest content with a line of defense which remained fundamentally vertical. Instead, the essence of federalism ought to consist in separating the federal ideal from its statist bathwater, to recover the original 'federal vision' as a construct which, as far as we can tell, has ordered human interactions for tens of thousands of years (Nicolaidis & Howse, 2001; Menon & Schain, 2006). Historically, *pace* Althusius, the 'federal' emerged prior to and in contrast with the 'state' before the two converged. The state-like attributes which federations acquired over the last two centuries, in the US but also Germany, Canada or even Switzerland, represent one contemporary variant of a more lasting federal vision which the EU can represent without becoming a state. Isn't this what Kant meant by his *foedus*, a covenant or contract achieved through a combination of self and shared rule (Elazar, 1987)? After all, it is hard to deny that the EU is, by essence, a 'federal construct': structurally, a governance system organized on different scales; functionally, a vertical division of power between the units and the whole; and institutionally, with these legal orders mutually involved with each other (Fossum & Menendez, 2011; Kelemen & Nicolaidis, 2007).

Unsurprisingly, such an understanding of federalism did not prevail on the Convention floor, neither for self-described federalists nor for those rejecting the F-word, whatever interpretative twist was on offer. After heated debates, the word was dropped from the draft Constitutional treaty. The 'essence' school was doomed by the capture of the federal label over time both by advocates of a 'European state' and, in mirror image, by all those using 'federal' to 'describe the centralized and state-like EU that they did not want, thus confirming the conflation of federalization with integration and centralization' (Fossum & Jachtenfuchs, 2017).

In this sense, while part of the same ideological cluster, federalism and constitutionalism temporarily parted course in 2001–2005 at a time when European elites sought the formal consolidation of the EU as a polity, bringing to fruition the prior 'constitutionalisation' of the Treaties. Constitutionalism beyond the state proved a more capacious concept, as 'essentialist' strategies invoked the ultimate value of Constitutions as means to safeguard individual liberty against encroachment by public authority, thus serving the liberal project of protecting citizens from the state Leviathan (Wind & Weiler, 2003; Isiksel, 2020). Accordingly, one can value a constitution as both a story, offering shared principles of legitimacy for a community, and as a blueprint, laying out a framework to distribute authority. Why would this understanding not be applied to an institution, the EU, that does not claim to be a state? Essentialists argue that it would be a waste not to exploit the legitimation potential of a process of democratic deliberation – the constitutional moment – above and beyond diplomatic bargaining, which could foster EU-level (constitutional) patriotism against the sirens of nationalism (Habermas, 2003; Ferry, 2005; Magnette & Nicolaidis, 2004). A commitment which flirted with nominalism at times – as with affirming that giving up an EU Constitution was the greatest catastrophe possible (Juncker) or that without one, Europe was politically emptying itself (Habermas).

But in the referenda campaigns that ensued in 2004-05 and the ultimate popular rejection, the essence argument was critically weakened on two counts. First, by the absence of its premise of popular assent – what is left of the constitutional ideal when a polity does not rely on each of its peoples to adopt a constitutional treaty? Second, by a diffuse intuition among the citizenry that the essence of constitutionalism was in the end elsewhere, namely to carve out a realm of principles untouchable by day-to-day politics, entrenched in the EU's 'economic constitution'. The day after the constitutional moment, constitutionalism would simply reinforce the EU's antipolitics of informal circles of like-minded and bureaucratized interaction, leading to less not more democratic authorisation (Kaiser, 2007).

It may not be surprising either then, that precisely as the federal and constitutional anchors were falling from grace, scholars and politicians sought refuge in a vaguer and perhaps more inclusive idea, namely cosmopolitanism, with federalism only one of its possible institutional translations. Accordingly, all human beings belong to a single community based on what we share, probably our destiny, possibly our morality, an ideal intuited by the likes of Diogenes in Antiquity, but never actual appropriated by an existing political construct before the EU (Kleingeld, 2009; Cheneval, 2005). Europeanism would be reinvested as an ideal not just for regional governance but as a beacon for a world enthralled by the nationalist fallout of 9/11.

Here the 'essence' of Kant's cosmopolitanism, that humanity ought to consist in 'united nations' sharing basic values and legal norms, lies in its open-endedness (Glendinning, 2011; Rumford, 2005). What this means in practice can be accommodated with various ideological variants – liberal, communitarian, republican, etc. – at the national level. Appropriating the Kantian mantle starts by freeing cosmopolitanism from its metaphysical origins as an expression of harmony between the universe and humans' aspiration to oneness, as well as its enlightenment rebirth as a cultural feature of individuals bent on philanthropy and worldliness. Instead, with

Kant's cosmopolitan law, the moral commitment that the boundary of your own state should not be the boundary of your concern turns into obligations which you owe non-nationals when they are within your own boundaries. The EU's Kantian path has reflected a legal-political understanding of cosmopolitanism seemingly perfectly suited to its ambition to entrench individual or corporate rights across borders by subjecting its states to external legal norms and dispute settlement bodies when it comes to how they treat these non-nationals. Such an ambition may have started as the core of the single market eco-system, but by the 2000s it had become the spirit of a more political ideal, European citizenship, which spoke to the relationship between Kant's formal legal cosmopolitanism having to do with rights, and the individual moral kind that preceded it.

Cosmopolitanism captured the mood of the times, as the EU motto of 'ever closer union' was progressively been supplanted by 'unity in diversity', with an increased emphasis on 'diversity'. For it is precisely this dialectic which cosmopolitanism speaks to, between the universal and differences, as an injunction to reflect on how the many facets of our diversity are coded to adjudicate between inclusiveness and exclusiveness of differences. And in doing so, an injunction to strike a balance between borderless hybridity and exclusive identity, ultimately a call altogether to promote, tolerate and constrain the many kinds of differences which are intrinsic to humanity. This in other words, is universalism as recognition of particularisms (Balibar, 2016). Or in Appiah felicitious phrase, the rooted cosmopolitanism of cosmopolitan patriots (Appiah, 1997). And this is not theory but 'bottom-up' sociological reality, argued Beck and Grande in their *Cosmopolitan Europe* (2007), pointing to Europeans increasingly comfortable with their neighbours, living 'unavoidably side by side' as Kant would say.

None of these takes however ultimately won the day, neither with the public at large nor the political class in its majority. First, without qualifiers, our 'isms' came to be perceived by many as covers for the protection of the privileged few from 'nowhere', and the rights of corporations to operate across borders, overriding nation-bound social protections linked to the commitment of individual states to supporting their specific version of the public interest. Second, while variations on the essentialist argument share a commitment to balancing unity and diversity, the ideological 'look-and-feel' of our isms remains teleological, prescribing an end-point to European togetherness. As programmes of action, they imply that the balancing act is unsustainable, that there will remain a need for transcendence, a moral direction for human progress beyond differences and conflict, as if these were simply contingent, there to be overcome, eventually. Thus, an essentialist pattern emerges: an abstract commitment to equilibrium leads to a drift in practice towards centralized steering, market preponderance and supranational rights, all serving particular entrenched interests, those of nomads against settlers.

Ultimately, if EU integration were to move only in one direction, a regional step towards 'the Kantian hope in a world *domestic* politics (*Weltinnenpolitik*)' in the words of Habermas and Derrida (2003), would this not simply amount to a change of scale towards a continental state, potentially relabelling 'inter-state' wars as 'civil' wars in the process? Why should people find this reassuring?

Composite Strategies

But while essentialist arguments cannot easily be corralled to support an idea of the EU faithful to the third way, the question arises: do we need to throw out the idealistic aspirations with the tainted bathwater? What I call here 'composite strategies' enter this ideological struggle to qualify, specify, attenuate, manipulate or otherwise tame our 'isms' and their pedigree as overly unitary.

While usually concocted in the academic realm, these strategies can be deciphered in political discourses, especially those seeking to explain and justify the institutional and policy remedies conjured up to address the poly-crisis in the EU triggered in 2008, remedies which have mostly consisted in enhancing EU powers. While theorists in turn seek to deconstruct them, these policy developments constitute the ambient material on which they build their critical constructs.

The first and most straightforward way to save Europeanism from its anti-pluralist demons has been to invoke empirical constraints, to set the ideal against the world as is. Pro-EU advocates admit that European citizens are not 'ready' and that such a state of unreadiness is to be respected. Isn't this the proper way to invoke Kant's mantle? By the time he wrote *Perpetual Peace*, Kant no longer found it desirable to establish a global cosmopolitan federation *de jure* but preferred to bet on citizen assent over time (Hurrell, 1990). He imagined a progressive democratization of states brought together by his permanent 'alliance between peoples', in accordance with extant inter-national law and reciprocity, norms freely embraced by citizens through an infinite process of 'gradual approximation' or what Cheneval calls *process cos-mopolitanism* (2005). After all, there are no immutable structures that demand that human loyalty be forever confined to bounded nation-states. If Kant's vision was predicated on observing the extraordinary acceleration of the uni-versalization of human history, what would he say today!

Indeed, Kant's modernity lies in part in his twin apprehension of time. On one plane, cosmopolitanism is a question of *habitus* and patience as mutual tolerance is built over time. It will be a slow process not an endgame, fluid not deterministic. It could even be reversible. The problem of course, is that, as Tocqueville lamented in his time, democracy is about the short term. Politicians and policy makers are creatures of their time and place. All the more so today in Europe, as we labour under what Jonathan White refers to as emergency politics (2019), or what van Middelaar identifies more neutrally as the politics of events (2018). And so we can do with Kant's second plane, whereby progress does happen in fits-and-starts, through crises and the ever-worsening danger of conflict which in turns justifies further inter-state integration.

Thus, a second, related, composite strategy consists in coopting an idea of Europe which both explains and justifies incremental reform in the here and now through the idea of (neo)functionalism, a more neutral 'ism' which affirms the open-endedness of the process of regional integration (Fossum & Jachtenfuchs, 2017). Here the 'functional federalism' features acquired by the EU during the eurocrisis through tightened macroeconomic coordination and the delegation of core powers are no longer the result of grand design, the *de jure* federation rejected by Kant, but have to do with identifying specific areas of 'EU value added', 'economies of scale', or un-internalized 'externalities', while drawing on theories of fiscal federalism, public goods and regulatory economics (Dabrowski, 2016). Yet, embedded in these 'functional fixes' are ideological positions testifying to the fact that ideologies are now frequently found in disaggregated form. To be sure, the EU has been operating under the dynamics of 'functional constitutionalism' for decades, whereby the treaties have been 'constitutionalised' by the ECJ, in particular through its direct effect doctrine, in order to achieve a relatively narrow set of substantive ends, namely promoting market integration (Isiksel, 2016). But since 2010, EU elites have managed to deepen 'functional federalism' and 'functional constitutionalism' under emergency imperatives presented as self-evident (Fossum & Jachtenfuchs, 2017). While 'functional' as a term may not often be used in everyday political language, scholars recognize as such the discursive legitimation employed by politicians to justify their actions as the product of necessity rather than political agency, a political agency that would presumably require the kind of citizen assent desired by a patient Kantian approach. In the process, critical scholars note, functionalism becomes a one-sided credo, amputated from its second, limiting, dimension, and conjured up simply to expand EU competence by stealth.

Is it surprising to find that this brand of composite strategy has engendered some degree of Eurosceptic backlash? More often than not, scholars question the discourse thus mobilized in the ideological arena, whereby the ruling class ended up tainting the very concept (functionalism) it sought to coopt. As a result of functionalism's narrow focus, Isiksel (2016) argues, the EU's constitutional order bears a tenuous relationship to the core emancipatory principle distinguishing modern constitutional rule since its eighteenth century origins, namely popular sovereignty and democratic authorship. The eurocrisis has demonstrated the limits of combining a purposive legal system with a constitutional device of entrenchment to insulate its teleological agenda from democratic challenge. As Borriello and Crespy (2015) note, EU leaders have legitimized the deepening of federal integration in a context where support for more European federalism is at its lowest, which in turn explains why federalism is both taboo and pervasive in French and German leaders' discourse. For many, functional motives have led to an ever more dysfunctional constitutionalism or federalism.

Hence the prevalence of a third, perhaps most widespread composite strategy, which addresses directly the *nature of the beast*. Here, the rhetorical path is more straightforward, namely to dispel the prospect that Europe's nation-states would eventually wither away as autonomous actors. Thus, politicians hardly ever utter the F word without the complementary nod, as with Jacques Delors' 'federation of nation-states', and its countless variants (Ricard-Nihoul & Delors, 2012). Against 'excessive cosmopolitanism akin to deterritorialisation', they embrace an 'open Europe'. After all, the failed constitutional moment was only about drafting a constitutional 'treaty', thus still an instrument of international law.

To be sure, cosmopolitans are not only wary of states but of *nation*-states which compound the exclusionary character of ethnic identity with the arbitrary potential of state power. But while this concern may warrant the transfer of some powers from the national to the supranational, it does not mean that they support a global or even European super-state (Archibugi et al., 1998). Hence the defence of what Ypi aptly termed statist cosmopolitanism, according to which 'political communities provide the unique associative sphere in which cosmopolitanism obtains political agency, may be legitimately enforced and cohesively maintained' (Ypi, 2008). Ypi's cosmopolitanism seeks to combine ethical universalism and political particularism, thus charting a third way between the orthodoxy of supranational law and of national cultural identity. Here, cosmopolitism can coexist with state sovereignty and therefore national political boundaries if this is predicated on the slow enlargement of moral boundaries, in particular through civic education, where the ties of bounded citizenship and the duties of cosmopolitan citizenship end up reinforcing each other.

Scholars have provided countless variations on this balancing act. (Euro)-constitutionalism can accommodate a statist cosmopolitan vision provided the contract and process leading up to it create the right democratic space. Critical theories of human rights stress the compatibility between European constitutionalism and national sovereignty, arguing that legal cosmopolitanism is compatible with democratic self-determination through a productive process whereby each level of governance interacts with the others to interpret and enhance the norms in question (Benhabib, 2016; Balibar, 2016). Given the fundamental incompleteness of cosmopolitan rights, self-government tends to be a precondition for enjoying them. Similarly, legal theorists have articulated a constitutional pluralist vision of an EU characterized by mutually conflicting claims of authority without the need to resolve them through hierarchy, but predicated on the mutual recognition of each other's claims (Maduro, 2003). In other words, if constitutional legitimacy were grounded on organizing collective self-rule by the people, why would it not accommodate the idea of joint sovereignty of peoples (Cheneval & Nicolaidis, 2017)? Musical metaphors seem to offer an apt referent for this multiplicity of time and space scales, from Bodei's cosmopolitan 'multitonality' to the contrapunctual of constitutional pluralists (Balibar, 2016; Maduro, 2003).

Here, we find the controversy over Kant exegesis at its more heated (Ferry, 2005; Archibugi et al., 1998). Suffice to say that proponents of a (nation)state-friendly reading of our 'isms' note that in his mature years of *Perpetual Peace*, Kant seemed more interested in thinking through the real-world process of recognition of separate polities within his *Völkerbund* (confederation of peoples) than elaborating on his *Völkerstaat* (polity of peoples) as an ultimate ideal (Kant, 1991[1795]). And even the latter, far from abolishing the existence of states, would transform them into law-abiding entities, considering that individual freedom depended to a large degree on legally orientated state sovereignty. Armed with this interpretative lens, Ferry for instance criticised Habermas for transforming the tension between Kant's *Völkerstaat* and his earlier presuppositions on universal human rights into an 'incompatibility', thus failing to acknowledge the mediating role played by states in sustaining cosmopolitanism (Habermas, 1997; Ferry, 2005). Not only does effective cosmopolitan law rely on the host state but Kant foresaw the risk that overbearing external intervention in the name of foreigners' rights can entail, at a minimum constraining host states' ability to defend the social economic rights of their own population, at worse justifying coercive colonialism (Hurrell, 2013).

In short, we need systematically to contrast the bright and dark sides of federal constitutional constraints or cosmopolitan designs. This is true from within but also from without Europe, where European-style cosmopolitanism can be seen to flirt with imperialism rather than emancipation. It matters, therefore, to ask who has the legitimacy but also the power to adjudicate in a cosmopolitan scheme. Which leads to a fourth kind of composite strategy relevant to those preoccupied with Europe's role in the world who would like to believe that cosmopolitan rights not only respect but also strengthen self-determination, including *against* Europeans. If 'we cannot not want' a cosmopolitan world, as Spivak famously proclaimed in her critique of what she calls post-colonial reason, this needs be a *post-colonial cosmopolitism* (Spivak, 1999; Pollock et al., 2000). Which in turn calls for the EU to acknowledge its own post-colonial condition (Fisher-Onar & Nicolaidis, 2015).

Can cosmopolitanism escape Eurocentric teleology? This would ultimately require inverting the relationship between unity and diversity in the Kantian worldview. When, in Kant's time, the Humboldt brothers promoted their pluralist version of cosmopolitism, a 'cosmopolitism of differences' in Marramao's felicitous phrase (2009) echoing Novalis' or Bloch's multiversum, they sought to start with the kind of radical pluralism which acknowledges the ways in which different cultures ground people's sense of human purpose, our relationship with nature and the cosmos. The free-floating use of the term cosmopolitanism is meaningless in a world where an array of cosmopolitanisms must be cobbled together through quite disparate histories (Baban et al., 2015). But if the cosmopolitanism of differences ends up being a stand against eurocentricism, inspired by the infinite multiplicity yet equal worth of human 'sites', taken to its ultimate logic, this stand means that each of these sites might itself require different degrees of closure to exist and survive as such. This includes the EU as a whole but also its constituent parts (Balibar, 2016). For cosmopolitanism from below to represent a revolutionary act of collective self-determination, all experiences of emancipation must be confronted in a process of mutual recognition of autonomy. Ultimately, we would need to observe the human race from *outside* in order to assess the merits of the cosmopolitan credo. Except, post-colonial cosmopolitans tell us, if the role of extra-terrestrials can be taken up by the extra-territorial, the subalterns, marginals, excluded or otherwise, who have so far failed to participate in the cosmopolitan design (Szendy, 2011). Excluded from without or from within, *même combat*!

This cursory probe into a sample of the composite strategies mobilized to bolster a third way understanding of Europeanism may offer horizons for our political imagination, but also suggests that these strategies can easily get lost in translation. Conceptual ambiguity does not easily work as mobilizing ideology. In fact, more often than not they provide a foil for taking the EU to task. It may be that EU politics is too messy to accommodate the Kantian mantle. In the end and whatever kind of composite rescue is attempted, cosmopolitanism is seen to pre-empt the local, federalism to pre-empt the state, and constitutionalism to pre-empt the political. And in the process we may sadly find that, as quipped by Peguy, 'Kant has such pure hands that he has no hand at all.'

Pollination Strategies

It was refreshing to hear Ursula von der Leyden explain when she became President of the Commission in 2019 that she no longer advocated the EU becoming a federal state or 'United States of Europe', that her dream for Europe had become 'more mature and more realistic', and that 'unity in diversity' was different from 'federalism'. Pollination strategies start with the intuition that the continued relevance of old labels might be better served by the presence of their absence, as only their evanescent 'pollen' is transferred from concepts to reality in order to fertilize new grounds. With these strategies, our isms may disappear as explicit referent but they remain part of the EU's DNA as adjectives, attributes, connotations, echoes.

In fact, the last two decades of politicization in the EU can be thought of as a coming-out, an unfolding understanding of our three isms as ideological constructs themselves. By bringing into sharper focus the distributional impact of EU policies, the multifaceted crisis has sucked the ideological Gini out of the bottle. In this context, our 'isms' become collateral damage in related ideological struggles, seen as conceptual props for the institutionalization in the EU of a certain brand of neoliberalism and for the disembedding of socio-economic contracts (Kaiser, 2007, Hien, in this special issue). They risk becoming so immiserated by their ideological appropriation that nothing might be left to save. Accordingly, no discursive or semantic treatment can rid cosmopolitanism of its connotation as an elite project (Vieten, 2018), federalism of its connotation as a centralizing ploy, or constitutionalism of its connotation as an attempt to dissolve Europe's many tribes into a single European people.

As a response to the critical onslaught, pollination strategies tend to facilitate paradigm shifts in defense of a third way for the EU and the bringing together of philosophical debates over normative arguments with the positive methods which prevail in the social sciences. We can ask what is lost and gained by selective rejection and appropriation of concepts, dropping existing frames, or endorsing conceptual innovations such as 'demoicracy'. The beauty of the philosophical traditions behind our 'isms' is that they come with baggage, insights, controversies, and exegesis; in short, intellectual gravitas. But with such baggage, we are also burdened with semantic argumentation, obfuscations, and interpretative turf battles. Pollination strategies enable us to extract insights from these alternative isms, while allowing the conversation to move on without the baggage of extant theory. If this is the case, pollination may be about valuing the questions raised by our isms, themselves inspired by the comparisons, histories and traditions they entail, without burdening the debate with the labels they provide. Thus, the question aptly put by Fossum and Jachtenfuchs (2017) can be extended to the challenges encountered by all three isms: is the EU unfit for them or does it bring up challenges that these theories do not have ready-made answers for? In effect, when you are told, 'I would not start from here', pollination strategies can help look for answers elsewhere. We could start for instance, by:

Bringing the state back in. It does not makes sense, does it, to leave the European project so vulnerable to sovereignist sirens when the EC was designed to rescue European states, and when to this day it finds its best *raison d'etre* in creating space for them to *exist* in a Hobbesian world (this article is written under the early shadow of the COVID-19 crisis). Say you argue that the EU is not a state in the coercive and symbolic Weberian sense, even if it constrains and coordinates core state powers. If so, the label 'EU federation', even of nation-states, will not do. Naming the beast, as treaty makers have done, is about other terms such as 'community' (pace Weiler), or better yet, 'union' in contradistinction with 'unity' (Nicolaidis, 2018). This union can be pollenized – as long as it remains a federal or cosmopolitan 'union' not a federal or cosmopolitan 'state'. And on the other side of the equation, 'statism' is reserved for member states, while the cosmopolitan pollen seeds the state itself – rather than pointing to what happens beyond it – a state which is expected to 'evince a cosmopolitan regard for the citizens of other states by treating them as moral equals and recognizing mutual cosmopolitan obligations' (Bellamy, 2019). After all, the EU has demonstrated how Kant's cosmopolitan law of trans-border rights can reach much deeper than his original notion of 'hospitality' without requiring a supranational state-like guardian or overrding national majority rights (Orgad, 2015).

Bringing politics back in. If Europeanism is to ward-off democratic scepticism, we need to extract from our 'isms' that which strengthens both national democracies and transnational democratic politics. It seems that the EU has taken too far Kant's idealized view that 'all politics must bend the knee before right' – as if morality could be subcontracted to philosopher kings, and law trump democratic political debate. In sustaining democracy, responsibilities on the ground and powers delegated upwards cannot diverge radically. But the argument does not boil down to sovereignty in the name of democracy. Instead the EU's ideal of other-regarding legal orders and legalized empathy must be embedded in the opening up of our democracies to each other. To those who argue against constraining state sovereignty in the name of democracy, offer another Kantian angle – the thought that popular and state sovereignty are not the same thing, that politics within and beyond the state are inseparable, with causality working in both directions, not only as democracies beget peace but as they are in turn perfected by the institutionalized gaze of other nations upon them. In a demoicratic EU therefore, we need to find ways for citizens to debate across borders the fundamental tradeoff: whether the EU's federal and cosmopolitan traits are worth the losses experienced in collective autonomy, cultural protection and economic self-determination. Sure, a renewed constitutional process could impose a greater burden of legitimation through deliberation. But let's ask, shall we, how this time around, it could be emancipatory and conducive to social and democratic innovation rather than ossifying – of hegemony, exclusion or injustice. This might require nothing less than a permanent citizens assembly to hold EU decision makers to account.

Bringing citizenship back in. Ultimately, reasserting the centrality of politics rests on a certain idea of citizenship, not that of the atomized individual of our dark modernity, but the individual as the new citizen of a digital era, mastering the politics as interconnection. From her viewpoint, cosmopolitan rights can suggest various kinds of 'democratic iterations' in Benhabib's apt formula, including through forum shopping, the forging of transnational alliances, the empowerment of minorities or the exploitation of hybrid citizenship (Benhabib, 2016). The cosmopolitan key is found in people's struggle among all levels of organization at once, whereby rights come to be contested and contextualized, invoked and revoked, posited and positioned. Irreducibly, as Hannah Arendt reminded us, these rights stand as shields against all potentially abusive and arbitrary power and as preconditions for our individual and collective emancipation (Lacroix & Pranchere, 2018).

Bringing power back in. To the extent that the EU has been an anti-hegemonic project *within* Europe as the key to peace, it rests on the collective memory that mitigating power asymmetries between states has historical been the key to peace in Europe. Think of the role of small buffer states in seventeenth and eighteenth century balance of power. Thus, if cooperative federalism relies on a compromise between the formal equality of unequal states and equality between citizens, there were good reasons for the EU to privilege the former (Magnette & Nicolaidis, 2004). Sadly, these lessons are slowly forgotten, as betrayed by the reforms in the weighting of votes in the Lisbon Treaty (Czaputowicz & Kleinowski, 2018), or by the asymmetric interference upon smaller states like Greece or Portugal practiced during the EU crisis. To be sure, it is fair to ask under what conditions the EU is to confront the reality of international anarchy where the capacity for effective power matters greatly. Indeed Kant never stopped wrestling with the problem that a legal constitutional order (of a state or in our case of the EU) depends on political conditions external to itself. But there is no reason to believe that a continued commitment to taming power asymmetries internally weakens the capacity collectively to assert power externally.

Bringing decentering back in. Federal covenants serve a fundamental purpose: to tame *horizontal* domination between states thanks to a 'shared centre', in contrast with empire-like polity where the centre belongs to a single ruler. But sadly, federal restraints generally end up trading horizontal for vertical domination in order to deal with states' disagreement over the interpretation of their mutual commitments. Binding rules above states become coercive in the absence of sufficient degrees of trust between states. If the EU system of constraining the nationalist excess of its member states has at least partially succeeded, is it not right to ask: what shall constrain it in turn? As Olstrom and others have argued, we can deliver Madisonian safeguards against the tyranny of factions, majorities, corrupt power and so on without an overbaring centre (Ostrom, 2008). Instead, the best way to square the circle between vertical and horizontal domination is to rely on polycentric, non-centralized structures, where the state or other sites of governance such as cities and regions support each other's governing capacity, a horizontal approach to sharing sovereignty predicated on the value of proximity, municipalism and localism, heterogenous preferences and the legitimacy of bounded social contracts (Nicolaidis & van Zeben, 2019; Hooghe & Marks, 2013).

Bringing the world back in. In the end, we need to ask under what conditions Europeans can sustainably cut the Kantian mantle to their regional measurements. The Kantian ideal for the progressive diffusion of liberal values and democratic interdependence to the entire world can still be rescued, but the charge of hypocrisy looms large. The idea of cosmopolitan Europe becomes an oxymoron if it is simply a unilateral strategy, predicated on the gradual expansion of the EU design to more states, through some kind of soft liberal crusading. It is hard to escape the colonial echoes of legitimizing interventionism in the name of safeguarding the economic freedoms of European or Western firms around the world, and the charge that Europe's cosmopolitan brand can appear to others as morally whitewashed imperialism (Walzer, 1989). And when it comes to opening our borders, the cosmopolitan view does not necessarily require the same borderlessness externally and internally, but at least a consistent reading between obligations to EU and non-EU citizens in terms of recognition (Strumia, 2013; Baban et al., 2015).

Some may argue that pollination strategies risk ending up stressing what the EU is not rather than what it is. Maybe pollinizers cannot escape the accusation of being too vague and non-committal. Or maybe there is a risk that the conceptual vacuum created by giving up the labels of not the spirit of our 'isms' would be filled by the appropriation of Europeanism by European populists who defend the 'real Europe' as the guardian of civilizational identity, Christianity, and 'true' European values. Yet it can also be argued that pollination strategies reflect not a tactical retreat but an intellectual commitment. Maybe there is nothing problematic for the EU in trundling along as different things to different people (Lacroix & Nicolaidis, 2010). Perhaps in the end, the *tabula rasa* approach finds its greatest merit in opening up our European imaginaries, keeping our politicians and citizens alike form relying on conceptual clutches, mindful of the fact that such a 'complex democracy' as the EU (Innerarity, 2018) cannot easily be labelled. Pollination strategies bring into focus the role of agency over the actual or desirable nature of the EU. Activists in particular do not need to defend an 'ism' wholesale in order to extract from it useful food for thought, conducive to their own democratic imagination ad appropriation of the European project.

Conclusion

To the extent that ideological struggles can be seen as competitions over the control of political language, debates about the nature of Europeanism have long clung to the 'isms' discussed in this article, transforming them in the process from philosophical concepts into ideologies. Yet, because ideologies are processed through filters of cultural understandings and misunderstandings, we must explore the recurring patterns of their changing content and popularized variants that secure success or failure for their public impact (Freeden, 1996). I have argued here that one way to go about teasing out such patterns is to ask what is gained and lost under alternative strategies, tentatively classified as essentialist, composite and pollination strategies. Specifically, in keeping with the transformative agenda of critical theory, I have asked whether and how these different strategies can contribute to articulating a 'demoicratic' third way for the EU (Manners, 2020).

To be sure, this exercise could be viewed as a kind of anti-politics, abstracting from the real world accounting of winners and losers. To the extent that the EU has been defended for its post-ideological character, focused on effectiveness as a 'regulatory state' or on fighting off the dangerous ideological revivals of 'nationalism' and 'populism', it may matter little whether we characterize it as cosmopolitan or not, federal or not, constitutional or not. Nevertheless, it is hard to deny that Europeanism is itself an ideologically motivated project, portrayed either from the left as a bastion of 'neo-liberal capitalism' or from the right as a 'socialist super-state'.

In assessing these competing claims, teasing out the truly ideological import of our philosophical placeholders is no bad place to start. Cosmopolitanism, Federalism and Constitutionalism. Each contains a universe of meanings in constant mutation, and with them the messages they are capable of transmitting. Decoding the ideological struggles they give rise to is an attempt to make the invisible discernible and thus to answer Camus' call for better naming the form of our global togetherness. Both Europe and our democratic health can only be better for it.

Acknowledgements

I would like to thank Michael Freeden, Andrew Hurrell and Jonathan White as well as two anonymous reviewers for their comments.

Disclosure statement

No potential conflict of interest was reported by the author(s).

References

Appiah, K. A. (1997). Cosmopolitan patriots. *Critical Inquiry*, *23*(3), 617–639.

Archibugi, D., Held, D., & Kohler, M. (Eds.). (1998). *Re-imagining Political Community: Studies in Cosmopolitan Democracy* (pp. 198–230). Polity.

Baban, F., Ponzanesi, S., Colpani, G., & 2015. (2015). Cosmopolitanism from the margins. Redefining the idea of Europe through postcoloniality. In S. Ponzanesi & G. Colpani (Eds.), *Postcolonial transitions in Europe. Context, practices and politics* (pp. 371–390). Rowman and Littlefield International.

Balibar, É. (2016). *Des universels: essais et conférences*. Éditions Galilée.

Beck, U., & Grande, E. (2007). *Cosmopolitan Europe*. Polity Press.

Bellamy, R. (2019). *A Republican Europe of States: Cosmopolitanism, inter governmentalism and democracy in the EU*. Cambridge University Press.

Benhabib, S. (2016). The new sovereigntism and transnational law: Legal utopianism, democratic scepticism and statist realism. *GlobCon*, *5*, 109.

Benz, A., & Broschek, J. (Eds.). (2013). *Federal Dynamics: Continuity, Change, and the Varieties of Federalism*. Oxford University Press.

Bohman, J., & Lutz-Bachmann, M. (Eds.). (1997). *Perpetual Peace: Essays on Kant's Cosmopolitan Ideal*. MIT Press.

Borriello, A., & Crespy, A. (2015). How to not speak the 'F-word': Federalism between mirage and imperative in the euro crisis. *European Journal of Political Research*, *54*(3), 502–524. https://doi.org/10.1111/1475-6765.12093

Cavallar, G. (1994). Kant's society of nations: Free federation or world republic? *Journal of the History of Philosophy*, *32*(3), 461–482. https://doi.org/10.1353/hph.1994.0057

Chalmers, D., Jachtenfuchs, M., & Joerges, C. (Eds.). (2016). *The end of the Eurocrats' dream*. Cambridge University Press.

Cheneval, F. (2005). *La Cité des Peuples*. Le Cerf.

Cheneval, F., & Nicolaidis, K. (2017). The social construction of demoicracy in the European union. *European Journal of Political Theory*, *16*(2), 235–260. https://doi.org/10.1177/1474885116654696

Cheneval, F., & Schimmelfennig, F. (2013). The case for demoicracy in the European union. *JCMS: Journal of Common Market Studies*, *51*(2), 334–350.

Czaputowicz, J., & Kleinowski, M. (2018). The voting systems in the Council of the EU and the Bundesrat – What do they tell us about European Federalism? *Perspectives on Federalism*, *10*(1), 176–201.

Dabrowski, M. (2016). The future of the European Union: Towards a functional federalism. *Acta Oeconomica*, *66*(s1), 21–48. https://doi.org/10.1556/032.2016.66.s1.2

Díez Medrano, J., (Eds.). (2010). Europe's political identity: Public sphere and public opinion. In J. Lacroix & K. Nicolaidis (Eds.), *European Stories: Intellectual Debates on Europe in National Contexts* (pp. 315–333). Oxford University Press.

Elazar, D. J. (1987). *Exploring Federalism*. University of Alabama Press.

Fabbrini, S. (2010). *Compound Democracies: Why the United States and Europe Are Becoming Similar* (rev. ed). Oxford University Press.

Ferry, J. M. (2005). *Europe, la voie Kantienne*. Humanité, Cerf.

Fisher-Onar, N., & Nicolaidis, K. (2015). Europe's post-imperial condition. In Behr, H. & Stivachtis, Y.A. (Eds.), *Revisiting the European Union as Empire* (pp. 115–133). Routledge.

Fossum, J. E., & Jachtenfuchs, M. (2017). Federal challenges and challenges to federalism. Insights from the EU and federal states. *Journal of European Public Policy*, *24*(4), 467–485. https://doi.org/10.1080/13501763.2016.1273965

Fossum, J. E., & Menendez, A. J. (2011). *The Constitution's Gift: A Constitutional Theory for a Democratic European Union*. Rowman & Littlefield.

Freeden, M. (1996). *Ideologies and Political Theory: A Conceptual Approach*. Oxford University Press.

Glencross, A., & Trechsel, A. H. (2010). *EU Federalism and Constitutionalism – The Legacy of Altiero Spinelli*. Lexington Books.

Glendinning, S. (2011). Europe, for Example, *LSEQ (31)*.

Habermas, J. (1997). Kant's idea of Perpetual peace, with the Benefit of Two hundred years' Hindsight. In B. a. Lutz-Bachmann (Ed.), *Perpetual Peace: Essays on Kant's Cosmopolitan Ideal* (pp. 113–153). MIT Press.

Habermas, J. (2003). Towards a cosmopolitan Europe. *Journal of Democracy*, *14*(4), 86–100. https://doi.org/10.1353/jod.2003.0077

Habermas, J., & Derrida, J. (2003). February 15, or what binds Europeans together: A plea for a common foreign policy, beginning in the core of Europe. *Constellations (Oxford, England)*, *10*(3), 291–297. https://doi.org/10.1111/1467-8675.00333

Hoffe, O. (1994). *Immanuel Kant*. Suny Press.

Hooghe, L., & Marks, G. (2013). Beyond federalism: Estimating and explaining the territorial structure of government. *Publius: The Journal of Federalism*, *43*(2), 179–204. https://doi.org/10.1093/publius/pjs029

Hurrell, A. (1990). Kant and the Kantian paradigm of international relations. *Review of International Studies*, *16*(3), 183–205. https://doi.org/10.1017/S026021050011246X

Hurrell, A. (2013). Kant and intervention revisited. In Recchia, S., & Welsh, J. M. (Eds.). *Just and unjust military intervention: European thinkers from Vitoria to Mill*. Cambridge University Press.

Innerarity, D. (2018). *Democracy in Europe: A political philosophy of the EU*. Palgrave Macmillan.

Isiksel, T. (2016). *Europe's Functional Constitution: A Theory of Constitutionalism Beyond the State*. Oxford University Press.

Isiksel, T. (2020). Cosmopolitanism and international economic Institutions. *The Journal of Politics*, *82*(1), 211–224.

Kaiser, W. (2007). *Christian Democracy and the Origins of European Union*. Cambridge University Press.

Kant, I. (1991). Perpetual peace: A philosophical sketch. In I. Kant, *Political writings* (pp. 93–130). H. B. Nisbet (Trans.). H. Reiss (Ed.), (2nd ed.). Cambridge University Press (Original work published 1795).

Kant, I. (1996). *The metaphysics of morals*. M. Gregor (Ed.). Cambridge University Press (Original work published 1797).

Kant, I. (1997). *Groundwork of the metaphysics of morals*. M. Gregor (Ed.). Cambridge University Press (Original work published in 1785).

Kelemen, R. D., & Nicolaidis, K. (2007). Bringing federalism back in. In *Handbook of European Union Politics* (pp. 301–316). Sage.

Kleingeld, P. (2009). Kant's changing cosmopolitanism. In Schmidt (Ed.), *Kant's Aim for a Universal History with a Cosmopolitan Aim* (pp. 171–186). Cambridge University Press.

Kurunmäki, J., & Marjanen, J. (2018). Isms, ideologies and setting the agenda for public debate. *Journal of Political Ideologies*, *23*(3), 256–282.

Lacroix, J., & Nicolaïdis, K. (2010). *European stories: Intellectual debates on Europe in national contexts*. Oxford University Press..

Lacroix, J., & Pranchere, J. Y. (2018). *Human Rights on Trial: A Genealogy of the Critique of Human Rights*. Cambridge University Press.

Lechner, S. (2017). Anarchy in International Relations. In *Oxford Research Encyclopedia of International Studies*.

Linklater, A. (1998). *The Transformation of Political Community: Ethical Foundations of the Post-Westphalian era*. Univ of South Carolina Press.

Maduro, M. P. (2003). Contrapunctual Law: Europe's Constitutional Pluralism in Action. In N. Walker (Ed.), *Sovereignty in transition*. Bloomsbury Publishing.

Magnette, P., & Nicolaidis, K. (2004). The European Convention: Bargaining in the shadow of rhetoric. *West European Politics*, *27*(3), 381–404.

Manners, I. (2020). Critical social theory approaches to European integration. In Y. Stivachtis, D. Bigo, T. Diez, E. Fanoulis, & B. Rosamond (Eds.), *The Routledge handbook of critical European studies*. Routledge.

Marramao, G. (2009). Passaggio a occidente: filosofia e globalizzazione, *Bollati Boringhieri*.

McCormick, J. (2010). *Europeanism*. Oxford University Press.

Menon, A., & Schain, M. A. (Eds.). (2006). *Comparative Federalism: The European Union and the United States in Comparative Perspective*. Oxford University Press.

Nicolaïdis, K. (2004). We, the Peoples of Europe. *Foreign Affairs*, *83*, 97.

Nicolaïdis, K. (2013). European demoicracy and its crisis. *JCMS: Journal of Common Market Studies*, *51*(2), 351–369. https://doi.org/10.1111/jcms.12006

Nicolaidis, K. (2018). Braving the waves? Europe's constitutional settlement at twenty. *JCMS: Journal of Common Market Studies*, *56*(7), 1614–1630.

Nicolaidis, K., & Howse, R. (Eds.). (2001). *The Federal Vision: Legitimacy and Levels of Governance in the United States and the European Union*. Oxford University Press.

Nicolaidis, K., & Van Zeben, J. (2019). Polycentric Subsidiarity. In J. Van Zeben & A. Bobić (Eds.), *Polycentricity in the European Union* (pp. 78–107). Cambridge University Press.

Orgad, L. (2015). *The Cultural Defense of Nations: A liberal theory of majority rights*. Oxford University Press.

Ostrom, V. (2008). *The Political Theory of a Compound Republic: Designing the American Experiment* (3rd ed.). Lexington Books.

Pollock, S., Bhahba, H. K., Breckenridge, C. A., & Chakrabarty, D. (2000). Cosmopolitanisms. *Public Culture*, *12*(3), 577–589. https://doi.org/10.1215/08992363-12-3-577

Ricard-Nihoul, G., & Delors, J. (2012). *Pour une Fédération européenne d'États-nations*. Larcier.

Risse, T. (2015). *European public spheres*. Cambridge University Press.

Rumford, C. (2005). Cosmopolitanism and Europe. Towards a New EU Studies agenda? *Innovation*, *18*(1), 1–9.

Schrag Sternberg, C. (2013). *The struggle for EU legitimacy, 1950–2005*. Palgrave MacMillan.

Spivak, G. C. (1999). *A critique of postcolonial reason: Toward a history of the vanishing present*. Harvard university press.

Strumia, F. (2013). *Supranational citizenship and the challenge of diversity: Immigrants, citizens and Member States in the EU*. Martinus Nijhoff Publishers.

Szendy, P. (2011). *Kant chez les extraterrestres. Philosofictions cosmopolitiques*. Minuit.

Van Middelaar, L. (2018). *Quand l'Europe improvise. Dix ans de crises politiques*. Editions Gallimard.

Vieten, U. M. (2018). Ambivalences of cosmopolitanisms, elites and far-right populisms in twenty-first century Europe. In Fitzi, G., Mackert, J., & Turner, B. S. (Eds.), *Populism and the Crisis of Democracy* (pp. 101–118). Routledge.

Walzer, M. (1989). *Nation and Universe*. The Tanner Lectures on Human Values.

White, J. (2019). *Politics of Last Resort: Governing by Emergency in the European Union*. Oxford University Press.

Wind, M., & Weiler, J. H. H. (2003). (Eds). *Constitutionalism beyond the State*. Cambridge University Press.

Ypi, L. L. (2008). Statist cosmopolitanism. *Journal of Political Philosophy*, *16*(1), 48–71. https://doi.org/10.1111/j.1467-9760.2008.00308.x

The European Union as a Christian democracy: a heuristic approach

Carlo Invernizzi Accetti ⓘD

ABSTRACT
While the historical role played by Christian Democrats in the construction of the European Union (EU) is well-known and amply documented, the impact this has had on the EU as it exists today has received virtually no attention in the relevant academic literature. This paper addresses the question by examining the heuristic purchase offered by distinctively Christian Democratic categories in describing the EU's current institutional framework. It argues that, in at least three respects, such categories appear more adequate than the ones that are more commonly used in the literature. First, the EU is more adequately described as a polity based on the principle of 'subsidiarity' than either a federation or a set of intergovernmental treaties. Second, its political regime is better understood as 'consociative' than either demo(i)cratic or technocratic. Finally, its socio-economic policies are closer to a model of 'social market economy' than either social democracy or neoliberalism.

Introduction

This paper explores the potential contribution of several key Christian Democratic concepts to the field of EU studies. The main argument is that looking at the European Union through the lens of these concepts can help to make sense of some its distinctive features that otherwise appear incomprehensible or difficult to reconcile with one another, thereby providing a useful heuristic framework for thinking about the EU's overall ideological character.

The paper builds on a broader body of literature that has recently highlighted the key role played by Christian Democratic actors and thinkers in driving the process of European integration from the start (on this point see for instance: Durand, 1995; Kalyvas, 1996; Lamberts, 1997; Kaiser, 2007; Kalyvas & Van Kersbergen, 2010; Muller, 2013). Its method is however rather different. Most of the existing literature on the relationship between Christian Democracy and the European Union has adopted a historical approach, focused on uncovering the *causal* impact of Christian Democratic actors and ideas on the process of construction of the European Union. In contrast, this paper adopts a heuristic approach, whose purpose is to establish the extent to which Christian Democratic concepts and categories offer an adequate *interpretive framework* for capturing the distinctive nature of the institutional framework that has resulted from the process of European integration.

More specifically, the paper focuses on three aspects of the European Union's current institutional framework that are the object of scholarly controversy: (1) the *type of polity* it instantiates; (2) the nature of its *political regime*; (3) the content of its *socio-economic policies*. In each case, I begin by examining the main conceptual categories that have been used in the existing academic literature to describe the relevant aspect of the EU's institutional framework, pointing to some limitations and interpretive problems they give rise to. I then suggest that concepts drawn from the Christian Democratic ideological tradition can help to solve these interpretive puzzles, and therefore shed a more revealing light on the distinctive nature of the EU's institutional framework. This leads to the (admittedly provocative) conclusion that the EU is better described as 'Christian Democratic' institutional framework than in terms of any of the other currently dominant descriptors – at least in the areas I will be focusing on.

One further preliminary remark is in order before delving into the substance of the analysis. This concerns the definition of Christian Democracy, and in particular of the specific concepts I will be extrapolating from this ideological tradition for the purpose of interpreting the EU's institutional framework. As in the case of all ideological traditions, there is an ongoing scholarly debate over what can be considered to count as a properly 'Christian Democratic' set of principles and values (on this point, see: Durand, 1995; Kalyvas, 1996; Kselman & Buttigieg, 2003; Kalyvas & Van Kersbergen, 2010). Adopting a 'morphological' approach drawn from Michael Freeden's seminal work on political ideologies, it nonetheless seems possible to identify a 'core' of reciprocally defining concepts which demarcate the Christian Democratic ideology as a specific constellation of meanings attached to key political notions (on this point, see for instance: Freeden, 1996, 2006). On this basis, I have recently attempted to systematize the substantive content of the Christian Democratic ideology in a book-length monograph entitled precisely *What is Christian Democracy?* which applies Freeden's methodology to the Christian Democratic ideological tradition (see: Invernizzi-Accetti, 2019). This paper therefore draws on my previous research on the topic, while also extending its scope by demonstrating the heuristic value of a morphological reconstruction of the Christian Democratic ideology's core concepts for the purpose of interpreting the distinctive nature of the European Union's institutional framework.

Polity Type: Beyond Federalism And Intergovernmentalism

The contemporary academic debate on the type of polity created by EU institutions is dominated by two conceptual categories: federalism and intergovernmentalism. On one hand, federalists maintain that the EU constitutes a distinct 'political system', which displays most of the key features traditionally associated with statehood, while at the same time devolving some of its functions to lower levels of administration, such as member states, regions and municipalities (see for instance: Hix, 2005; Schmidt, 2005). To be sure, most federalists also recognize that the European Union has not yet reached the level of political and institutional integration characteristic of more established federations – such as the United States or Germany – so the European Union is more often described as a 'quasi federal' (Hix, 2005), 'partially federal' (Piris, 2012), or 'sui generis' (Tömmel, 2011) type of federation, rather than a full-blown federal state.

At the opposite end of the spectrum, Andrew Moravcsik has suggested that 'the EC can be analyzed as a successful intergovernmental regime, designed to manage economic interdependence through negotiated policy coordination' (Moravcsik, 1993, p. 474). From this point of view, the EU is ultimately nothing more than a set of international treaties negotiated by independent sovereign states, each pursuing their own separate self-interest, for the purpose of coordinating their policy responses to specific issues or problems that are better managed together (on this point, see also: Hoffman, 1995; Milward, 2000; Moravcsik, 1998, 2002).

While intergovernmentalists usually contend that the specific political competences assigned to the European Union in its founding treaties fall short of those assigned to (either federal or national) states by domestic constitutions, federalists usually respond by pointing out that its assigned competences far exceed those of any other intergovernmental organization, both in terms of scope and capacity of securing compliance from member states. The debate between federalists and intergovernmentalists therefore boils down to a disagreement over whether European institutions or member states ultimately have the upper hand in an ongoing struggle of power between them (on this point, see: Eising & Poguntke, 2011). As several commentators have noted, however, this may well be an 'insoluble question' as long as it is posed in a 'binary' and 'exclusive' way, since the answer clearly depends on the specific policy area and political conjuncture that is being considered (on this point, see: Magnette, 2017).

In addition, there are also a number of deeper conceptual problems which challenge the descriptive adequacy of *both* the notions of federalism and intergovernmentalism for capturing the specific type of polity instantiated by the European Union. To begin with, it is worth pointing out that neither of these notions is ever mentioned explicitly in the founding Treaties of the

EU, and both also appear to be studiously avoided in its secondary legislation and official documents. At a minimum, this tells us that the European Union neither understands itself, nor wants to be perceived, as either a federation or a set of intergovernmental treaties (or even something in between), but rather as something else.

Secondly, it is also worth highlighting how implicitly dependent on the paradigm of *sovereignty* both the notions of federalism and intergovernmentalism remain, even while pointing to a variety of possible displacements, transformations and interactions. If a federal Europe is essentially a supranational political system that transfers at least some of the traditional prerogatives of state sovereignty to the European level, an intergovernmental Europe is nothing but a collection of interacting and reciprocally constraining sovereign states. This poses a problem if we are to take seriously the one insight that almost all commentators on the EU's institutional framework seem to agree on. Namely, that it constitutes a new type of 'post-sovereign' political order, which disaggregates sovereignty into a variety of separate 'competence areas' and 'layers of governance' (on this point, see: Hooghe & Marks, 2001; Bache & Flinders, 2004).

While descriptively adequate in a negative sense, this notion of a 'post-sovereign' EU still has the problem that it doesn't positively name the specific type of polity that replaces the previous paradigm of sovereignty, giving unity and coherence to the various 'layers of governance' that constitute the European Union's institutional framework. In this respect, I contend that the concept of *subsidiarity* – which emerges directly out of the Christian Democratic ideological tradition, and also has the advantage of being mentioned explicitly in the EU's founding treaties and jurisprudence – offers a more powerful interpretive lens.

As an extensive academic literature has already pointed out, the concept of subsidiarity stems precisely from a critique of the concept of state sovereignty, which was developed in the middle part of the twentieth century by a number of different Christian – and in particular Christian Democratic – authors, in order to formulate an overarching vision of the nature and function of public authorities which would prove less inimical to spontaneous forms of social (and in particular religious) organization compared to traditional nation states (on this point, see: Delsol, 1992, 1993; Follesdal, 1998; Van Kersbergen & Verbek, 2004; Barroche, 2012; Invernizzi-Accetti, 2019).

Its first recorded usage occurs in a papal encyclical of 1931, where the term subsidiarity is employed in the context of a critique of the presumptive 'overreach' of state power pursued by both liberal and authoritarian regimes of the time, which according to Pope Pius XI threatened the 'rich associational life' of existing polities, and in particular the 'eternal rights' of the Catholic Church itself. The positive vision of the nature and function of state power that results from these premises was spelled out most clearly by the French

Catholic intellectual and political activist, Jacques Maritain, in his 1951 treatise on *Man and the State*. This text begins from a critique of the notion of 'state sovereignty', which Maritain associates with an 'absolutist' tradition, said to have laid the conditions for the emergence of modern 'statolatry' and ultimately 'totalitarianism' (Maritain, 1951, pp. 50–52). On this basis, Maritain goes on to suggest that the state ought not be seen as a 'separate and transcendent entity' standing above civil society, but rather as an 'organic expression' of society's own organizational structure. This vision of the state therefore ultimately proves indissociable from a broader conception of human society as a 'natural order' composed of a multitude of functionally integrated sub-groups radiating outwards from the human 'person', to the 'family', the 'neighborhood', the 'professional associations' and ultimately 'humanity as a whole' (Maritain, 1951, pp. 10–13).

Despite these rather obscure origins, it is striking to note that the notion of subsidiarity is now assigned a rather prominent place in the founding treaties of the European Union, as well as in the rest of its official political discourse. Already in the Preamble to the Treaty on the European Union (TEU), for instance, we find that the famous reference to the goal of creating an 'ever closer union' is qualified by an appeal to this principle, since the full text recites that its signatories are 'resolved to continue the process of creating an ever closer union … in which decisions are taken as closely as possible to the citizen in accordance with the principle of subsidiarity'. Article 5 of the same Treaty then states that:

> The European Union's competences are governed by the principles of *subsidiarity* and *proportionality* … Under the principle of subsidiarity, in areas which do not fall within its exclusive competence, the Union shall act only if and in so far as the objectives of the proposed action cannot be sufficiently achieved by the member states, either at central level or at regional and local level, but can rather, by reason of the scale or effects of the proposed action, be better achieved at union level.

Even though the degree to which the principle of subsidiarity has proved juridically effective in the substantive application of European law by the European Court of Justice has been a matter of some disagreement (on this point, see: Craig & De Burca, 2008, pp. 94–100), my contention is that it still offers the most adequate interpretive lens for making sense of the specific kind of polity instantiated by the European Union's 'multilevel system of governance', since it provides a framework of intelligibility for a number of its distinctive features that otherwise appear incomprehensible or difficult to reconcile with one another.

First of all, looking at the European Union through the lens of the Christian Democratic concept of subsidiarity can help to make sense of that fact that its institutional framework is neither purely federal (since it doesn't fully transfer political sovereignty to the European supranational level) nor merely inter-governmental (since it doesn't leave sovereignty in the hands of member states either), but rather based on a disaggregation of the category of sovereignty itself, through the distribution of different political functions or 'competences' to different administrative levels. For, as I indicated above, the core political significance ascribed to the concept of subsidiarity by the Christian Democratic ideological tradition lies precisely in an overcoming of the paradigm of sovereignty through a functional distribution of state competences to a variety of different institutionalized bodies assumed to emanate out of an organically structured civil society.

As Julien Barroche has insightfully pointed out, this implies that, from the point of view of the principle of subsidiarity itself, there is strictly speaking no juridical way of resolving a conflict of competences that emerges between two different levels of administration, since such conflicts are assumed to be already resolved in advance by the overarching conception of the 'natural order' in which the principle of subsidiarity is assumed to be inscribed (see Barroche, 2012, pp. 448–479). Thus, in effect, the principle of subsidiarity functions as a mechanism of 'self-limitation of positive law' (on this point, see Invernizzi-Accetti, 2019, pp. 121–125). This resonates with the fact that, within the framework of the European Union's juridical order, there is strictly speaking no overarching criterion that can determine whether European or member state law takes precedence in cases of conflict between them.

The same reasoning can also help to make sense of another peculiar feature of the European Union's legal order, which appears difficult to comprehend otherwise. That is, the specific role its founding treaties and jurisprudence assign to religious principles and values in providing a unifying political identity to the European institutional framework. It is in fact striking that the European Union's founding documents contain no explicit or implicit reference to the idea of separation between church and state, but on the contrary explicitly mention religion as a source of 'inspiration' for European legislation (Preamble to the Treaty on the European Union) and later also recognize the 'specific contribution' offered by 'religious associations' in the process of European integration (Article 17 of the Treaty on the European Union).

Although the controversial reference to the 'Christian roots' of Europe was ultimately excised from the proposed draft of the European constitutional treaty, which was ultimately ratified in reduced form as the Lisbon Treaty in 2007, these remaining formulations still assign religious principles and values a specific political role which would be unthinkable in the context of any constitutional framework that actually did recognize the principle of separation of church and state, such as the French or American ones (on this point see: Willaime, 2010; Zucca, 2012). Looking at the European Union's institutional framework through the lens of the principle of subsidiarity offers a key for making sense of this because – as I have noted above – this principle is indissociably tied to the idea that political institutions are the emanations from an organically structured 'natural order', whose theoretical foundations lie in the Christian (and specifically Catholic) idea of the 'temporal common good'. Thus, whenever it is a matter of defining the basic grounds of its unity and coherence, a juridical order founded on the principle of subsidiarity *must* appeal to an extra-juridical (and ultimately inherently religious) set of principles and values, just like the EU's founding treatise and jurisprudence end up doing.

The point was in fact made explicitly by François Foret in his insightful analysis of the relationship between the process of European integration and Europe's complex religious history. Although he still uses the (in my opinion misleading) notion of 'federalism' to express this point, if we substitute that term for the notion of 'subsidiarity' in the following passage by Foret, it expresses precisely the point am trying to make:

> A [polity based on the principle of subsidiarity] is not merely a label with which to describe the allocation of power. It suggests a moral dimension, a global ethic for politics. It is at this level that there is a junction with religion, concerning two points. First, the aim is to articulate levels of governance in order to ensure peaceful political regulation and to respect cultural diversities, including religious diversity. Second, the delimitation of competences also concerns the divide between political and religious institutions. Here, federalism must be understood in its interaction with the notion of subsidiarity. Rooted in the Catholic doctrine of personalism but reappropriated by other denominations and turned into a key principle of the European institutional order, the competing versions of subsidiarity heavily influence the nature and functions of the EU (Foret, 2015, p. 24).

On this basis, I advance the suggestion that the notion of a *polity based on the principle of subsidiarity*, as defined in particular by the Christian Democratic ideological tradition, offers a more adequate interpretive lens for grasping the specific type of polity established by the EU's institutional framework, compared to the notions of federalism and intergovernmentalism which are more commonly used for this purpose.

Regime Form: Neither A Democracy Nor A Technocracy

Alongside the long-standing debate on whether the EU's institutional framework instantiates a federal or an intergovernmental polity, there has also been an equally vivid controversy over whether the political regime created by these institutions is (or was ever even meant to be) democratic. Advocates of the idea that the EU suffers from a 'democratic deficit' implicitly presuppose that its political regime is democratic to some extent, and that it is intended to be *more* so. The most prominent exponent of this idea is the German legal and political philosopher, Jurgen Habermas. In an article explicitly entitled 'Democracy in Europe', for instance, Habermas claims that: 'The European treaties already prefigure an at once federally and democratically constituted supranational polity' (Habermas, 2015). Of course, Habermas also notes that, in its actual functioning, the EU falls short of such an idealized model. However, this is precisely why he denounces its 'democratic deficit', making a case for the idea that this is something that needs to be 'overcome' (Habermas, 2015, p. 547).

The opposite view is that the EU both isn't – and was never even meant to be – a democratic political regime. For instance, in a series of highly influential books and articles, Giandomenico Majone has argued that the EU should be understood as a 'regulatory state', whose function is to deal with the specific set of policy areas where 'Pareto improvements' are possible, and therefore no intrinsically 'political' – i.e., 'redistributive' – decisions need to be made (Cf Majone, 1996, 1999). On this basis, Majone contends that the very idea that the European Union suffers from a 'democratic deficit' is conceptually confused, since the latter was not (or, at least, should not) have ever intended to be a democracy. A 'regulatory state', in Majone's sense, is only supposed to find the most 'efficient' solutions for the specific set of policy areas with which it is entrusted, which doesn't require 'democratic legitimacy' but 'technocratic competence' (Majone, 1996, 1999, p. 20).

Despite the interesting and in many ways pertinent theoretical insights developed on either side, both the idea that the EU is a 'supranational democracy' in-the-making and that it is an inherently technocratic 'regulatory state' suffer from serious limitations. Even if we take into account that proponents of the idea that the EU is indeed a 'democracy' recognize that its actual institutional structure falls short of the posited ideal in many significant respects, there must still be a point at which the gap between the ideal and reality becomes so large that it no longer makes sense to describe the EU in terms of that ideal. In this respect, Andreas Follesdal and Simon Hix have pointed out that 'meaningful political contestation over leadership and policy ... is an essential element of even the 'thinnest' theories of democracy. Yet, it is conspicuously absent from the EU' (Follesdal & Hix, 2006, p. 533).

At the same time, also the characterization of the European Union as a technocratic 'regulatory state' falls short in many significant respects. First of all, this interpretation is incapable of accounting for the fact that the specific competences delegated by Member States to the EU level are far from being restricted exclusively to those areas where 'Pareto efficient' policy improvements can be achieved in relatively uncontroversial ways. Most importantly, however, it seems inappropriate to describe the EU as a purely 'technocratic' institution since all of its treaties and relevant policy documents manifest a clear intention for it to be (or at least become) a 'democratic' institution.

As in the case of the dilemma between federalism and intergovernmental-ism discussed above, some concepts and categories stemming from the Christian Democratic ideological tradition may help us to overcome this conundrum. In particular, here I will be focusing on the heuristic purchase offered by the concept of 'consociational democracy' employed by Arend Lijphart to describe several continental European regimes (in particular: Austria, Belgium, the Netherlands and Switzerland), and whose core feature is 'a strategy of conflict management by cooperation and agreement among elites rather than by competition and majority decision' (Lijphart, 1977, p. 5). More specifically, Lijphart, spells out the distinctive features of what he calls the 'consociational model of democracy' in terms of four institutional dimensions: (i) 'A grand coalition of the political leaders of all the significant members of a plural society'; (ii) 'The mutual veto or concurrent majority rule, which serves as additional protection of vital minority interests'; (iii) 'Proportionality as the principal standard of political representation, civil service appointments and allocation of public funds'; (iv) 'A high degree of autonomy for each segment to run its internal affairs' (Lijphart, 1977, p. 25).

The strong degree of overlap that exists between this specific model of democracy and the particular type of political regime instantiated by EU institutions has already been pointed out by several commentators. In an article specifically devoted to the question of whether the EU can be interpreted as a 'consociation', for instance, Paul Magnette and Olivier Costa have written that: 'Once a specific version of the consociative theory has been precisely defined, it seems plausible to propose a comprehensive interpretation of the EU as a new form of consociation, distinct from both classical federal and unitarian consociations' (Magnette & Costa, 2003, pp. 1–2). Similarly, in a separate contribution, Paul Magnette and Yannis Papadopoulos have suggested that 'The social-cultural structure, institutional system and political practices of the European Union share much with the consociational polities we are more familiar with; i.e., the Netherlands, Belgium and Austria' (Papadopoulos & Magnette, 2010, p. 716).

What is striking about these contributions, however, is that they seem to all but ignore the Christian Democratic roots of the consociational model of democracy itself. The latter emerge first of all historically, if we consider that all the countries which Lijphart refers to in order to develop his abstract model were dominated, not just politically but also culturally, by Christian Democratic parties at the time he focuses on. To this effect, for instance, Lijphart himself writes that:

> We shall be concerned here with the four countries in their consociational phase of development. This means that 'Austria' will usually mean Austria during the time of the Catholic-Socialist elite cooperation embodied in the grand coalition; whereas 'the Netherlands' will refer to the Dutch case of consociationalism in the second post-war period. (Lijphart, 1977, p. 2)

Most importantly, however, the Christian Democratic roots of the concept of 'consociational democracy' emerge if we consider that the underlying logic uniting the various institutional features Lijphart identifies is one of social and political 'reconciliation', oriented towards the 'integration of various sectors of society' through the practice of 'compromise and accommodation' (Lijphart, 1977, pp. 25–44). This is precisely the core feature of what the Christian Democratic ideological tradition has historically identified as the political kernel of the notion of 'popularism' – that is, the overcoming of (especially class, but also regional and religious) social tensions through the appeal to an overarching vision of the people, based on reciprocal compromise and accommodation. Already in his 1897 article on 'The Christian Conception of Democracy', for instance, Giuseppe Toniolo stated that: 'Democracy, in its essential concept, can be defined as that system of civil government in which all the social, juridical and economic forces that constitute a 'people' … cooperate proportionally in the pursuit of the common good' (Toniolo, 1897, p. 330). Similarly, in their 2010 review essay on the concept of Christian Democracy, Stathis Kalyvas and Kees Van Kersbergen write that:

> Christian Democracy's problem has not been whether to seek support exclusively in one class or to rely on multi- or even non-class forces, but rather how to formulate and implement a feasible *mediation* between the various layers of society, whether these are defined as classes or not … The key concepts that made Christian Democracy distinctive are [accordingly] integration, class compromise, accommodation and pluralism … In this framework pragmatism and accountability can be interpreted as effects of principled value commitments rather than mere opportunism. It is likely that it was this dimension of the Christian Democratic movement that made it so hard to grasp (Kalyvas & Van Kersbergen, 2010, pp. 187–189).

In this light, we can return to the EU's political regime in order to show that the Christian Democratic concept of 'consociationalism' offers a better interpretive framework of its distinctive features than both the Habermasian ideal of a 'transnational deliberative democracy' and Majone's conception of a technocratic 'regulatory state'. To begin with, the notion of consociational democracy can help make sense of the multiplicity of veto points and countermajoritarian procedures that notoriously characterize the EU's 'ordinary legislative procedure' (Hix, 2005). While these institutional complexities are frequently interpreted as a deviation from the ideal of a pure democracy (in particular by authors keen to emphasize the EU's presumptive 'democratic deficit') from the point of view of the consociational model of democracy I outlined above they appear both natural and justified since, as Lijphart himself points out: 'Mutual veto points are the key mechanism through which the consociational model of democracy ensures that compromise and broad agreement over government policy are always required' (Lijphart, 1999, pp. 34–35).

Secondly, the consociational model of democracy can also help to make sense of the elite-driven and weakly responsive nature of the political process that takes place in the so-called 'Brussels bubble'– which is another feature routinely pointed out by critics of the EU's presumptive 'democratic deficit'. In this respect, it is worth recalling that Lijphart explicitly maintained that 'elite cooperation is the primary distinguishing feature of consociational democracy'; but also what the French Christian Democratic politician and public intellectual, Pierre-Henri Teitgen (who collaborated closely with Robert Schuman in drafting the latter's famous Declaration, which ultimately lead to the creation of the European Coal and Steel Community in 1950) wrote concerning his party's conception of democracy in 1961:

> Democracy – and this is its paradox – needs elites. This must never be forgotten. Democracy cannot exist or survive without the devotion of a small number of awakeners of conscience, educators and apostles of the spiritual values of freedom, dignity and fraternity … It cannot survive, in other words, without the work of elites capable of constituting, in the face of the unjust hierarchies created by power and wealth, a more just hierarchy of prophets of the people (Teitgen, 1961, p. 91).

Finally, a further piece of evidence substantiating the heuristic utility of interpreting the EU's political regime in light of the Christian Democratic model of 'consociational democracy' lies in the rarely noted but still striking fact that almost all the references to the notion of democracy in the European treaties and jurisprudence involve two separate components: a procedural and a substantive one, which Scharpf (1999) has famously referred to respectively as 'input' and 'output' legitimacy. As I already pointed out above, for instance, in the Preamble to the Treaty on the European Union (TEU) we read that its goal is to 'enhance further the *democratic and efficient* functioning of the institutions, so as to enable them to better carry out … the tasks entrusted to them' (emphasis added). Similarly, in the 'White Paper on Governance' published by the European Commission in 2001, we read that 'Democratic institutions and representatives of the people at both national and European levels can and must try to connect to its citizens … [since] this is the starting condition for more effective and relevant policies' (EC, 2001, p. 3).

This insistence on the fact that there must be some kind of 'substantive' or 'objective' counterpart to the 'subjective' element of popular choice for a system to qualify as truly democratic is also a characteristic feature of the consociational model of democracy developed by the Christian Democratic ideological tradition. At several junctures in his writings, for instance, Lijphart point out that the consociational model of democracy aims at achieving a 'kinder, gentler form of society', in which 'everyone's interests are taken into account', through the mechanism of an 'inclusive welfare system' (see for instance: Lijphart, 1999, pp. 293–300). Even more explicitly, in a comment he wrote on Romolo Murri's first Christian Democratic association, the Italian cleric and Christian Democratic political activist, Luigi Sturzo, wrote that:

> The democracy we want as Catholics is not simply a political form of society in which the people play a role in deciding who rules them. After all, even today the people already participate in the political lives of their nations ... Such acts of power are only 'popular' in name but not in fact, because the action of those we call the representatives of the people, just because the latter have put a piece of paper in a ballot box, most often develops in an 'anti-popular' sense, both in its laws, in its economic purposes and in its concrete social effects ... In contrast, Christian Democracy means a 'popular' organization of the whole structure of society, whether that concerns politics, law, economics, finance or concrete social practice (Sturzo, 1900, p. 58)

To be sure, the Christian Democratic ideological tradition is not the only one to have maintained the necessity of a substantive counterpart to democracy's procedural dimension. The Social Democratic ideology also of course maintains something comparable. For this reason, in the ensuing section I turn to the actual content of the socio-economic policy regime either actively supported or constitutionally enshrined by the EU, in order to establish whether the latter is more adequately described as neo-liberal, Social Democratic, or Christian Democratic.

Socio-Economic Policy: Between Neoliberalism And Social Democracy

As might be expected, the debates concerning the content of the EU's socio-economic policies are even more polarized than those over its polity type and regime form. On one hand, as Andrew Moravcsik has noted that: 'Many view the EU as a throwback to the nineteenth century: a fiscally weak, neoliberal state' (Moravcsik, 2002, p. 605). On the other hand, it is interesting to note that there also exists a competing set of views, according to which the European Union entrenches very *high* levels of state regulation and income redistribution, especially when compared to other areas of the world. As Christopher Bickerton has noted, for instance, the firm stance adopted by the European Commission in several high-profile cases of tax avoidance by large multinational corporations – such as Apple, Google and Amazon – have fed into a relatively widespread concern that the European Union is an intrusive 'Superstate', and even 'Europe's Robin Hood' (Bickerton, 2016, p. 77).

What appears rather unconvincing, however, both in the picture of the EU as a neoliberal steamroller and a Social Democratic super-state, is that such marked policy orientations would seem to have a hard time emerging out of the EU's notoriously complex decision-making procedures. In this respect, for instance, Andreas Follesdal and Simon Hix have noted that:

> The EU's elaborate system of checks and balances ensures that an overwhelming consensus is required for any policies to be agreed ... As a consequence, EU policies are inevitably very *centrist*: the result of a delicate compromise between a wide variety of interests, from all the Member States and all the main partisan positions. (Follesdal & Hix, 2006, pp. 540–541)

Along similar lines, Kalypso Nicolaidis has recently written that: 'The EU's transformative potential lies not in pursuing an ideal to its extreme, but in a kind of *fanatic moderation* by which political actors unrelentingly pursue compromise under the shadow of consensus' (Nicolaidis, 2013, p. 357, emphasis added).

The question, however, remains: what is the specific nature of the 'compromise' unrelentingly pursued by political actors within the EU in the domain of socio-economic policy? Here too, some characteristically Christian Democratic concepts and categories may prove heuristically useful. As Kees Van Kersbergen has noted in a book devoted specifically to this theme (1995), the Christian Democratic ideological tradition has been historically tied to the elaboration and implementation of a particular model of 'social capitalism', broadly understood as constituting a 'third way' between liberal capitalism on one hand and state socialism on the other. Its core component elements are two:

- First, a conception of private property as an article of 'natural law', from which is assumed to follow a commitment to free enterprise and the market mechanism as organizing principles of economic production and distribution. To this effect, for instance, the compendium of Christian Social teaching authored by the German Cardinal and CDU political adviser Josef Hoffner in 1959 states that:

> The natural-law character of private ownership follows from the weight of the reasons advanced by Christian social teaching ... By 'private ownership' one here understands not only the legally recognized and exclusive power of disposal of a natural or legal person or body of persons over things (chattels and real estate), but also the obligatory rights which are gaining ever greater importance in the modern economy (membership rights such as stocks and bonds, etc.) ... Thus, an active economic exchange is proper to the system of private ownership and connects branches of the economy and peoples with one another peacefully and voluntarily and not through the official intervention of functionaries. (Hoffner, 1959, pp. 107–110)

- Second, a conception of 'distributive justice' predicated on the assumption that every individual must be granted sufficient material conditions to be able to offer an adequate contribution to the collective pursuit of the 'temporal common good', in his or her particular capacity as a member of a particular social group. Thus, the same document I just quoted from above also maintains that:

> Even if commercial justice is extremely important for human coexistence, an even greater importance, nevertheless, attaches, especially today, to those fundamental forms of justice that regulate the strained relations between individuals and society. Here is to be named first that fundamental form of justice, which orders the relation of the social body to its members from above, as it were: *justitia distributiva*. Its goal is to allow individual people to participate in the common good through a just distribution, so that spiritual and moral development becomes possible for all. (for a further elaboration of both these points, see: Invernizzi-Accetti, 2019, pp. 139–168)

As Kees Van Kersbergen has emphasized, the combination of these two organizing principles translates into a particular conception of the welfare state that is significantly different from the standard Social Democratic one, as theorized for instance by Esping-Andresen (1990), inasmuch as it is not predicated on a principle of 'decommodification' which involves the universal provision of certain basic goods on an egalitarian basis, but rather functions as a form of 'repair work' that compensates those left behind by the system of private property, supplying them with a minimum amount of resources deemed necessary for participating adequately in the market economy itself. 'Christian Democracy' Van Kersbergen writes

> promotes what has been identified empirically as passive or reactive social policies. Such a practice typically moderates the outcome of the logic of the market by transferring considerable sums of money to families and other social institutions in need, but is hesitant in changing the logic itself. (Van Kersbergen, 1995, p. 189)

On the basis of this, we can return to the specific socio-economic policy regime constitutionally enshrined and actively supported by the EU, in order to establish whether it is more adequately described with reference to the Christian Democratic notion of 'social capitalism' or the competing notions of neo-liberalism and Social Democracy. The first thing to note in this respect is that all references to socio-economic policy contained in the EU's founding treaties are placed under the aegis of the notion of a 'social market economy'. In particular, Article 3 of the TEU states that the Union 'shall work for the sustainable development of Europe based on balanced economic growth and price stability, a highly competitive *social market economy*, aiming at full employment and social progress, a high level of protection and improvement of the environment'.

This notion of a 'social market economy' is unmistakably of Christian Democratic origin, since the term itself was coined by the German CDU Finance Minister, Ludwig Erhard, in the aftermath of the Second World War, precisely in order to name the 'compromise' between neoliberal market principles and Social Democratic demands for economic redistribution he pursued in order to relaunch the German economy, which at the same time containing the social tensions that rapid capitalist growth might generate. In his 1958 book of political memoirs, for instance, Erhard wrote that:

> The social market economy practiced in the Federal Republic can claim recognition by politicians as an important and formative factor in the reconstruction of our democratic state ... My constant endeavor to direct all efforts towards expansion, without endangering the healthy basis of the economy or currency, rests on the belief that only thus can a suitably decent standard of living be guaranteed to those who, through no fault of their own, but because of age, sickness, involuntary unemployment, or as victims of the two world wars, could no longer participate in production. (Erhard, 1958, pp. 4–8)

A second element which also suggests that the specific kind of socio-economic policy regime enshrined in the EU treaties and fostered by it is best understood in terms of the Christian Democratic category of 'social capitalism' is that the two core sets of socioeconomic rights mentioned in the EU's founding treaties correspond substantively to the two main pillars of this model I mentioned above. For instance, in the Charter of Fundamental Rights that is annexed to the TEU we find explicit mention of the 'right to free enterprise' (Article 16) and 'private property' (Article 17). The latter, however, is qualified by a dual 'public interest' clause specifying that: 'No one may be deprived of his or her possessions ... except in the public interest'; and that 'The use of private property may be regulated by law insofar as is necessary for the general interest' (Article 17.1).

This would seem hard to reconcile with the idea of a purely 'neo-liberal' EU, inasmuch as neo-liberalism is normally assumed to be based on the assumption that whatever socio-economic distribution of private property emerges from the free operations of the market is *ipso facto* just (on this point, see for instance: Harvey, 2007; Slobodian, 2018). Moreover, later in the European Charter of Fundamental Rights we find that the same document also grants a number of social or 'solidarity' rights, which are clearly intended to temper the outcomes of the market economy, by compensating those that are left behind. Article 34, for instance, states that:

> The Union recognizes and respects the entitlement to social security benefits and social services providing protection in cases such as maternity, illness, industrial accidents, dependency or old age, and in cases of loss of employment ... Everyone residing and moving legally within the European Union is entitled to social security benefits and social advantages in accordance with Union law and national laws and practices.

Two features of this right to 'social security' are particularly worth emphasizing, because they mark an important difference with the way social rights are generally understood in the Social Democratic ideological tradition, while resonating with the Christian Democratic model of 'social capitalism' I have outlined above. The first is that social security is not granted here to all citizens of the Union on the basis of a principle of equality, but rather reserved for specific categories of people who are singled out as requiring 'protection' because of their particular circumstances: 'maternity, illness, industrial accidents, dependency, old age, and ... loss of employment'. The second is that the conception of social justice that constitutes the foundation for this right ultimately boils down to a form of 'sufficientarianism', rather than egalitarianism, since the overarching goal is to provide all citizens with sufficient material resources for participating effectively in the market economy. This transpires for instance from the further clause added to the article I just quoted, which states that: 'In order to combat social exclusion and poverty, the Union recognizes and respects the right to social and housing assistance, so as to ensure a *decent* existence for all those who lack *sufficient* resources' (Article 34.3, emphasis added).

Both the ideas of compensating those that are left behind and of doing so by providing minimal conditions for effective participation in social activity are at the heart of the Christian Democratic model of 'social capitalism', inasmuch as the latter is predicated on an overarching conception of the 'natural order' which sees society as a functionally differentiated whole, in which different categories of citizens are assigned specific purposive tasks in pursuit of the 'temporal common good'.

To be sure, the extent to which these kinds of provisions included in the European Union's founding documents have been faithfully implemented in the concrete policies pursued or fostered by European institutions in the socio-economic domain remains open to question. Especially in the aftermath of the 2008 economic crisis, there has been a widespread perception that European officials and institutions have played an instrumental role in imposing an 'endless austerity regime', more focused on shoring up the principles of 'economic competition', 'balanced budgets' and 'sound money' within the framework of the common market, than in making sure that all sectors of society benefit from it in a distributively just way (on this point see for instance: Moss, 2008; Schafer & Streeck, 2013; Blyth, 2013).

Even if we restrict ourselves to the substantive socio-economic policies that have been actually pursued by European agencies in the aftermath of the 2008 economic crisis, however, there remain several elements that simply do not fit the picture of the EU as a 'neoliberal steamroller'. To begin with, it is worth pointing out that European institutions are both directly and indirectly responsible for a pretty extensive degree of economic redistribution, both between its member states and within them. The largest single item within the European Union's budget, for instance, remains the Common Agricultural Program, which provides direct subsidies to farmers and other businesses in the agricultural sector through a general tax levy on member states. Together with the so-called Structural and Cohesion Funds – which aim specifically at 'reducing regional disparities in income, wealth, and opportunities' within the European Union – these programs have reallocated a total of more than 775 billion Euros for the period between 2014 and 2020.

Finally, even the specific way in which the European Central Bank (ECB) has been attempting to stimulate economic recovery within the Eurozone, at least since the beginning of 2015, appears highly unconventional from the point of view of standard 'neoliberal' (or at least 'ordoliberal') orthodoxy, inasmuch as the practice of quantitative easing through which the ECB has been buying bonds issued directly by the governments of its member states effectively amounts to a subsidy for public and private lending and therefore implicitly investment (on this point, see: Tooze, 2018).

None of these specific policy pursuits appear consistent with the image of a purely neoliberal EU, since they all constitute violations of the core neoliberal principle that public authorities ought to restrict themselves to that institution of market systems, while refraining as much as possible from interfering with their operations and outcomes. At the same time, the elements I have high-lighted also clearly fall short of the Social Democratic standard of 'decommo-dification' of key sectors of the economy in the interest of universal equality and the protection of certain basic rights, since they all continue to presup-pose a market-based economy, and only really interfere with its functioning on a remedial and *ad hoc* basis.

For this reason, I maintain that the so-called 'European Social Model' is better understood as occupying some kind of middle ground between the ideal types of a purely neoliberal and a truly Social Democratic policy regime. Since this is precisely the conceptual space occupied by the Christian Democratic notion of a 'social market' or 'social capitalist' economy (which, as we saw, was elaborated explicitly as a 'third way' between liberal capitalism and socialist collectivism), this notion ultimately appears to offer a more adequate interpretive framework for grasping the specificity of the European Union's socioeconomic policy regime than either neoliberalism or Social Democracy.

Conclusion

The overall purpose of the analysis conducted in this paper has been to examine the heuristic purchase afforded by concepts and categories drawn from the Christian Democratic ideological tradition in capturing the distinctive nature of the EU's institutional framework. In at least three respects, it has been shown that such concepts and categories appear more descriptively adequate to the object in question than the ones more commonly used for this purpose in the relevant academic literature. More specifically, I have shown that: (1) the Christian Democratic notion of 'subsidiarity' offers a more adequate interpretive framework for understanding the specific type of polity that is created by EU institutions than either the notions of federalism or intergovernmentalism; (2) the originally Christian Democratic model of 'consociational democracy' offers a better description of the EU's political regime than either the idea that the EU constitutes a supra-national democracy in-the-making or that it is an inherently technocratic regulatory state; (3) the Christian Democratic model of 'social capitalism' more closely approximates the content of the socio-economic policies enshrined in EU treaties and fostered by it than either the notions of neo-liberalism or Social Democracy. On this basis, I submit that the EU's current institutional framework is better described as 'Christian Democratic' than any other of the currently available descriptive categories.

Disclosure statement

No potential conflict of interest was reported by the author(s).

ORCID

Carlo Invernizzi Accetti ⓘ http://orcid.org/0000-0002-2867-1557

References

Bache, I., & Flinders, M. (2004). *Multi-level governance*. Oxford University Press.
Barroche, J. (2012). *Etat, Libéralisme et Christianisme. Critique de la Subsidairité Européenne*. Dalloz.
Bickerton, C. (2016). *The european union: A citizen's guide*. Penguin.
Blyth, M. (2013). *Austerity. The history of a dangerous idea*. Oxford University Press.
Craig, P., & De Burca, G. (2008). *EU law. Text cases and materials*. Oxford University Press.
Delsol, C. (1992). *L'Etat subsidiaire*. Cerf.
Delsol, C. (1993). *Le Principe de Subsidiarité*. Presses Universitaires de France.
Durand, J.-D. (1995). *L'Europe de la Démocratie Chrétienne*. Complexe.
EC (European Commission). (2001). *White paper on governance*. https://ec.europa.eu/commission/presscorner/detail/en/DOC_01_10
Eising, R., & Poguntke, T. (2011). Government and governance in Europe. In E. Jones, P. Heywood, M. Rhodes, & E. Sedelmeier (Eds.), *Developments in european politics* (pp. 83–107). Palgrave.
Erhard, L. (1958). *Prosperity through competition*. Praeger.
Esping-Andresen, G. (1990). *The three worlds of welfare capitalism*. Polity.
Follesdal, A. (1998). Subsidiarity: Survey Article. *Journal of Political Philosophy*, 6(2), 190–218. https://doi.org/10.1111/1467-9760.00052

Follesdal, A., & Hix, S. (2006). Why there is a democratic deficit in the EU: A response to Majone and Moravcsik. *JCMS: Journal of Common Market Studies, 44*(3), 533–562. https://doi.org/10.1111/j.1468-5965.2006.00650.x

Foret, F. (2015). *The secular canopy. Religion in the European Union*. Cambridge University Press.

Freeden, M. (1996). *Ideologies and political theory*. Oxford University Press.

Freeden, M. (2006). *Taking ideology seriously. 21st century reconfigurations*. Routledge.

Habermas, J. (2015). Democracy in Europe: Why the development of the EU into a transnational democracy Is necessary and How It Is possible. *European Law Journal, 21*(4), 546–557. https://doi.org/10.1111/eulj.12128

Harvey, D. (2007). *A brief history of neoliberalism*. Oxford University Press.

Hix, S. (2005). *The political system of the European Union* (2nd ed.). Palgrave.

Hoffman, S. (1995). *The European sisyphus. Essays on Europe*. Westview Press.

Hoffner, J. (1959). *Christian social teaching*. Ordo Socialis. [1997].

Hooghe, L., & Marks. (2001). *Multi-level governance and European integration*. Rowman and Littlefield.

Invernizzi-Accetti, C. (2019). *What is christian democracy? politics, religion and ideology*. Cambridge University Press.

Kaiser, W. (2007). *Christian democracy and the origins of the European Union*. Cambridge University Press.

Kalyvas, S. (1996). *The rise of christian democracy in Europe*. Cornell University Press.

Kalyvas, S., & Van Kersbergen, K. (2010). Christian democracy. *Annual Review of Political Science*. https://doi.org/10.1146/annurev.polisci.11.021406.172506

Kselman, T., & Buttigieg, J. (Eds.). (2003). *European christian democracy. historical legacies and comparative perspectives*. University of Notre Dame Press.

Lamberts, E. (Ed.). (1997). *Christian democracy in the European Union (1945/ 1995)*. Leuven University Press.

Lijphart, A. (1977). *Democracy in plural societies*. Yale University Press.

Lijphart, A. (1999). *Patterns of democracy*. Yale University Press.

Magnette, P. (2017). *Le Régime Politique de l'Union Européenne*. Presses Universitaires de Sciences Po.

Magnette, P., & Costa, O. (2003). The European Union as a consociation? A methodological assessment. *West European Politics, 3*, 1. https://doi.org/10.1080/01402380312331280568

Majone, G. (1996). *Regulating Europe*. Routledge.

Majone, G. (1999). The regulatory state and its legitimacy problems. *West European Politics, 22*(1), 1–24. https://doi.org/10.1080/01402389908425284

Maritain, J. (1951). *Man and the state*. University of Chicago Press. [1998].

Milward, A. (2000). *The european rescue of the nation state*. Routledge.

Moravcsik, A. (1993). Preferences and power in the European Community: A liberal Intergovernmentalist approach. *JCMS: Journal of Common Market Studies, 31*(4), 473–524. https://doi.org/10.1111/j.1468-5965.1993.tb00477.x

Moravcsik, A. (1998). *The choice for Europe. Social purpose and state power from messina to maastrict*. Cornell University Press.

Moravcsik, A. (2002). In defence of the democratic deficit: Reassessing legitimacy in the European Union. *Journal of Common Market Studies, 40*(4), 603–624.

Moss, B. (2008). *Monetary union in crisis. The European Union as a Neo-Liberal construction*. Palgrave.

Muller, J.-W. (2013). Towards a new history of Christian democracy. *Journal of Political Ideologies, 18*, 2. https://doi.org/10.1080/13569317.2013.784025

Nicolaidis, K. (2013). European democracy and its critics. *Journal of Common Market Studies, 51*(2), 351–369.

Papadopoulos, Y., & Magnette, P. (2010). On the politicisation of the European Union: Lessons from consociational national polities. West European Politics, *33*(4), 711–729. https://doi.org/10.1080/01402381003794571

Piris, J.-C. (2012). *The future of Europe: Towards a Two-speed EU?* Cambridge University Press.

Schafer, A., & Streeck, W. (2013). *Politics in the age of austerity*. Polity Press.

Scharpf, F. (1999). *Governing in Europe: Efficient and democratic?* Oxford University Press.

Schmidt, V. (2005). *Democracy in Europe. The impact of European integration*. Oxford University Press.

Slobodian, Q. (2018). *Globalists: The End of Empire and the Birth of Neoliberalism*. Harvard University Press.

Sturzo, L. (1900). Il Nostro Programma. In *La Croce di Costantino*. Edizioni di Storia e Letteratura (pp. 58–65). [1958].

Teitgen, P.-H. (1961). Notre Conception de l'Ordre Social. In A. Fosset (Ed.), *Le MRP, Cet Inconnu* (pp. 77–96). supplement to *MRP Vous Parle*.

Tömmel, I. (2011). The European Union – A Federation Sui Generis?. In Finn Laursen (Ed.), *The EU and Federalism: Polities and Policies Compared*. Ashgate Publishing.

Toniolo, G. (1897). Il Concetto Cristiano della Democrazia. *Rivista Internazionale di Scienze Sociali e Discipline Ausiliarie, 14*, 55.

Tooze, A. (2018). *Crashed. How a decade of financial crisis changed the world*. Harvard University Press.

Van Kersbergen, K. (1995). *Social capitalism. A study of christian democracy and the welfare state*. Routledge.

Van Kersbergen, K., & Verbek, B. (2004). Subsidiarity as a principle of governance in the European Union. *Comparative European Politics, 2*, 2. https://doi.org/10.1057/palgrave.cep.6110033

Willaime, J.-P. (2010). European integration, Laïcité and religion. In L. Leustean, & J. Madeley (Eds.), *Religion, politics and law in the European Union* (pp. 17–30). Routledge.

Zucca, L. (2012). *A secular Europe. Law and religion in the European constitutional landscape*. Oxford University Press.

The social democratic case against the EU

Fabio Wolkenstein

ABSTRACT

Until the 1980s, many European social democratic parties had reservations about the project of European integration. But what exactly is the status of Euroscepticism within the broader ideology of social democracy? Does honouring social democratic commitments demand rejecting European integration and membership of the EU? This article investigates this question, using debates around Europe in the social democratic parties of Great Britain, Sweden and Denmark as primary cases. Employing Freeden's morphological approach to political ideology, the article argues that there is no necessary connection between social democracy's core commitments and opposition to European integration. The analysis also unveils the indeterminacy of the concept of sovereignty in social democratic thought, as well as how particular national imaginaries shaped centre-left opposition to European unity.

Introduction

Since the mid 1980s or so, social democratic parties across Europe have gradually adopted pro-European positions, supporting European integration and membership in the EEC and later the EU (Balley, 2005; Heffernan, 2001; Forster, 2002; Lightfoot, 2005). Prior to that, however, many social democratic parties were ambivalent about the project of European integration; especially in Great Britain and in the Scandinavian countries, enthusiasm was not the dominant sentiment.

Today, social democratic arguments against European integration are regaining traction in some parts of Europe. Especially in Britain, left-leaning intellectuals with and without formal party affiliation (Bickerton & Tuck, 2018; Lapavitsas, 2019; see also the programmatic website *thefullbrexit.com*), as well as certain elected Labour MPs (Stringer, 2019), increasingly express support for a more or less radical break with the EU. And quite often, a 'long tradition within Labour to oppose the EU' (Stringer, 2019) is invoked, as if honouring the true core of social democracy demanded rejecting EU membership.

The recurrence of such arguments raises questions about what ideas exactly this social democratic 'tradition' of opposing European integration rests upon. Arguably the most important question is whether there is any necessary connection between social democracy's ideological core and a rejection of European integration. Exploring this issue is relevant not just because of the relative success of 'social democratic Euroscepticism' in contemporary Britain, but also in relation to the more general evolution of centre-left politics in the EU. Is, as many social democratic Eurosceptics would have it, opposition to European integration the most coherent social democratic position?

To answer these questions, I want to investigate the main ideas that underpin traditional social democratic opposition to the EU. I begin by looking at their emergence in Great Britain and the Scandinavian countries, specifically Denmark and Sweden, who unlike Norway eventually joined the EU and are today considered important member states. These countries are typically thought to be the paradigmatic 'reluctant Europeans' (Olesen, 2000, p. 147; also see Aylott, 1999; Raunio, 2007), and have a long-standing social democratic legacy. This makes them critical cases for understanding the phenomenon of social democratic Euroscepticism.

I then go on to investigate the relationship between social democratic Euroscepticism and the ideological core of social democratic ideology. I draw here on Freeden's (1998, pp. 47–91) morphological model of political ideologies, which distinguishes between an ideology's 'core concepts', 'adjacent concepts' and 'peripheral concepts'. This three-fold distinction usefully allows us to determine the distinctive functions particular ideas perform, and the status they possess, within an ideological formation. It permits us to examine social democratic Euroscepticism with enhanced systematicity and precision, clarifying how the relevant concepts hang together and relate to each other.

I argue that there is ultimately no necessary connection between social democratic 'core concepts' and a rejection of European integration: the different arguments for why European integration should be opposed hinge on 'adjacent' or 'peripheral' concepts, notably specific sovereigntist interpretations of the state and certain ideas about the distinctiveness of the respective countries' national culture and history. This conclusion instructively re-orients our focus to the contingent nature of social democratic Euroscepticism, most importantly to the fact that claims about state sovereignty rely on a liberal, rather than distinctively social democratic, understanding of the state.

Before embarking, three clarifications are necessary. First, I will in what follows define social democracy as a political ideology that is marked by a commitment to the primacy of politics over markets and the democratisation of all spheres of society. I here follow key historical accounts of social democracy (e.g., Berman, 2006; Jackson, 2013), and accept the potentially controversial implication that social democrats' gradual 'acceptance of market forces … as beyond their control' (Mudge, 2018, p. 55) in the 1980s and 90s eventually transformed social democracy into something other than itself.

Second, although I acknowledge that 'Euroscepticism' is a term that is often used imprecisely and with polemical intention (Leconte, 2010), I will throughout describe the social democratic positions in question as 'social democratic Euroscepticism'. I use the term mainly for want of better terminology and will take it to connote being initially opposed to joining the Europe-wide cooperative ventures like the EEC and, once a member, resisting all attempts at further integration if not supporting outright withdrawal.

Finally, I will prioritise analysing the main substantive ideas behind social democratic Euroscepticism over analysing the cross-temporal development of these ideas, though I of course situate the different ideological debates in space and time. Readers interested in detailed analyses of how social democratic thinking about European integration has changed over time may turn to case studies that take a close look at this (e.g., Aylott, 1999; Bailey, 2005; Heffernan, 2001), as well as to more general accounts of how social democratic ideology changed in the last decades of the twentieth century (e.g., Mudge, 2018).

The emergence of social democratic Euroscepticism

Social democratic Euroscepticism originally emerged in the immediate postwar era, when the objective of intensified cooperation between the war-torn countries of Western Europe was widely discussed by political elites around the continent, and many of them considered integration desirable. The first strands of social democratic Euroscepticism were essentially a reaction to this. I take these different strands as my point of departure, since they allow us to get a good sense of the structure and content of this branch of social democratic thinking.

The first thing to note is that it was particularly the British and Scandinavian social democratic parties that expressed reservations against European integration. As one post-war historian writes, 'the French and Dutch socialists especially, but also the Belgians and the Socialist party of Italian Workers, called for decisive steps towards a European federation … [but the British] Labour Party … , while admitting the need for closer co-operation, pointed to the numerous difficulties that stood in the way of a supranational Europe; and the Scandinavians took advantage of British scepticism to avoid being involved in binding obligations' (Loth, 1990, p. 441). The Swedish SAP was especially wary of the sorts of 'federalist' ideas several of the 'continental' parties promoted, and insisted that the proposed new political institutions for European cooperation – such as the Council of Europe –

must not acquire too much importance (Misgeld, 1992, p. 59). The Danish social democrats likewise exhibited a dismissive attitude toward European federalism: for example, at the famous Congress of Europe in 1948, sometimes described as the first major 'federalist moment' in European history, social democratic delegates from Denmark were completely absent, as the party 'would not endorse [its members'] participation' (Olesen, 2000, p. 150).[1]

What animated the British and Scandinavian parties' hesitancy about or disinterest in European integration? Beginning with the British Labour party, which assumed office in 1945, it is important to note that the party was elected on the basis of a radical manifesto that promised a wide extension of welfare provision and economic planning. As Croft (1988:, p. 619) argues, for Labour it was accordingly 'clear that any attempt to take these powers away from London – whether to a supranational authority or through a return to the dominance of market forces – would clearly be opposed. Economic sovereignty had to remain in London in order to implement the socialist transformation of society. This was particularly so given the problems faced by other European socialist parties in obtaining governmental power'. In addition, the Labour government was committed to maintaining and indeed strengthening the bonds with the Commonwealth. This was powerfully reflected in the party's 1951 pamphlet 'European Unity', which stated that 'in every respect except distance, we in Britain are closer to our kinsmen in Australia and New Zealand on the far side of the world, than we are to Europe' (cited in Davis, 2017, p. 4). Taken together, these commitments meant that 'it was never politically possible for Britain to go beyond the concept of union and accept the concept of unity' in the post-war period (Croft, 1988, p. 619).

The Scandinavian social democratic parties shared the British view that cooperation between the European states should at most be 'functional and intergovernmental' (Olesen, 2000, p. 151). A large part of the explanation is that – in a way that has clear parallels with the British case – the Scandinavian social democratic parties each in their own way endorsed an 'exceptionalism thesis'. For instance, Hans Hedtoft, Denmarks social democratic prime minister from 1947–1953, appealed in a speech to 'the Nordic peoples' mutual descent, common linguistic heritage and the rest of the cultural affinity binding the area together for more than a thousand years; an affinity which has found its special expression in the Nordic peoples' common ideals concerning democracy and the conception of law' – and he went on to argue that intensified cooperation between the Nordic countries, rather than with the countries of the continent, is the way forward (quoted in Laursen & Olesen, 2000, p. 64; Olesen, 2006, p. 40; on Swedish exceptionalism, see Ringmar, 1998, pp. 45–47).

Notably, this emphasis on Nordic exceptionalism was closely bound up with a strategic judgment about the capacity to implement political

agendas: in a way similar to the British Labour party, the Danish social democrats entered the post-war period with an 'ambitious programme inspired by
Keynesian demand management … with the aim of securing economic
growth, a sustained process of industrialisation and full employment'
(Laursen & Olesen, 2000, p. 63). These goals dovetailed with the goals of
their Norwegian and Swedish sister parties, which formed majority governments and possessed significant structural power within their respective
countries. They seemed at odds, however, with the political ambitions of
the Christian democratic parties that dominated most continental European
democracies, notably the countries of 'the Six'. In short, just like in Britain,
opposition to European unity was in important ways driven by considerations
about the feasibility of realising social democratic political projects. As Misgeld
(1992:, p. 61) notes in this connection, in Swedish social democratic circles the
ambitious integration plans of 'the Six' were even regarded as representing an
'attempt of the catholic and conservative forces on the continent to exclude
protestant Great Britain and the equally protestant Scandinavia from European cooperation'. This suspicion was not entirely off the mark, given that
some of the influential continental Catholic parties saw 'core Europe' as coex-
tensive with the *Catholic* regions of Europe only (Forlenza, 2017, pp. 267–271
and 273-276). But whether it was true or not, things were *perceived* in this way,
and political alliances with parties on the 'continent' were therefore widely
deemed undesirable, presenting an obstacle to implementing social democratic ends.

An additional reason for why the Swedish social democrats were rather
negative about European unity had to do with Sweden's neutrality policy –
a position that marked the country off from its Scandinavian neighbours
Denmark and Norway. The policy of neutrality defined Swedish foreign
policy since the early nineteenth century, leading Sweden to stay out of the
two World Wars and avoid taking sides in the Cold War (Andrén, 1996). It
'was universally regarded as a success and as the fundamental reason why
Sweden had remained at peace for nigh on two hundred years' – which
was deemed 'a conclusive argument for why Sweden could not join the
EEC in the 1960s and 70s' (Ringmar, 1998, p. 49). Thus, the distinctively
Swedish version of early social democratic Euroscepticism added to a more
general sense of not belonging to 'core Europe' – due to the latter's conservatism and Catholicism, which in the eyes of the social democrats all in all 'represented the opposite of the Swedish model' (Silva, 1997, p. 379) – an
emphasis on the ultimate importance of remaining neutral (and ideally a
'bridge builder' between East and West). This position had nothing less
than hegemonic status within the party until about the mid-1980s.

It is worth underlining that the parties I mentioned so far were not the only
major social democratic parties who initially had reservations about European
integration. In the immediate post-war period, the German SPD was equally

unexcited about more ambitious integration plans. Indeed, the then-relatively isolated SPD 'staunchly opposed several measures often seen as steps on the road to a united Europe, most notably the creation of the International Authority of the Ruhr, the Schuman Plan (the European Coal and Steel Community), and the European Defence Community' (Imlay, 2017, p. 225). Kurt Schumacher, who dominated the SPD's leadership until his death in 1952, was the driving force behind this: though he in principle supported the idea of a Western economic-political bloc as a counter-weight to the Soviet Union, he also insisted on a maximally tough oppositional strategy vis-à-vis the Christian Democratic Adenauer government. Accordingly, he rejected the latter's proposals for Europe, dismissing the '*Kleineuropa*' (small Europe) of 'the Six' – Belgium, France, Italy, Luxembourg, Netherlands, and West Germany – as 'conservative, clerical, capitalist and cartelist' (Brandt, 1996, pp. 52–53). It was only Schumacher's death in 1952 – and the gradual intensification of exchanges between the SPD and other European social democratic parties – that 'created an opening for the more pro-European forces within the SPD', leading to a shift towards an integrationist stance (Imlay, 2017, p. 225).

Towards a morphology of social democratic Euroscepticism

With this overview in place, we can now proceed to get a clearer sense of the concepts and beliefs that comprised the British and Scandinavian traditions of Euroscepticism. To that end, it is useful to engage with Freeden's (1998, pp. 47–91) morphological model of political ideologies. As I have already noted, this model sees ideologies as comprised of three primary components, namely core, adjacent and peripheral concepts, each of which have a different status and perform distinctive functions within an ideological formation. *Core concepts* are those elements of an ideology that determine central objectives and maintain a stable meaning. Think, for example, of the status of the notion of 'freedom' within the conceptual structure of liberalism. This informs liberals' conceptions of a desirable social order, as well as mediating how they engage with other elements of their ideology. For example, concepts such as 'community' are typically conceived in ways that are compatible with a core commitment to freedom; the latter simply forms a baseline value all other concepts must be brought in resonance with.

Adjacent concepts, in turn, are defined by Freeden as compatible with core concepts and serving the end of furnishing ideologies with additional meanings. At the same time, adjacent concepts are not an integral and ineliminable part of an ideology, and their meaning and status might be modified and adapted in response to social, cultural and political change. To illustrate, let us revisit again the example of liberalism and the adjacent concept of 'community'. 'Community' may be conceived by liberals as having a local relationship with the concept of 'freedom', say in the sense that an individual's autonomy hinges on her integration into the community within which she lives. Yet, community is in this view only considered desirable because it is seen as compatible with freedom, so its status within the liberal ideological formation is contingent. It has no intrinsic value and getting rid of it would not harm liberalism's essential meanings.

Finally, *peripheral concepts* are conceived as those concepts that are located at the margins of an ideological formation, allowing practitioners of an ideology to relate their ideological commitments to very concrete contexts. These concepts often take what may be called a 'programmatic' form and operate on specific political events. One example is trade-unionism in the context of socialist ideologies. Many a socialist party regarded trade unions as 'crucially involved with the organizational aspects of working-class politici-zation', but once we look at 'socialist conceptualizations of [trade unions'] functions and attributes' it emerges that their relationship to socialism's con-ceptual core is negligible (Freeden, 1998, p. 451). To the extent that trade unions are valued by socialists, they are valued as a pragmatic response to particular political challenges, not as a central ideological commitment.

The virtue of Freeden's three-tiered framework is that it helps shed light on the complex relationships that exist between the different concepts that com-prise an ideological formation, as well as on the status of individual concepts within that formation. To see why this is relevant, it suffices to reflect for a moment on one of the points mentioned in the previous section, namely that neutrality was a major reason why the Swedish social democrats initially rejected EEC membership. Applying Freeden's conceptual apparatus here permits us to establish whether neutrality was an 'adjacent' concept that was logically linked to the core values of social democracy without itself con-stituting such a core value, or merely a 'peripheral' one, without any note-worthy logical relationship to social democratic core commitments.

Before turning to this and other questions, it is worth noting that it would be misleading to assume that the abstract morphological structure of a par-ticular ideological tradition is neatly replicated by all the parties or move-ments that claim allegiance to it. Not least because political actors are often required to adapt their message to a specific socio-historical context, the exact structure of their conceptual foundations is often difficult to trace. Nonetheless, I want to argue in what follows that there are clearly distinguish-able features within British and Scandinavian social democracy that also adhere to the conceptual morphology of the broader ideological family of social democrats.

When social democratic ideologies are located within Freeden's conceptual framework, it is most plausible to regard as their most central core concept a commitment to what Berman (2006) has called the 'primacy of politics', or perhaps more accurately: the primacy of collective democratic self-determi-nation in virtually all spheres of society, especially the economic sphere. As

Jackson (2013:, p. 349) puts it, social democracy 'prescribes the use of demo-cratic collective action to extend the principles of freedom and equality valued by democrats in the political sphere to the organisation of the economy and society, chiefly by opposing the inequality and oppression created by laissez-faire capitalism'. While it is possible to identify specific con-cepts and values that figure in different social democratic bodies of thought, their meaning is typically determined by their relationship to this principal commitment. (This was so at least before many social democratic parties departed from their traditional core commitments in the 1980s and 1990s, making a 'concession to the primacy of the market over democratic politics' [Faucher-King and Le Galès, 2010; Jackson, 2013, p. 360; Mudge, 2018].)

The central commitment to the democratisation of 'economy and society' was shared also by the British and Scandinavian social democrats in the post-war era, when their scepticism toward European integration originally devel-oped. Most visible is this perhaps in the Swedish social democrats' (SAP) party manifestos from 1944 and 1960 – the party's two main post-war manifestos. Each begins by stating that the party's primary goal is to 'rebuild' society (in the 1944 manifesto it explicitly says 'bourgeois society') in such a way that 'the right to decide over production' and the distribution of associated gains should 'lie in the hands of the whole people' (the two manifestos use almost the same formulation, see Arbetarrörelsens arkiv och bibliotek, 2001, p. 40 and 52). This should 'liberate citizens from their dependence on any sort of market actors that are beyond their control' and ensure that 'a societal order built on [different] classes, makes space for a community of people who cooperate on the basis of liberty and equal status' (Arbetarrörelsens arkiv och bibliotek, 2001, p. 52). Statements of this kind continued to preface the party's manifestos, and be voiced by major figures within the party, for decades to come (cf. Brandt et al., 1976).

The Danish social democrats rarely made such emphatic programmatic statements in the immediate post-war period, even though – as noted – they had quite ambitious political reform plans. Nonetheless, in multiple party documents a fundamental commitment to 'democratic socialism' and an 'anti-capitalist' politics that should 'break down class differences' is under-lined, which must be realised through 'cooperation among the labour market's different parties (arbejdsmarkedets parter)' and on the 'basis of parlia-mentary democracy' (Socialdemokraterne, 1953: n.p.). And Hedtoft – Den-mark's social democratic prime minister after the war – is quoted (in Laursen & Olesen, 2000, p. 64) saying that the 'consequence of political democracy is economic democracy'. By contrast, the Labour party was unam-biguously clear about its principled commitment to public ownership, especially in the 1945 election. The 1945 manifesto – recently described as the basis for 'the most radical economic programme ever implemented in Britain' (Guinan and Hanna, 2018, p. 123) – indeed promised 'drastic policies and keeping a firm constructive hand on our whole productive machinery' as a strategy of no tolerance against 'the sectional interests of private business', putting 'community first' (Labour Party, 1945). More specifically, the proposal was to bring the Bank of England, coal, steel, civil aviation and the major utilities into public hands. In line with social democracy's core concept of extending democratic principles to the organisation of the economy and society, this should help secure 'freedom for the ordinary man and woman, whether they be wage-earners or small business or professional men or housewives' (Labour Party, 1945).

The remainder of this article investigates how the main ideational components of social democratic Euroscepticism in Great Britain, Denmark and Sweden relate to social democracy's core concept of the primacy of politics, understood in the just-described terms. The components I examine in turn have already briefly been touched upon: sovereignty, neutrality, and national identity.

Sovereignty as adjacent concept

As Freeden (1998: 438) notes, all ideologies' core concepts 'are vacuous unless situated in a constraining idea-environment. They are surrounded by an intricate and sophisticated body of adjacent concepts' that endow them with meaning. Some of these adjacent concepts 'display durability of presence, others are interchangeable, but all will, through subtle or less subtle decontestations of their own, react back on the core concepts to impart to the latter the further specificity'. The perhaps most important such adjacent concept in the context of social democratic Euroscepticism is the concept of *sovereignty*, more specifically national sovereignty.

The country where the notion of national sovereignty played the most central role in social democratic opposition to European integration was – and arguably still is – the UK. Indeed, from the outset the relevant debates about Europe within the Labour party 'hinged on conceptions of sovereignty' (Hickson & Miles, 2018, p. 867). These debates began in the post-war period and took up pace as the UK joined the European Communities, and eventually continued all the way into the 1980s, when the Labour party still was 'the anti-European party' in British politics (O'Rouke, 2019, p. 153). The main concern voiced by those Labour members who rejected 'more Europe' was that membership in the EEC effectively meant the end of national sovereignty residing in the Westminster Parliament and, thereby, the end of meaningful popular self-rule. As Labour MP Peter Shore put it in 1972, 'I did not come into socialist politics in this country to connive in the dismantling of the power of the British people as represented in their parliament and in their government' (Labour Party, 1972, p. 205). Several other Labour politicians, such as Anthony Wedgwood and Tony Benn, echoed the concern.

This position was closely entwined with several other arguments against membership in the European Communities and a deepening of European integration more generally. There was for one thing the popular view that the EEC is a fundamentally capitalist institution, 'membership of which would make it difficult or impossible to pursue socialist policies in Britain' (O'Rouke, 2019, p. 74; cf. Croft, 1988). As we saw, this was a major concern in 1945, but it remained lingering and was never entirely dispelled. National sovereignty was accordingly a pre-requisite for implementing a social democratic political agenda, since the dominant political forces on the continent pulled in the opposite direction, aiming to shape Europe and its common institutions of cooperation in a conservative and capitalist image (recall Schumacher's 'four c's'). For another thing, the sovereignty argument was also justified with arguments to do with Britain's national identity and particular history. (I will look more closely at these ideas in the subsequent section, arguing that they have a 'peripheral' status in relation to social democratic core concepts.)

However, the sovereignty debate within the Labour party proved highly divisive. Several important figures within the party resisted the interpretation of sovereignty advanced by those opposed to European integration and British Communities-membership. One of them, John Mackintosh, argued in the Commons debate on entry into the European Communities in 1971 that 'no nation has un-tramelled sovereignty, no nation has complete power to do as it likes, and what matters to the public is not the legal power to act but whether the consequences may mean anything', and accused his intra-party opponents of endorsing a 'very restricted and old-fashioned concept of sovereignty' (Hansard, 1971). Mackintosh believed that the states of Europe were increasingly becoming interdependent, and that membership in the EEC in particular would therefore not diminish sovereignty but in some respects even enhance it. In his own words: 'the decision to join with the other powers was not in fact a derogation or loss of sovereignty; it was in reality an increase in the effective power of this House' (Hansard, 1971).[2]

To mention these disagreements is important because they unveil the 'adjacent' status of the concept of sovereignty. By this I mean that the notion of sovereignty is only assigned instrumental value in relation to the social democratic core concept of the primacy of politics: sovereignty may be interpreted in radically different ways, the point of the distinct interpretations being only to demonstrate how sovereignty can serve social democratic ends. As such, however, sovereignty has no intrinsic value. This helps explain why, as we saw, both those who opposed *and* those who favoured membership in the EEC, argued that their preferred path forward (i.e., national vs. 'pooled' sovereignty) would *strengthen* the 'effective power' (Mackintosh) of the UK parliament, thereby also increasing Labour's capacity to pursue its preferred policies in Britain.

To fully understand why two diametrically opposed interpretations of sovereignty are logically compatible with social democracy's ideological core, it is useful to remember that social democrats – in contradistinction to Orthodox Marxists – never developed a self-standing theory of the state. Instead, they endorsed the sovereign liberal state as they found it as a unitary system of cooperation, suggesting that its institutions of collective government – above all, representative parliamentary democracy – should be used to advance social democratic ends (Jackson, 2013, pp. 351–352; Berman, 2006: ch. 3; for a famous critique, see Luxemburg, 1970). This is true not only for the British social democrats, many of whom from the mid-twentieth century regarded this approach as 'justified by events' as they managed to form a parliamentary majority and implement their goals (Hickson & Miles, 2018, p. 867). The Danish and Swedish social democrats were likewise committed to what Berman (2006:, p. 166) calls 'reform-based social transformation' within the institutional framework of the liberal-democratic state. The Nordic social democratic parties were in fact generally heavily influenced by liberal thought, especially compared with their continental counter-parts: it was for instance not uncommon in Sweden to see 'socialism as a form of making liberalism complete' (Müller, 2011, p. 65).

Yet, the sovereign liberal state was a contingent historical configuration that was accepted by social democrats mainly for pragmatic reasons, and so it was also possible for some of them to re-interpret the meaning of sovereignty in ways that responded to the 'changing facts' of growing interdependence and increased economic cooperation between the states of Western Europe. This was essentially the approach taken by Mackintosh in his aforementioned defence of Communities-membership as potentially 'increasing', rather than undermining, the power of the UK parliament. (And, at a more theoretical level, it is also reflected in the so-called 'pluralist' tradition within Labour thought that goes back to the writings of G.C.H. Cole and Harold Laski, and regards 'the state as one, but only one, way of implementing socialism' [Hickson & Miles, 2018, p. 868]. This tradition was rediscovered in the 1980s by writers such as Paul Hirst [1989] and David Marquand [1988], who viewed sovereigntist statism as discredited.)

In Denmark and Sweden, debates around national sovereignty within the social democratic parties took a quite different shape. Notably, the issue did not prove as divisive as in the UK. In Sweden in particular, there was for a long time a relatively broad agreement among social democrats that national sovereignty ought to be preserved, and that that spoke against membership in the European Communities – although already in 1960 the SAP highlighted in its party manifesto that Sweden must adapt to a 'world, where national borders and national sovereignty lose much of their old meaning or where governments and peoples (*folk*) to an increasing extent must submit to new rules for international coexistence' (Arbetarrörelsens arkiv och bibliotek, 2001, p. 61). Nor was sovereignty as strongly connected to democratic self-rule in the Swedish context as it was the case in the UK. Perhaps because the SAP all but completely dominated domestic politics up until the 1970s, it limited itself to portraying national sovereignty as a necessary prerequisite for preserving the specific (social-, economic-, agrarian-, etc.) policy regime that comprised the 'Swedish model', as well as emphasising that Swedish foreign traditionally policy demanded *alliansfrihet* (neutrality) (Misgeld, 1992, p. 64). I return to this latter issue shortly. The former concern – preserving the 'Swedish model' – may meanwhile be interpreted as analogous to the worry, held by many in the Labour party, that the EEC is a capitalist institution, membership of which would hamstring the pursuit of social democratic ends.

The notion that membership in the European Communities would obstruct or make impossible the implementation of social democratic goals was also *the* major fear the Danish social democrats harboured – at least in the immediate post-war period. Insofar as they proposed an intensification of Nordic cooperation with Sweden and Norway, however, they seemed in principle ready to renounce some of their national sovereignty so long as it did not mean ceding it to conservative 'core Europe'. Indeed, as Laursen and Olesen (2000:, p. 72, my emphasis) note, the social democratic vision of strengthened 'Nordic co-operation and integration' was repeatedly invoked from the late 1950s onwards 'as a defensive weapon aimed at safeguarding and fending off *European* challenges to Danish sovereignty and independence'. In the end, though, the Danish social democrats quickly – and quite pragmatically – came to regard Communities-membership as desirable. Already in the late 1940s they began giving in to pressures from right-leaning parties to engage more actively in the debate about the future of Europe (Olesen, 2006, p. 40), and despite some internal resistance they eventually supported the decision to join the Communities together with Britain in 1973. The priority, as the social democratic prime minister Jens Otto Krag put it in 1971, was to ensure that Denmark is capable of 'exercising voice on the future development of Europe, which we will under all circumstances be affected by' (Socialdemokraterne, 1971, p. 9). The defence of national sovereignty thus became a secondary issue.

Peripheral components of social democratic Euroscepticism

The conclusion to take from the previous section is that sovereignty as an adjacent concept played an important role in social democratic Euroscepticism, though the emphasis put on its value and its centrality to social democratic debates differed quite a lot across the three countries. In Britain, sovereignty proved absolutely central to the discussion on how social democracy should relate to European integration, and it was a divisive issue at that. In Sweden, the social democrats largely agreed that sovereignty ought to be safeguarded in order to protect Swedish neutrality and the specific social democratic policy achievements – an agreement that eventually lasted up until the 1990s – while the Danish social democrats were altogether less insistent on sovereignty, proposing first a Nordic cooperation and then relatively swiftly accepting European Communities membership.

To complete the picture, I turn in this section to the politically important peripheral concepts that filled social democratic Euroscepticism with additional contextual meaning. To recall: following Freeden's morphological framework for studying political ideologies, 'peripheral' concepts are concepts that can be located at the margins of an ideological formation. They typically lack a logical connection to the ideology's core concepts but are important inasmuch as they allow the practitioners of an ideology to relate their commitments to concrete social and political contexts. Their 'permutations and responsiveness to cultural constraints' are accordingly 'virtually infinite' (Freeden 1998: 450). The particular peripheral concepts I will focus on are *national identity* and *neutrality*, the latter being relevant only in the Swedish case. These concepts were often evoked in tandem with core and adjacent concepts (like sovereignty), but can be analytically distinguished from them.

Firstly, arguments from national identity were advanced in all three countries in question, again perhaps most emphatically in Britain. Earlier I briefly mentioned the Labour party's 1951 pamphlet 'European Unity', which stressed that Britain has more in common with the countries of the Commonwealth than with continental Europe. This is a good indication of the nature of the identity-based ideas held by Labour's Eurosceptic wing. Arguably the most influential manifestation of this strand of Labour thinking was then-party leader Hugh Gaitskell's 1962 party conference speech – sometimes called the 'high watermark of social democratic Euroscepticism' in Britain (Hickson & Miles, 2018, p. 871). In this speech, Gaitskell famously argued that Labour should pursue closer ties with the Commonwealth, rather than European Communities membership and European integration. His argument underlined the distinctiveness of the UK's particular, historically grown identity:

> [W]e are not just a part of Europe – at least not yet. We have a different history. We have ties and links which run across the whole world, and for me at least the Commonwealth, the modern Commonwealth, which owes its creation fundamentally to those vital historic decisions of the Labour Government, is something I want to cherish (Labour Party, 1962, p. 12).

Like many other Labour Eurosceptics, Gaitskell regarded European integration as a fundamentally federal project, warning that participation in it would imply Britain becoming 'no more than a state … in the United States of Europe, such as Texas and California … it does mean the end of Britain as

an independent state' and thus also 'the end of a thousand years of history …
and … the end of the Commonwealth' (Labour Party, 1962, p. 11 and 12).
(Note that Danish PM Hedtoft, in an earlier-quoted passage, also refers to a
'thousand years' of shared Scandinavian history.) In sum, Gaitskell made the
case for resisting European integration on the grounds that Britain's national
identity as an empire that had to 'think of global not regional problems; of the
interest of all races not just of one' precluded it (O'Rouke, 2019, p. 74). His
famous speech significantly 'influenced the next generation of Labour's …
Eurosceptics including Bryan Gould, Austin Mitchell and Gwyneth Dunwoody'
(Hickson & Miles, 2018, p. 874), and it is still appealed to by present-day critics
of European integration within the party (Stringer, 2019).

What seems clear is that these arguments have a negligible logical relationship to social democracy's conceptual core of advancing the democratisation
of all domains of society. True, Gaitskell also linked his idea of Britain's exceptionalism to a particular interpretation of national sovereignty that sees the
pursuit of social democratic goals as presupposing a sovereign nation state
and may be classified as an adjacent concept; but the identity-focused
claims I discuss in this section are clearly peripheral to British social democracy's system of ideas. They are, to speak with Freeden, best understood as
a 'cultural constraint' imposed on Labour ideology by the fact that practitioners of that ideology were operating in a particular historical context.

The same may be said about Scandinavian identity-based arguments against
European integration, though these took a very different shape compared with
the British ones. At a general level, claims to the effect that the particularities of
Danish or Swedish national identity would rule out membership in the European Communities were not animated by a sense that the responsibility of
Nordic countries was more global than European, as in the British case;
rather, as Olesen (2000:, p. 162) notes, it was underpinned by the worry 'that
encroachments from Brussels will affect the Nordic way of life and endanger
basic Nordic values'. In Denmark, this view was widespread among social democrats up until their gradual acceptance of EEC membership in the mid to late
1960s. An emblematic example is the following statement made by Niels Mat-
thiasen, a social democratic party secretary and later minister, in 1957:

> As a member of the Common Market we would become the seventh country in
> a union dominated by the Catholic Church and Right-Wing political movements.
> It serves no purpose to claim that the Danish concept of democracy is the same
> as the German, the French or the Italian. It is evident that Danish democracy and
> political life are based on a different foundation equalling to some extent what
> you find in Britain, and in certain respects in Canada and the USA, but first and
> foremost in the other Nordic countries (quoted in Engberg, 1986, p. 68).

Such sentiments were not uncommon at that time, neither in Denmark nor in
Sweden. They were further reinforced by a 'widespread belief' shared by

voters and political elites 'that the Nordics had created a welfare state system of unique and superior standard to all others' – a system that, to repeat, thoroughly shaped a particular Nordic form of life, and that was threatened by the core Europe of the Six with its ostensibly conflicting political leanings (Olesen, 2000, p. 165). The logical connection of these claims to social democracy's ideological core is very weak, however; it seems again plausible to speak of ideology-shaping 'cultural constraints', distinctive national perceptions of reality that had a great impact on Danish and Swedish social democratic thinking. For it was certainly not the case that the social democratic parties in the countries that were 'dominated by the Catholic Church and Right-Wing political movements' had fundamentally different goals than their Nordic sister parties (cf. Brandt et al., 1976). (Nor did the Catholic parties who were in power in the larger part of 'core Europe' refuse to implement relatively generous welfare states; see Berman, 2006: ch. 8.)

This leads to the final peripheral concept of social democratic Euroscepticism: neutrality. As already noted, this concept is centrally important only to the Swedish case, where social democrats insisted almost up until the country's EU accession in 1995 that the long-standing neutrality policy 'precluded Swedish membership in the EC' (Silva, 1997, p. 376). One reason why neutrality is but peripheral to the structure of social democratic ideology is simple: Sweden's neutrality policy defined Sweden's relations to foreign powers since the early nineteenth century, preceding the age of social democracy (Andrén, 1996; Ringmar, 1998, p. 49). It was not 'invented' by social democrats, nor was it adequately theorised by them. Yet neutrality was extremely popular across partisan divides, and so the SAP had little choice but to accept it as a core pillar of their own foreign policy. Indeed, even their attempts to rationalise neutrality 'as one of the constitutive pillars of the Swedish welfare state' in the *folkhem*-era of the mid-twentieth century cannot distract from the fact that neutrality policy had a status 'close to a semi-ideology or mentality' that permeated the whole country, and was generally associated with all imaginable benefits (Olesen, 2000, pp. 156–157). So, while a principled commitment to a 'firm (*fast*) and neutral (*alliansfri*) foreign policy' (Arbetarrörelsens arkiv och bibliotek, 2001, p. 88) was close to the heart of most Swedish social democrats, it would be misleading to say it was more than a peripheral concept in relation to social democracy's core concepts; indeed, it is difficult to see how any other governing party could have deviated from it.

Conclusion

This article examined the ideological tradition of social democratic Euroscepticism in Great Britain, Denmark and Sweden, using Freeden's morphological model of political ideologies as a framework for analysis. There are two main takeaways. First, there is no necessary logical relationship between social democracy's core commitments and a rejection of European integration. Second, reflecting on the 'adjacent' status of the notion of sovereignty in social democratic ideology draws our attention to the challenging question of what role the liberal state can and should play in the pursuit of social democratic ends.

How social democrats relate to European integration seems to depend in important ways on how they answer this question. In the past, social democratic Eurosceptics have justified their commitments by pointing out that European integration threatens the sovereign liberal state as a unitary system of cooperation that historically enabled social democrats to achieve so many things. Social democratic integrationists have in turn advanced a contrasting position that emphasises the need for pooling sovereignty in an interconnected world, and presents European integration as a successful and hence desirable attempt of doing so. Both of these positions still figure in contemporary debates on the left.

Yet, neither position is without drawbacks. The view that European integration should be opposed because state sovereignty is a precondition for implementing social democratic policies seems spurious, given how difficult it is to 'domesticise' capitalism after decades of dis-embedding it from statist political structures (cf. Roos, 2019). But the same may be said about the view that European integration should *generally* be affirmed as a way of pooling sovereignty, given that the EU by design subordinates democratic politics to markets (Isiksel, 2016: ch. 4). To move forward, social democracy perhaps needs a new theory of the state, one that does not merely accept existing liberal arrangements as given. Acknowledging that its traditional understanding of the state can be replaced without undermining core commitments is a productive first step.

Notes

1. All of this must be seen in light of the more general tendency of social democratic and socialist parties to prioritise national considerations over international ones after 1914 (e.g. Misgeld, 1984, pp. 18–19; Sassoon, 1996, p. 29). This is not to say that internationalism ceased to exist in the post-1914 period (Imlay, 2017, p. 218), but it is arguably the case that many social democratic parties were more strongly oriented toward their nation. And, as the Danish social democrats' calls for stronger Nordic cooperation – instead of more cooperation with continental states – illustrates, even where they sought to knit cross-national ties, this was not necessarily driven by genuinely internationalist aims.
2. Mackintosh's primary example was monetary policy. As he put it in the 1971-debate: 'We in this Parliament have the sovereign power to regulate many things in connection with sterling as a currency, its control and the rates of exchange at which we offer to trade in sterling. If other forces outside the country result in a serious run on our sterling reserves we cannot continue to

operate the system; we do not have the sovereignty to carry out economic policies through to the conclusion that our people want' (Hansard, 1971).

Acknowledgements

A previous draft of the paper was presented at the Universidad Carlos III de Madrid. The comments received on this occasion proved immensely helpful. In addition, I would like to thank Josef Hien, Philip Rathgeb, Antoinette Scherz, Glyn Morgan and two anonymous reviewers for further important observations and criticisms.

Disclosure statement

No potential conflict of interest was reported by the author(s).

Funding

This work was supported by Nederlandse Organisatie voor Wetenschappelijk Onderzoek: [Grant Number 016.Veni.185.084].

References

Andrén, N. (1996). *Maktbalans och alliansfrihet: svensk utrikespolitik under 1900-alet*. Norstedts juridik.
Arbetarrorelsens arkiv och blbllotek. (2001). *Socialdemokratins Program: 1897–1990*.
Aylott, N. (1999). *Swedish Social Democracy and European Integration: The People's Home on the Market*. Ashgate.
Bailey, D. J. (2005). Obfuscation through integration: Legitimating "New" social democracy in the European union. *JCMS*, *43*(1), 13–35. https://doi.org/10.1111/j.0021-9886.2005.00544.x.
Berman, S. (2006). *The Primacy of Politics*. CUP.
Bickerton, C., & Tuck, R. (2018). A Proposal for Brexit. Retrieved May 10, 2019 from https://briefingsforbrexit.com/a-brexit-proposal-by-christopher-bickerton-and-richard-tuck/.
Brandt, P. (1996). Demokratischer Sozialismus - Deutsche Einheit - Europäische Friedensordnung: Kurt Schumacher in der Nachkriegspolitik (1945–1952). In D. Dowe (Ed.), *Referate und Podiumsdiskussion Eines Kolloquiums des Gesprächskreises Geschichte der Friedrich-Ebert-Stiftung in Bonn* (pp. 35–56). Forschungsinstitut der Friedrich-Ebert-Stiftung.
Brandt, W., Kreisky, B., & Palme, O. (1976). *Briefe und Gespräche, 1972-1975*. Büchergilde Gutenberg.
Croft, S. (1988). British policy towards Western Europe, 1947-9: The best of possible Worlds? *International Affairs*, *64*(4), 617–629. https://doi.org/10.2307/2626046

Davis, R. (2017). Euroscepticism and opposition to British entry into the EEC, 1955-75. *French Journal of British Studies XXII*, 2, 1–15. https://doi.org/10.4000/rfcb.1364.

Engberg, J. (1986). *I minefeltet: Træk af arbejderbevægelsens historie siden 1936*. Arbejderbevægelsens Erhvervsråd.

Faucher-King, F., & Le Galès, P. (2010). *The New Labour Experiment: Change and Reform Under Blair and Brown*. Stanford UP.

Forlenza, R. (2017). The politics of the *Abendland*: Christian democracy and the idea of Europe after the Second world War. *Contemporary European History*, *26*(2), 261–286. https://doi.org/10.1017/S0960777317000091

Forster, A. (2002). Anti–Europeans, anti–marketeers and Eurosceptics: The evolution and Influence of Labour and conservative opposition to Europe. *Political Quarterly*, *73*(3), 299–308. https://doi.org/10.1111/1467-923X.00470

Freeden, M. (1998). *Ideologies and Political Theory: A Conceptual Approach*. OUP.

Guinan, Joe, & Hanna, Thomas M. (2018). Democratic Ownership in the New Economy. In John McDonnell (Ed.), *Economics for the Many* (pp. 108–125). London: Verso.

Hansard. (1971). *Hansard 27th October 1971*. https://api.parliament.uk/historic-hansard/commons/1971/oct/27/european-communities.

Heffernan, R. (2001). Beyond Euro-scepticism: Exploring the Europeanisation of the Labour Party since 1983. *Political Quarterly*, *72*(2), 180–189. https://doi.org/10.1111/1467-923X.00356

Hickson, K., & Miles, J. (2018). 'Social democratic Euroscepticism: Labour's neglected tradition'. *British Journal of Politics and International Relations*, *20*(4), 864–879. https://doi.org/10.1177/1369148118787148

Hirst, P. (1989). *After Thatcher*. Collins.

Imlay, T. (2017). Socialist Internationalism after 1914. In G. Sluga & P. Clavin (Eds.), *Internationalisms: A Twentieth-Century History* (pp. 213–243). CUP.

Isiksel, T. (2016). *Europe's Functional Constitution: A Theory of Constitutionalism Beyond the State*. OUP.

Jackson, B. (2013). Social democracy. In M. Freeden, & M. Stears (Eds.), *The Oxford Handbook of Political Ideologies* (pp. 348–363). OUP.

Labour Party. (1945). *Let Us Face the Future*.

Labour Party. (1962). *Britain and the Common Market*.

Labour Party. (1972). *Report of the Seventy-First Annual Conference of the Labour Party*.

Lapavitsas, C. (2019). *The Left Case Against the EU*. Polity.

Laursen, J. N., & Olesen, T. B. (2000). A Nordic Alternative to Europe? The interdependence of Denmark's Nordic and European policies, 1945-1998. *Contemporary European History*, *9*(1), 59–92. https://doi.org/10.1017/S096077730000103X

Leconte, C. (2010). *Understanding Euroscepticism*. Palgrave.

Lightfoot, Simon. (2005). *Europeanizing Social Democracy? The Rise of the Party of European Socialists*. Abingdon: Routledge.

Loth, W. (1990). The socialist international. In W. Lipgens, & W. Loth (Eds.), *Documents on the History of European Integration, Vol. 4: Transnational Organizations of Political Parties and Pressure Groups in the Struggle for European Union, 1945-1950* (pp. 436–476). De Gruyter.

Luxemburg, R. (1970). *Reform or Revolution*. Pathfinder.

Marquand, D. (1988). *The Unprincipled Society*. Fontana.

Misgeld, K. (1984). *Sozialdemokratie und Außenpolitik in Schweden: Sozialistische Internationale, Europapolitik und Deutschlandfrage*. Campus.

Misgeld, K. (1992). Den svenska socialdemokratin och Europa från slutet av 1920-talet till början av 1970-talet. *Arbeiderhistorie*, *1992*(2), 55–80.

Mudge, S. L. (2018). *Leftism Reinvented: Western Parties from Socialism to Neoliberalism*. Harvard University Press.

Müller, J.-W. (2011). *Contesting Democracy: Political Ideas in Twentieth-Century Europe*. Yale University Press.

Olesen, T. B. (2000). Choosing or Refuting Europe? The Nordic countries and European integration, 1945-2000. *Scandinavian Journal of History*, *25*(1-2), 147–168. https://doi.org/10.1080/03468750050115645

Olesen, T. B. (2006). Dansk europapolitik 1945-2005: Hovedtræk og hovedbrud. *Økonomi & Politik*, *79*(2), 38–53.

O'Rouke, K. (2019). *A Short History of Brexit: From Brentry to Backstop*. Penguin.

Raunio, R. (2007). Softening but Persistent: Euroscepticism in the Nordic EU countries. *Acta Politica*, *42*(2-3), 191–210. https://doi.org/10.1057/palgrave.ap.5500183

Ringmar, E. (1998). Re-Imagining Sweden: The Rhetorical Battle over EU membership. *Scandinavian Journal of History*, *23*(2), 45–63. https://doi.org/10.1080/03468759850116016

Roos, J. (2019). From the Demise of social democracy to the "End of capitalism": The Intellectual Trajectory of Wolfgang Streeck. *Historical Materialism*, *27*(2), 248–288. https://doi.org/10.1163/1569206X-00001599

Sassoon, D. (1996). *One Hundred Years of Socialism*. The New Press.

Silva, C. (1997). Europe or Bust? European integration in Recent Swedish Historiography. *Scandinavian Studies*, *69*(3), 376–381.

Socialdemokraterne. (1953). *Vejen til fremskridt: En henvendelse til det danske folk*. Det Kongelige Bibliotek.

Socialdemokraterne. (1971). *Socialdemokratiet og EF*. Det Kongelige Bibliotek.

Stringer, G. (2019). There is a strong leftwing case against the EU. *The Guardian* 9 January 2019. Retrieved February 10, 2019, from https://www.theguardian.com/politics/2019/jan/09/there-is-a-strong-leftwing-case-against-the-eu.

European integration and the reconstitution of socio-economic ideologies: Protestant ordoliberalism vs social Catholicism

Josef Hien

ABSTRACT

Christian Democratic socio-economic ideology underwent a paradigm shift through the Europeanization of its party networks. Christian Democratic networks started with a distinctive Catholic socio-economic ideology emphasizing corporatism, welfare transfers and a coordination of the economy. This institutional blueprint influenced the early years of European socio-economic integration. The original social Catholicism was gradually replaced by Protestant and secular inspired socio-economic ideology, emphasizing undistorted market competition with successive enlargements of the European Union and the European People's Party (EPP). The article empirically reconstructs the contested process of transformation of the EPPs socio economic ideology through the inclusion of mainstream conservative and Protestant Christian Democratic parties and its impact on European Christian Democracy and the European integration process.

Introduction

Christian Democratic ideology had a core formative function in the early stages of European integration. Christian Democratic parties were hegemonic in the six founding states and the Catholic 'founding fathers' Adenauer, Schumann, and De Gasperi were all Christian Democrats. Pillars of Christian Democratic ideology like subsidiary, the reservations against the nation-state and federalism shaped the direction of European integration in the 1950s and 1960s. These state concepts of Catholic ideology – and the transnational Christian Democratic networks binding them together – have been well documented (Invernizzi-Accetti, 2019; Johansson, 2002; Kaiser, 2007). Yet, few studies pay attention to the socio-economic ideology of Christian Democracy (exception: Hanley, 2002).

This contribution gives an answer to the question why European Christian Democracy shifted its socio-economic ideology from its original social Catholic pro-welfareist and corporatist position in the 1950s and 1960s towards a neoliberal socioeconomic ideology from the 1990s onwards. The article argues that successive enlargement rounds of the European Union (EU) and the European People's Party (EPP) brought in new centre right parties in Spain, Portugal, Greece and Italy that embraced more secular forms of conservatism which were closer to the neoliberal socio-economic ideological orientation of Protestant Christian Democrats, especially in Germany but also in Denmark or Sweden. The new secular conservatives formed alliances with the existing Protestants within European Christian Democracy, marginalizing social Catholics and shifting the programme of European Christian Democracy from welfareist corporatism to neoliberal capitalism. The tripartite relationship between Catholics, more secular conservatives and Protestants brought about the ideological shift of the EPP.

The study breaks new ground in three ways: First, for the literature on EU integration, it highlights the 'other side' of the relation between ideologies and the EU. It shows not just how specific ideological traditions affected European integration, but also how these ideological traditions were themselves altered by this process in return. Second, for the literature on Christian Democracy in general, and Christian Democracy and the EU in particular, it shows that Christian Democracy does not only have a Catholic ideological core but also a Protestant one, which has so far been neglected in most contributions. Third, it offers a novel interpretation of the European Union's drift away from an originally corporatist and welfareist socio-economic institutional lay-out, congruent with Catholic social ideology, towards a neo-liberal inspired socio-economic institutional set-up congruent with Protestant socio-economic concepts. This understanding adds a crucial explanatory layer to known factors behind the neo-liberal turn, such as the stagflation crisis of the 1970s, the rise of various forms of neoliberalism in the 1980s, the end of the Cold War and developments in Social Democratic party ideology (Blyth, 2013; Bremer & McDaniel, 2019; Scharpf, 1991).

Section 1 proceeds with a discussion of methodological considerations and the existing literature. Section 2 reconstructs the socio-economic core concepts of Catholicism and Protestantism. Section 3 traces how the different socio-economic ideologies of Christian Democratic parties interact during the institutionalization of the European Christian Democratic party network. Section 4 concludes.

Studying ideology through morphology

The paper uses the morphological approach developed by Michael Freeden. Morphology allows to map 'temporal' (Freeden, 1994, p. 146) change in ideologies 'as a scientific endeavour' (Freeden, 2006, p. 7) which makes it a suitable analytical tool to assess change in European Christian Democratic socio-economic ideology.

According to Freeden ideologies consist of core, adjacent and peripheral concepts. The core concepts of ideologies maintain a stable, almost 'ineliminable' (Freeden, 1994, p. 147), meaning over time. Core concepts include a 'unit of political analysis, a view of human nature, a notion of social structure, a concept of moral ends' (Freeden, 1994, p. 150). Adjacent concepts add political meaning to the core concepts. They have to be compatible with the core concepts but can alter with social, cultural or political change. Peripheral concepts are located on the outer borders of the ideology and translate the ideological core and adjacent concepts into policy proposals.

To analyse the change in Christian Democratic ideology between the 1970s and 2000s, the article relies where possible on primary sources. The core concepts of European Christian Democratic socio-economic ideology are mapped through the Papal encyclical Quadragesimo Anno and the writings of the influential Catholic socio-economic thinkers of the inter- and post-war period Giorgio La Pira, Giuseppe Dossetti, Joseph Höffner, Friedhelm Hengsbach and Walter Kerber. For the mapping of the Protestant socio-economic core concepts key thinkers from the German ordoliberal school like Walter Eucken and his political allies in the Christian Democratic party Alfred Müller-Armack are analyzed.

Party platforms from conservative and Christian Democratic parties document the adjacent categories. Party platforms (called basic programmes by the EPP) are, in contrast to electoral manifestos and party programmes, issued scarcely (the EPP has so far only issued three in 1978, 1992, 2001). They reflect long-term ideological positions of parties. The adjacent concepts are further documented by the analysis of memoires and editorials, interviews and books written by central Christian Democratic politicians. These have been collected from the oral history holdings of the Historical Archives of the European Union in Florence (cited as HAEU), the Archiv für Christlich Demokratische Politik (cited as ACDP) in Sankt Augustin and the Oral History of European Integration Collection of the Centre Virtuel de la Conaissance sur L'Europe in Luxemburg (cited as CVCE). To map the peripheral concepts the study relies on election manifestos. The article considers all European Christian Democratic and conservative parties that have become members of the EPP.

Previous analysis of Christian Democratic socio-economic ideology

The best morphological mapping of Christian Democratic ideology has been made by Carlo Invernizzi-Accetti (2019). Invernizzi-Accetti identifies five core concepts: anti-materialism, personalism, populism, subsidiarity, social capitalism and Christian inspiration. These are reconstructed with ideas from Catholic Christian Democratic thinkers (Sturzo, Maritain, Schumann, La Pira, Leo XIII) in line with the Catholic layout of the Christian Democratic movement before WWII. Invernizzi-Accetti's chapter on social capitalism does not feature the word Protestantism. This exclusive focus on Catholicism is common in the literature on Christian Democracy and European integration.

The sociologist Etzioni (1963) pointed out already in the 1960s that European integration was possible because the founding states were Catholic. Early historiography argued that the integration project was a creation of Catholic Christian Democrats in search for peace (Lipgens, 1977). The historian Kaiser (2007) brought in attention to the role of the Nouvelle Equipes Intenationales (NEI), gatherings of Catholic politicians from all over Europe in the 1940s and 1950s as a driver for European integration. In the past decade, historians shifted the focus from network interaction between politicians to the role of symbols, ideas and values ideas in these networks (Acanfora, 2015; Cellini, 2018; Forlenza, 2017). The focus is on subsidiarity, federalism and anti-communism, in short the Christian Democratic concept of the state, but not on the socio-economic ideology (Cellini, 2018; Forlenza, 2017).

These contributions occasionally mention the call for a unified socio-economic ideology by Christian Democrats in the early phases of European integration. The Italian Christian Democratic leader Luigi Sturzo commented on the Sorrento congress that 'a positive doctrine' of socio-economic ideology is needed for European integration and the French Christian Democratic leader Henri Teitgen seconded on the Bad Ems congress in 1951 that it has to be 'aimed at emancipating the proletariat' (cited in Acanfora, 2010, p. 380, 387). The closing remarks of the NEI congress in Sorrento expressed that European integration should promote 'the subordination of economics to human interests' (cited in Cellini, 2018, p. 82). These quotes show that the transnational Christian Democratic socio-economic ideology discussed in the early phases of European integration was indeed connected to social Catholic socio-economic core concepts.

If Christian Democracy was based exclusively on Catholic and social-Catholic concepts and prescriptions of the economy as most of the literature suggests, then the union would be more corporatist than it is today. It would not have an independent central bank, hard currency, a strict competition policy that goes harshly against cartels and a strive for a free market (all not compatible with social-Catholic ideology). The union would not be accused of being neo- or ordoliberal (Blyth, 2013; Streeck, 2013). Instead, it would embrace corporatist interest mediation, peak level bargaining, and a transfer-oriented welfare state. This begs the question: what has happened to the formerly social-Catholic pro welfareist and corporatist socio-economic core ideology of European Christian Democracy?

Research on the socio-economic ideology of Christian Democracy and European integration has neglected that in some countries, Christian Democratic socio-economic ideology is not only based on Catholic but also on Protestant socio-economic core concepts. Catholic and Protestant socio-economic ideology developed in the 1930s in diametrically opposite directions (Bösch, 2001; Hien, 2019; Manow, 2001). While social Catholicism, with its pro-welfareist and corporatist ideology has been attributed a major role in continental welfare state restructuring after WWII, Protestant socio-economic thought has been associated with the establishing of anti-welfareism, anti-corporatism and pro market competition (Van Kersbergen, 1995). These insights have not yet been adequately reflected in studies of the socioeconomic structuring of the European integration process and the trans-nationalization of Christian Democracy in the European People's Party.

The paper argues that successive rounds of enlargement led to a shift of Christian Democratic socio-economic ideology from its early Catholic pro-welfareist and corporatist leaning to a neo-liberal socio-economic ideology more compatible with Protestant socio-economic thought. The enlargement of the Union and of the EPP did not directly alter the power balance in favour of Protestantism by including more Protestants and Protestant Christian Democratic parties. Instead, the northern, southern and eastern enlargement rounds brought in Protestant and Catholic countries that did not have a strong social Catholic Christian Democratic tradition in the way the original six member states had. The new parties joining the EPP stood in the tradition of secular conservative parties (especially the new Spanish PP and the FI in Italy). This conservatism, whether originating from Catholic or Protestant countries, tapped into the existing Protestant socio-economic ideology of some of the original Christian Democratic parties (the German CDU and Dutch Christian Democracy). The new conservative members formed alliances with these Protestant parts of the traditional Christian Democratic parties, progressively marginalizing social Catholics in the EPP and leading to an overall shift from welfare corporatism towards undistorted economic competition.

The socio-economic core concepts of Christian Democracy

Catholicism and Protestantism have diverging ascendance models that lead to different socio-economic ideologies (Sombart, 1902; Weber, 1905). Ascendance models and socio-economic ideologies are linked through the ethical status they ascribe to work. Before the split into different branches, unified medieval Christianity considered work a toil and a worldly plague (Kahl, 2005, p. 95). The rich did not work because their status forbid them to do so and the poor only worked in order to avoid starvation. Medieval (Catholic) Christianity did not attach any virtue to work as such, emphasizing that the here and now was anyhow only a waiting period towards the transcendental realm.

Through the Reformation, work was liberated from its status as toil and became central to Protestant doctrine (Gorski, 2003). Fulfilling one's vocation, not almsgiving, altruism or praying, became essential for ascendance. Weber claims that amongst 'Latin-catholic people', the terminology of vocational calling did not exist before Reformation (Schluchter, 2014, p. 57; Weber, 1920/1988, pp. 178–179). The work ethos of Protestantism stands in sharp contrast to the 'Communism of the ancestral Christianity and its derivates' (Weber, 1920/1988, pp. 100–101). The difference that Catholicism and Protestantism ascribe to work led to diverging socio-economic ideologies in the twentieth century.

After the world economic crisis of the late 1920s, both confessions reinforced their respective positions. The central document of modern Catholic socio-economic ideology was the social encyclical Quadragesimo Anno (Misner, 2004). Issued in 1931 it argued that 'the free market has destroyed itself' (Quadragesimo Anno: 109). The encyclical states that 'economic life cannot be left to a free competition of forces' (Quadragesimo Anno: 87) and proposes to embed capitalism through a transfer-heavy welfare state and a corporatist organization of the economy (Hengsbach, 2010; Kerber, 2013).

At the same time as Quadragesimo Anno was launched, German Protestant economists and lawyers developed ordoliberalism, the German branch of neo-liberalism, as a reply of German Protestantism to the world economic crisis (Krarup, 2019; Manow, 2001; Petersen, 2008). At its core is an argument against corporatism, extensive redistribution through the welfare state and state involvement in the economy (Eucken, 1949, p. 113; Müller-Armack, 1947, p. 130). Instead, ordoliberal Protestants argued in favour of a system of undistorted market competition protected through strong legal institutions that can break up the concentration of economic power of cartels or monopolies.

These two positions became the bases for the core concepts of European Christian Democratic socio-economic ideology after WWII. Depending on which confession prevailed, these core concepts translated into different socio-economic platforms (adjacent concepts) of European Christian Democratic parties. In Catholic countries, Christian Democracy adopted a social-Catholic inspired corporatist pro-welfare core concept (Italy, Belgium, Luxemburg, Netherlands until the unification of three Christian Democratic parties in the 1980s). In countries where Christian Democracy had to incorporate both confessional lines, like in Germany and the Netherlands after 1980, the adjacent concepts had to reflect both the Protestant and Catholic core concepts.

In the 1940s, the socio-economic peripheral and adjacent concepts of the German CDU ping-ponged back and forth with each programme between Ordoliberal Protestant and Social Catholic thought (Bösch, 2001, p. 35). The Ahlen party programme drafted in March 1946 pulled the CDU in the direction of Social Catholicism. Under the title 'CDU overcomes Marxism and Capital-ism', the programme opens with the assessment that 'The capitalist economic system did not live up to the state and social interests of the German people' (CDU, 1947, p. 3). Moreover, it calls for codetermination in industry and rigid state control of money, bank and insurance systems (CDU, 1947, p. 13). The Düsseldorfer Leitsätze, adopted by the CDU only three years later, pointed into a market-liberal direction. The document opens with the statement that 'he who wants to be free has to subordinate himself to competition' (CDU, 1949, p. 20). After the fluctuations of the 1940s and 1950s the party adopted a middle ground in its adjacent concepts between the two cores.

In contrast, the Italian DC was all-Catholic and had one ideological socio-economic core. The DCs founding father De Gasperi emphasized in his early writings the centrality of the Catholic corporatism of Quadragesimo Anno (Cau, 2009, p. 441). The DC had an influential social Catholic fraction: the 'dos-setians' named after Giuseppi Dossetti, a social philosopher at the Catholic Uni-versity of Milan (Masala, 2004, p. 101) who developed a synthesis of Keynesianism and social Catholicism. The reliance on Catholic-inspired core concepts is also evident in the adjacent concepts. The first party platform pre-scribes the establishment of an 'assembly of the organized interests' (DC, 1943, p. 1) next to parliament echoing the corporatism of Quadragesimo Anno.

Monoconfessional Catholic Christian Democratic parties like the Italian DC called for the implementation of a trans-European platform in line with their socio-economic core pushing for a 'coordination of the European Economy' (Acanfora, 2010, p. 213). On the NEI congress in Sorrento in 1950, the Italian Christian Democrat Lodovico Benvenuti argued that a 'missionary objective would fall to European Christian Democracy: the achievement of a real eman-cipation of the proletariat' (cited in Acanfora, 2010, p. 209).

Catholic and Protestant social ideology within European Christian Democracy

The differences between the socio-economic ideologies of Catholic and split denominational Christian Democratic parties grew in the 1970s. The Italian DC started to collaborate with the Partita Comunista Italiano (PCI) leading to a support of the DC government through the PCI in 1978.

The collaboration with the Communists reinforced the left social-Catholic socio-economic positions within the DC, leading to strong tensions with the German Christian Democrats. Henning Wegener, the head of the bureau for foreign relations of the CDU, described the drift to the left of the DC to party secretary Heiner Geissler, pointing out that the new party secretary Benigno Zaccaginis was now more eager to meet with the Social Democratic chancellor Schmidt than with the CDU leadership when visiting Germany (ACDP, 1977). The frictions became so tangible that the new party president

Flaminio Piccoli had to conclude his (Italian) speech on the CDU party congregation in Ludwigshafen in 1978 in German stating: 'You can relax, we have stayed the same – the Christian Democracy of Luigi Sturzo, of Alcide De Gasperi, of Aldo Moro'. (CDU, 1978, p. 22). While the developments were less extreme than in Italy, also the social-Catholic inspired socio-economic ideology of the Christian Democratic parties in the Benelux countries was reinforced through the political coalitions with Social Democratic parties in these countries. In the late 1960s and early 1970s the social-Catholic welfareist and corporatist socio-economic core reached the apex of its ideological strength in European Christian Democracy.

That the German Christian Democrats with their Protestant wing based on ordoliberal socio-economic ideology disapproved of the left-turn in the socio-economic ideology of other European Christian Democratic parties showed in the run-up to the northern enlargement of the EU in 1973. For the first time, countries that were neither Catholic (Britain, Denmark) nor had traditional Christian Democratic parties (Britain, Denmark, Ireland) became members of the EU. German Christian Democrats pushed for a collaboration with the British conservatives. Italian, Belgian and Catholic-Dutch Christian Democrats were afraid that an opening towards conservative parties from Protestant countries would dilute the social Catholic core concepts of European Christian Democracy and make it harder to align with Social Democratic, Socialist and Communist coalition partners at home (Gehler et al., 2018, p. 33; Jansen & Van Hecke, 2011). The head of the political academy of the Konrad Adenauer Stiftung, Bernhard Gebauer, briefed the president of the German parliament, the Christian Democrat von Hassel, on the reservations of the Italian and Benelux Christian Democrats in February 1972 stating that:

> in the domain of economic- and social policy the conservatives diverge form the principles of Christian social teaching. The conservatives emphasize private initiative so much that the obligations concerning the common good fall short and that necessary state intervention, even of limited scope, would be rejected programmatically. Always emphasized are the alleged reservations of conservatives to modern forms of planning and co-determination. (ACDP, 1972)

The German Christian Democrats that already 'integrated social Catholic, liberal-conservative and Protestant and Catholic conservative traditions' (Kaiser, 2013, p. 21) had no problem with incorporating conservative mainstream parties with neo-liberal socio-economic ideology (see also: Gehler et al., 2018, p. 31). The ordoliberal core of the socio-economic ideology of German Christian Democracy made it easier for the German CDU to accommodate the neo-liberal agenda of Thatcher than it was for purely Catholic Christian Democratic parties (Kaiser, 2013, p. 26).

When Thatcher got elected party leader of the British conservatives in 1975, tensions between Catholics and Protestants within the European

Christian Democratic movement peaked. As a guest speaker on the CDU party congregation in Hannover in 1976, Thatcher argued that 'the Christian Democratic, Conservative, and Centre parties in Europe should now join together in an effective working alliance'. (cited in Dörr, 2017, p. 78). Kurt Biedenkopf, then secretary general of the German Christian Democrats, Protestant and a student of the Ordoliberal founding father Franz Boehm, sided by clarifying that the German Christian Democrats were no longer only interested in a 'collaboration with the Christian parties in Europe, but in a full collaboration with the conservatives' (Biedenkopf cited by Kohl, 2015, p. 1870). Consequently, Kohl and Thatcher tried to initiate a network between European Christian Democratic and conservative parties. When this was discussed in a meeting of the party leadership of the CDU on 16 February 1976, Hans Katzer, an exponent of the left social Catholic employee wing of the CDU, voiced concerns pointing out how important a clear Christian Democratic commitment to the social-Catholic socioeconomic core would be for the union wings of Christian Democracy in Italy and the Benelux countries (ACDP, 1976). Katzer was right, in 1976 the Italian DC, together with the Dutch and Belgian Christian Democrats vetoed the accession of the British and other conservative parties to the foundational formation of the EPP.

Socio-economic adjacent concepts in the first EPP platform

On the 8th of July 1976, the EPP was founded. The discussion about the accession of the British conservatives had set in motion a discussion on the purity of Christian Democracy that slowly strengthened the neoliberal Protestant core embedded in German Christian Democracy. This can be seen in the first party platform, launched in 1978, that balanced between the social-Catholic and the Protestant core concepts of European Christian Democracy (EPP, 1978). The EPP aims to 'transcend[s] capitalism and collectivism' (EPP, 1978, p. 11.2) by adopting the Protestant ordoliberal concept of the social market economy. In line with the Protestant ordoliberal core of the German Christian Democrats, the EPP platform now emphasized 'the initiative of the individual', 'efficiency' and 'competition on the free market' next to the social Catholic core positions of 'active solidarity' and a 'better' distribution of economic 'decision making powers as well as property' (all EPP, 1978, p. 11.2).

The inclusion of both Protestant ordoliberal and social Catholic core concepts made the programme acceptable for both sides. German Christian Democrats, like the secretary of the CDU Heiner Geissler, emphasized the congruence with the socio-economic content in the party platforms of conservative parties in the UK and Denmark (Gehler et al., 2018, p. 47). The Catholic Dutch Prime Minister Dries van Agt argued that it included many social Catholic core positions since questions on 'the distribution of wealth' in society were central (ACDP, 1975).

The southern enlargement of the EU between 1981 and 1986 brought in three countries with center-right parties without a Christian Democratic position (Hanley, 2002, p. 469). While the German Christian Democrats argued in favour of a quick integration of the Greek *Nea Dimokratia*, the Spanish *Partido Popular (PP)* and the Portuguese *Partido Social Democrata* into the EPP, the Benelux parties opposed it (Kaiser, 2013, p. 25).

The Social Democrats had already included the Irish (1973), Danish (1973), Spanish (1979) and Portuguese (1979) parties into their party federation (Hix, 1999, p. 208). This made the EPP lose its dominance in the EP for the first time in 1980. The structural majority of Social Democrats softened the opposition towards the integration of conservative parties. In addition, after the assassination of the left-wing social-Catholic Aldo Moro in 1979, the new party leader Giulio Andreotti abandoned the rapprochement between the DC and the Communist PCI, decreasing the influence of the social-Catholic wing in the DC.

This paved the way for the inclusion of the Greek *Nea Dimokratia* in 1981 and the Spanish *Partido Popular* in 1991. Jose Maria Aznar, the leader of the PP, was a 'liberal conservative having been influenced by the liberal economists' (Gilmour, 2005, p. 426). According to him, the PP should be 'transformed into a modern, mainstream, European center-right party like those in power in Britain' (Gilmour, 2005, p. 426). The inclusion of the Spanish PP influenced the socio-economic adjacent concepts of the EPP.

While the 1978 platform was still accommodating between calls for free market competition and corporatism, the new party platform issued in 1992 included more market-liberal positions. The EPP now has 'trust in solutions which go hand in hand with the market economy' (EPP, 1992, p. 251) and 'pseudo-solutions' like 'increased public sector activity, more bureaucratic planning or more direct state intervention' (EPP, 1992, p. 251) are rejected. These neoliberal catch phrases can be attributed to the influence of the socio-economic ideology of the Spanish PP. The influence of the ordoliberal Protestant core of the German Christian Democrats can be felt in passages that stress the concept of the 'social market economy' (EPP, 1992, pp. 239–253) and argue to be 'vigilant with regards to the dangers of economic power' as well as to 'safeguard competition between market forces' (EPP, 1992, p. 139). All corporatist passages which featured in the 1978 EPP platform are gone.

However, even in the early 1990s the skepticism towards inclusion of more mainstream conservative parties remained. Kohl analyzed the religious character of the opposition in a meeting of the presidency of the CDU, pointing out that

> the Italians are always used as a pretext but the truth is that the main problem is in Den Haag, where with absolute severity of the Calvinist and Dutch-catholic strengthened fate, decisions are taken as who is conservative and who is not.

This cannot be our policy. We must be able to become the strongest party in the European parliament or more or less, so that we can take part in future decisions. (Kohl, 2012, p. 259)

Gérard Deprez, Belgian EPP member and European parliamentarian between 1984 and 2009, recalls how the German Christian Democrats pressed for the inclusion of conservative parties while he, as a Belgian Catholic EPP member, opposed it (CVCE, 2010a). The Catholic Christian Democrats could bar the British conservatives from entering the EPP but they could not prevent them from collaboration with the MEPs of the EPP. From 1992 onwards, British Tories and conservatives voted together. The shedding of some of the social Catholic positions from the EPP programme in 1992 paved also the way for the admission of a series of mainstream conservative parties without Christian Democratic traditions, like the Finnish (1995), Danish (1995), Swedish (1995), Portuguese (1996) conservatives and the Protestant Christian Democrats from Sweden (1995).

Aznar came to power in Spain in 1996 and was, after Kohl lost elections in 1998, the only conservative heavyweight left in government in Europe. Aznar was convinced that the EPP 'should move away from its original Christian Democrat ideology by adopting a more reformist agenda and implementing policies that would cut back the powers of the state' (Gilmour, 2005, p. 427).

Aznar was helped by the coincidence that, at the beginning of the 1990s, Italy experienced a corruption scandal leading to the implosion of the DC, the strongest all-Catholic Christian Democratic party. To fill the void, Silvio Berlusconi launched Forza Italia as a counter-image to the old DC. Berlusconi organized his party with strong managerial overlaps between his holding Fininvest and the party (HAEU, 1998, p. 13). Not only was the strong centralization and virtually nonexistent membership structure of the party very different from the DC, but also ideologically the party was a new beast (McDonnell, 2013). Berlusconi was eager to present himself as 'il nuovo' and distanced himself from the DC (Farrell, 1995; Poli, 1998). Instead of developing an ideological platform through deliberation with members he used 'professional marketing experts in designing the party's political message' as a 'Forza Italia product' (Hopkin & Paolucci, 1999, p. 326). The '4000 Forza Italia Clubs, aimed at mobilizing public opinion in favour of a vaguely neo liberal project' (Hopkin & Paolucci, 1999, p. 322). The first party platform's socioeconomic ideology was one 'of new right liberalism, with talks of slimming down the role of the state, measures to encourage private enterprise and tax cuts' (Hopkin & Paolucci, 1999, p. 325). The man put in charge to develop the economic side of the party platform was Antonio Martino, an economist trained by Milton Friedman in Chicago, and between 1988 and 1990 president of the Mont Pelerin society (HAEU, 1998, p. 10). Consequently, in the run-up to the elections Berlusconi expressed more than once 'the need to put the state on a diet' (Berlusconi cited in Semino & Masci, 1996, p. 257) and he was proud to tell the *Times* in 1994 that he had a portrait of Thatcher in his office (Berlusconi, 1994). The only overlap with a Christian Democratic ideology were appeals to 'Catholic commonplaces of family life' (Hopkin & Paolucci, 1999, p. 325). Aznar's and Berlusconi's new conservative parties were in their socio-economic ideology much closer to the British conservatives than to traditional Christian Democratic positions.

This explains why Forza Italia was first refused admission to the EPP group in 1994. Aznar continued to push to 'open up the EPP to Silvio Berlusconi's *Forza Italia*' generating fierce protest from the original EPP members arguing that the 'EPP's basic principles of social justice and Christian humanism were being abandoned in favour of FI's populist and liberal ideology'. (Gilmour, 2005, p. 427). There was also resistance from within Forza Italia to join the EPP. The cofounder of FI and leading FI European parliamentarian Luigi Caligaris protested in a phone call with Berlusconi that 'the Italians have voted for this movement because it is liberal' and that 'all of us, after passing a week there, we will become Christian Democrats' (HAEU, 1998, p. 18). In 1996 Berlusconi wrote a letter to Wilfried Martens, the head of the EPP, trying to diffuse the Christian Democratic resistance against his party in the EPP arguing that his party would be the true representative of the Catholic heritage of Italian Christian Democracy (ACDP, 1996a, p. 2). In the next meeting of the party presidency where the letter was discussed vice president Graziani found it 'ironic on part of mister Berlusconi to pretend that his movement has common roots with Christian Democracy' and that Berlusconi has 'no redeeming qualities to pretend to reunite the Catholics' (ACDP, 1996b, p. 2).

Being refused entry into the EPP, Berlusconi gave Caligaris free hands to negotiate an entry into the liberal or conservative party group in the EP. Caligaris recalled that the talks with liberals and conservatives 'went very well' (HAEU, 1998, p. 19). Berlusconi used the negotiations to threaten the EPP to found a new conservative European transnational party. Martens and his party secretary Poettering were 'dumbstruck' (Martens, 2006, p. 143). Martens recalls in an interview in 2010 that he had tried to avoid Berlusconi's entry for five consecutive years but that after the threat it was no longer possible (CVCE, 2010b).

Kohl feared a split of the EPP and invited the important leaders to an emergency meeting in his cottage. With conservative party presidents like Bildt from Sweden and Aznar from Spain present, the circle concluded to propose a vote on Forza Italia's membership to the EPP group. It also prepared a document which under point two spelled out that 'we are no longer exclusively Christian Democratic (Christian Social) but also adhere to conservative and liberal values' (Martens, 2006, p. 143). Full membership was granted to *Forza Italia* in 1999, making it the second largest contingent after the

German MEPs in the EPP. Pierre Bernard-Reymond, the former president of the French delegation within the EPP, argues that with the opening towards the Spanish PP and later FI, the EPP shifted away from its original position for which the 'social doctrine of the church' was central (CVCE, 2009). Bernard-Reymond argues that this enabled the PPE to keep up with the Socialists but it came at the price that there are now 'people in the party that have nothing to do with Christian Democracy' (CVCE, 2009). Thomas Jansen, the secretary general of the EPP between 1983 and 1994 summarizes:

> the incorporation of Conservative and other like-minded parties was a delicate process that took more than a decade. [...] it transformed the EPP from an inclusive federation of western European Christian Democratic parties into a pan European political family of the center-right. (Jansen & Van Hecke, 2011, p. 50)

Aznar got reelected in 2000 and assembled the EPP party leaders in Madrid where they received a document from him outlining the 'EPP's basic aims and ideological development for the new millennium. His ideas on reform of social welfare systems, full employment and greater flexibility in the work-place became the basis of the EPP's economic policies'. (Gilmour, 2005, p. 428). In 2001 Aznar succeeded Wilfried Martens in the leadership of the Christian Democratic International. In 2001 the new EPP platform, which was largely congruent with Aznar's ideas was approved at the congress in Berlin.

In an interview with *Der Spiegel* in 2001 at this occasion, Berlusconi put forward that

> I feel very comfortable here. We, the Forza Italia, have contributed to the remodeling of the party platform. Many of our positions have been adopted one to one. Our party program in Italy concerning economic and social policy, our support for companies and especially enterprises, has been inscribed word for word into the program of the European People's Party. (Berlusconi, 2001)

Indeed, while the term Christian Democracy still featured prominently in the 1978 and 1992 manifestos, now the manifesto embraces 'secular humanism' next to 'Juedo-Christian values' (EPP, 2001, p. 105). In the 1978 manifesto, economic integration and the strive for a single currency was still backed by a call for a complementary socio-economic policy. The 2001 manifesto explicitly states that 'budget surpluses should primarily be used to reduce debt and taxation' (EPP, 2001, p. 205). The EPP now argues for 'increased liberalization' (EPP, 2001, p. 208), 'more competition', better access to 'risk capital' and the 'use of venture capital' (EPP, 2001, p. 213). Subsidizing 'distorts the market' (EPP, 2001, p. 212) and 'burdens need to be reduced by cutting social expenditure and by reducing people's tendency to think in terms of what entitlements that they can claim' (EPP, 2001, p. 216). The labour market has to be 'deregulated' and 'labour flexibility is essential in a fast-moving and unpredictable global economy' (EPP, 2001, p. 218). The section on the 'European social model' boils down to 'individual responsibility' with a minimum social protection floor (EPP, 2001, pp. 228–233). The basic programme has changed the adjacent concepts of European Christian Democracy which now reflects the socio-economic ideology of the original Protestant core concepts fused with new secular neoliberal conservative socio-economic ideology.

The eastern enlargement and its effects on EPP ideology

The 2001 platform had with its neo-liberal socio-economic ideology 'created the programmatic basis for its own eastern enlargement' (Freudenstein, 2012, p. 136) since the party platform was now fully compatible with conservative socio-economic ideology. In 2004, 19 East and Central European parties joined the EPP (Jansen & Van Hecke, 2011, p. 74). The new conservative parties in eastern Europe had no Christian Democratic heritage. When asked whom the greatest western politicians that had contributed to European unification were, the Estonian Prime minister Martin Laar did not answer Schumann, Adenauer or De Gasperi but Thatcher, Reagan and Kohl (Laar, 2010).

The 2009 declaration from the Bonn congress shows how far the EPP has shifted away from its social Catholic core concepts. In the declaration, the EPP presents a detailed account of ordoliberal socio-economic ideology, fusing it with Anglo-Saxon, Austrian and French branches of neoliberalism. Instead of citing earlier social-Catholic thinkers or politicians as the core of its ideology, the EPP now refers to the gatherings in the Walter Lippmann Colloquium in 1938 and the writings of neo-liberal economist like Ludwig von Mises, Lion Robbins, Jaques Rueff and Friedrich von Hayek. When defining its 'normative value fundament' (EPP, 2009) the manifesto refers to 'Immanuel Kant, the Scottish philosopher David Hume and in our days the Austrian economist and Nobel laureate Friedrich A. von Hayek' (EPP, 2009, p. 3). In its policy advice, the manifesto emphasizes 'framework conditions', 'stable money' and 'sound public finances' and Hayek's 'discovery process' with 'decentralized and spontaneous knowledge' leading to 'prosperity for all' (EPP, 2009, p. 3). Social policy 'should never be in contradiction to the basic principles of personal responsibility in a competitive market system' (EPP, 2009, p. 4). The programme argues that the social policies in many EU states 'do not provide enough incentives for unemployed people to get back to work' (EPP, 2009, p. 6) and encourages policies that 'point out the moral obligation to work' (EPP, 2009, p. 9). The manifesto uses many reference points to the ordoliberal fraction of the CDU in the 1950s like Erhard's quote that 'low taxes and stable money supply are the best social policies' (EPP, 2009, p. 9).

Since the EPP congress is held every three years, the declaration form 2009 only displays a change in the peripheral concepts of the EPPs socio-economic ideology. These, however, indicate a shift towards social policy concepts based on workfare that stand in opposition to traditional social-Catholic socio-economic thought. Moreover, the emphasis on economic competition is not compatible with social Catholicism. Not the social encyclicals of Popes, but the Protestant philosophers Hume and Kant are mentioned as the inspiration for the EPPs socio-economic core concepts.

After the world financial crisis, the EPP toned down these neo-liberal positions. The 2014 electoral manifesto argues for the primacy of 'growth and jobs' through 'growth friendly budget consolidation' (EPP, 2014, p. 3). The 2019 electoral manifesto even proposes 'industrial policy' to 'create the conditions for at least 5 million new jobs in the coming years' (EPP, 2019, p. 8). While it seemed that during the 1990s and 2000s, the EPP had in its adjacent and peripheral concepts abandoned the original social Catholic socio-economic core, the electoral manifestos of the 2010s indicated that this was not fully achieved. Social Catholic thinkers and core concepts are not explicitly mentioned but many traits are again compatible with the pro-welfareist and corporatist social Catholic ideological core.

Yet, all in all, the adjacent (party platforms) and peripheral concepts (election manifestos) today rely much stronger on the Protestant socio-economic core than ever before. Whether the abandoning of the social-Catholic core will continue in the aftermath of the world economic and epidemic crisis can only be speculated here; but the trend identified indicates that.

The contribution argued that the social Catholic core lost influence in the EPP because the Protestant core is more compatible with the socio-economic ideologies of the new conservative party members accumulated through the northern, southern, and eastern enlargements. A objection against this argument would be that social Catholicism had already started to disappear on the national level way before the EPP expanded (Hien 2017). The Catholic subcultures, the role and political resources of the Catholic Church in society all decline at end of the 1960s also in countries with strong Christian Democratic traditions. Hence, we have to see Europeanization as an accelerator of the domestic decline of social Catholicism. National Christian Democratic parties like the German CDU saw the success of theconservative-secular EPP on the European level, which allowed them to shed some of the more antiquated parts of Catholicsocial teaching like the male breadwinner model (Hien, 2013; Hien & Schroeder, 2018).

Conclusion

This article has analyzed the socio-economic ideology of European Christian Democracy. It has argued that European Christian Democracy was based not only on social-Catholic but also on Protestant socio-economic core concepts. While the social Catholic core had from the 1950s to the 1970s the upper-hand, it lost influence to the Protestant ordoliberal core afterwards. Since the Protestant socio-economic core was compatible with neoliberal socio-economic ideology of mainstream conservative parties, its existence enabled the integration of ever more conservative parties into the EPP. Each enlargement round of the EU and EPP diminished the influence of the original social-Catholic core and led to a strengthening of the Protestant ordo-liberal core and new strands of neoliberal conservative socio-economic ideology. The existence of a Protestant core made it easier for conservative parties to enter the EPP since there was a certain elective affinity between the new conservative liberal socio-economic ideology of the new parties and the old ordoliberal Protestant core of European Christian Democracy. This explains also why the EPP ideology did not just dilute into a shapeless amalgam. The conservative-liberal socio-economic thinking of the new members like the PP or FI fit with the already existing Protestant branches in European Christian Democratic socio-economic thought.

Acknowledgement

I want to thank the four anonymous reviewers as well as Carlo Invernizzi-Accetti, Jonathan White, Elin Hellquist and Fabio Wolkenstein for great comments. Thanks also to the JEPP editors for the excellent process. Maurizio Ferrera for intellectual stimulation and Stefan Svallfors and Gustav Arrhenius for hosting me at the Institute for Future Studies. The research is part of the ERC project 'Reconciling Economic and Social Europe: the role of ideas, values and politics' (Uni Milan, PI Maurizio Ferrera, grant number: 340534).

Disclosure statement

No potential conflict of interest was reported by the author(s).

References

Acanfora, P. (2010). The Italian Christian Democratic Party within the international Christian Democratic organizations: Nationalism, Europeanism, and religious identity (1947–1954). *Journal of Modern Italian Studies, 15*(2), 200–231. https://doi.org/10.1080/13545711003606602

Acanfora, P. (2015). Christian Democratic Internationalism: The *Nouvelles Equipes Internationales* and the Geneva Circles between European unification and religious Identity, 1947–1954. *Contemporary European History, 24*(3), 375–391. https://doi.org/10.1017/S0960777315000211

ACDP. (1972). *Dokument 87, Bernhard Gebauer an Kai-Uwe von Hassel, 8.2.1972, [ACDP, Nachlass Kai-Uwe von Hassel, I-157-162-2].* Archiv für Christlich Demokratische Politik, Konrad Adenauer Stiftung.

ACDP. (1975). *Dokument 158, Entwicklung zur Europäischen Volkspartei, 17./18.11.1975 [ACDP, Nachlass Kai-Uwe von Hassel, I-157-139-1].* Archiv für Christlich Demokratische Politik, Konrad Adenauer Stiftung.

ACDP. (1976). *Dokument 200, Protokoll der Sitzung der CD-Fraktion am 1./2. Juli 1976 in München, 5.10.1976 [ACDP, Nachlass Egon Klepsch, I-641-006-1].* Archiv für Christlich Demokratische Politik: Konrad Adenauer Stiftung.

ACDP. (1977). *Vermerk über die Schwierigkeiten im Verhältnis der DC zur CDU von Henning Wegener an Helmut Kohl und Heiner Geissler, 5. Dezember 1977, in ACDP 07-001-16032.* Archiv für Christlich Demokratische Politik, Konrad Adenauer Stiftung.

ACDP. (1996a). Letter from Silvio Berlusconi to Wilfried Martens, Rome 25. Spetember 1996. In *ACDP 09-001-207.* Archiv für Christlich Demokratische Politik, Konrad Adenauer Stiftung.

ACDP. (1996b). Minutes from the meeting of the presidency of the EPP 15 October 1996. In *ACDP 09-001-207.* Archiv für Christlich Demokratische Politik, Konrad Adenauer Stiftung.

Berlusconi, S. (1994, November 14). Interview with William Rees-Mogg. *The Times.*

Berlusconi, S. (2001, January 13). Interview: Wir sind die Kinder Helmuth Kohls. *Der Spiegel.*

Blyth, M. (2013). *Austerity: The history of a dangerous idea.* Oxford University Press.

Bösch, F. (2001). *Die Adenauer CDU: Gründung, Aufstieg und Krise einer Erfolgspartei 1945–1969.* Deutsche Verlags Anstalt.

Bremer, B., & McDaniel, S. (2019). The ideational foundations of social democratic austerity in the context of the great recession. *Socio-Economic Review.* https://doi.org/10.1093/ser/mwz001

Cau, M. (2009). Alcide De Gasperi: A political thinker or a thinking politician? *Modern Italy, 14*(4), 431–444. https://doi.org/10.1080/13532940903237516

CDU. (1947). CDU überwindet Kapitalismus und Marxismus: Das Ahlener Wirtschafts und Sozialprogramm der CDU. Retrieved April 15, 2020, from https://www.kas.de/de/web/geschichte-der-cdu/grundsatzprogramme

CDU. (1949). Düsseldorfer Leitsätze. Retrieved April 15, 2020, from https://www.kas.de/de/web/geschichte-der-cdu/grundsatzprogramme

CDU. (1978). Christlich Demokratische Union Deutschlands, Bundesgeschaeftsstelle (Hg.): *Protokoll des 26. Bundesparteitags der CDU vom 23. Bis 25. Oktober 1978 in Ludwigshafen.* Union Betriebs Gmbh: Bonn.

Cellini, S. (2018). The idea of Europe at the origins of the European people's party. The making of the European manifesto and of the EPP's political programme. *Journal of European Integration History, 24*(1), 79–94. https://doi.org/10.5771/0947-9511-2018-1-79

CVCE. (2009). Interview with Pierre Bernard-Reymond, Oral History of European Integration Collection of the Centre Virtuel de la Conaissance sur L'Europe in Luxemburg, Video-interview, (Paris, 11 March 2009). Retrieved March 15, 2020, from https://www.cvce.eu/collections/unit-content/-/unit/en/da53c3f9-6a19-4c52-8802-26206906f253/d9918c07-f0e6-4df6-845f-d55a725b791b

CVCE. (2010a). Interview with Gérard Deprez, Oral History of European Integration Collection of the Centre Virtuel de la Conaissance sur L'Europe in Luxemburg, Video-interview (Brussels, 20 May 2010). Retrieved March 15, 2020, from https://www.cvce.eu/collections/unit-content/-/unit/en/da53c3f9-6a19-4c52-8802-26206906f253/c45b9a82-e0fb-4a1a-9953-a0a38d82f0e9

CVCE. (2010b). Interview with Wilfried Martens, Oral History of European Integration Collection of the Centre Virtuel de la Conaissance sur L'Europe in Luxemburg, Video-interview (Brussels, 20 May 2010). Retrieved March 15, 2020, from https://www.cvce.eu/collections/unit-content/-/unit/en/da53c3f9-6a19-4c52-8802-26206906f253/b2e838fd-9ca9-4b45-94ee-366598f6a313

DC. (1943). *Le Idee Ricostruttive della Democrazia Cristiana.* In W. Lipgens (1985, Ed.), *Documents on the History of European Integration.* de Gruyter, 503.

Dörr, N. (2017). Der „Historische Kompromiss" als Belastung für die Beziehungen der Democrazia Cristiana zur CDU und den britischen Konservativen. *Historisch-Politische Mitteilungen, 24*(1), 59–86. https://doi.org/10.7788/hpm-2017-240104

EPP. (1978). Political programme, Adopted by the First EPP Congress in Brussels on 6–7 March 1978.

EPP. (1992). Basic Programme, Adopted by the Ninth EPP Congress in Athens on 12–14 November 1992.

EPP. (2001, January). A union of values – final text agreed at the XIV EPP Congress Berlin.

EPP. (2009, December 9–10). The social market economy in a globalised world. Congress document adopted by the EPP Statutory Congress Bonn.

EPP. (2014). *Why vote for the European People's Party.* Election Manifesto.

EPP. (2019). EPP manifesto. Lets Open the next Chapter for Europe Together.

Etzioni, A. (1963). European unification: A strategy of change. *World Politics, 16*(1), 32–51. https://doi.org/10.2307/2009250

Eucken, W. (1949). *Die Sozialpolitische Frage.* Weber.

Farrell, J. (1995). Berlusconi and Forza Italia: New force for old? *Modern Italy, 1*(1), 40–52. https://doi.org/10.1080/13532949508454757

Forlenza, R. (2017). The politics of the *Abendland*: Christian Democracy and the Idea of Europe after the second world War. *Contemporary European History, 26*(2), 261–286. https://doi.org/10.1017/S0960777317000091

Freeden, M. (1994). Political concepts and ideological morphology. *Journal of Political Philosophy, 2*(2), 140–164. https://doi.org/10.1111/j.1467-9760.1994.tb00019.x

Freeden, M. (2006). Ideology and political theory. *Journal of Political Ideologies, 11*(1), 3–22. https://doi.org/10.1080/13569310500395834

Freudenstein, R. (2012). Unity in diversity: The EPP's two and a half decades of expansion. *European View, 11*(2), 133–140. https://doi.org/10.1007/s12290-012-0218-2

Gehler, M., Gonschor, M., & Meyer, H. (2018). Einleitung: Von der europaeischen Union Chrsitlicher Demokraten (EUCD). In M. Gehler, M. Gonschor, M. Hinnerk, & H. Schönner (Eds.), *Transnationale Parteienkooperation der europäischen Christdemokraten und Konservativen: Dokumente 1965–1979* (pp. 1–64). De Gruyter.

Gilmour, J. (2005). Losing its soul: The changing role of Christian Democracy in the development of Spain's new right. *South European Society and Politics, 10*(3), 411–431. https://doi.org/10.1080/13608740500282223

Gorski, P. S. (2003). *The disciplinary revolution: Calvinism and the rise of the state in early modern Europe.* University of Chicago Press.

HAEU. (1998). Interview with Luigi Caligaris recorded in 27 July 1998 – 29 July 1998 Roma, Interview by G. Malgeri in Italian, reference code: INT582, Historical Archives of the European Union, Florence, Italy.

Hanley, D. (2002). Christian Democracy and the paradoxes of Europeanization: Flexibility, competition and collusion. *Party Politics, 8*(4), 463–481. https://doi.org/10.1177/1354068802008004006

Hengsbach, F. (2010). *Kapitalismuskritik bei Joseph Höffner und Oswald von Nell-Breuning* (Working Paper 07.10). Oswald von Nell-Breuning Institut.

Hien, J. (2013). Unsecular politics in a secular environment: The case of Germany's Christian Democratic family policy. *German Politics*, *22*(4), 441–460. https://doi.org/10.1080/09644008.2013.853041

Hien, J. (2017). From private to religious patriarchy: Gendered consequences of faith based welfare provision in Germany. *Politics and Religion*, *10*(3), 515–542. http://doi.org/10.1017/S1755048317000086

Hien, J. (2019). The religious foundations of the European crisis. *JCMS: Journal of Common Market Studies*, *57*(2), 185–204. https://doi.org/10.1111/jcms.12635

Hien, J., & Schroeder, W. (2018). Ökonomisierung und Religion in Deutschland. Was bleibt? Einleitung zum Sonderheft des Sozialen Fortschritts. *Sozialer Fortschritt*, *67* (6), 407–413. http://doi.org/10.3790/sfo.67.6.407

Hix, S. (1999). The party of European socialists. In R. Ladrech & P. Marliere (Eds.), *Social democratic parties in the European Union* (pp. 204–217). Palgrave.

Hopkin, J., & Paolucci, C. (1999). The business firm model of party organisation: Cases from Spain and Italy. *European Journal of Political Research*, *35*(3), 307–339. https://doi.org/10.1111/1475-6765.00451

Invernizzi-Accetti, C. (2019). *What is Christian democracy? Politics, religion and ideology.* Cambridge University Press.

Jansen, T., & Van Hecke, S. (2011). *At Europe's service: The origins and evolution of the European People's Party.* Springer.

Johansson, K. M. (2002). Party elites in multilevel Europe: The Christian Democrats and the single European Act. *Party Politics*, *8*(4), 423–439. https://doi.org/10.1177/1354068802008004004

Kahl, S. (2005). The religious roots of modern poverty policy: Catholic, Lutheran, and reformed Protestant traditions compared. *European Journal of Sociology*, *46*(1), 91–126. https://doi.org/10.1017/S0003975605000044

Kaiser, W. (2007). *Christian Democracy and the origins of the European Union.* Cambridge University Press.

Kaiser, W. (2013). Europeanization of Christian Democracy? Negotiating organization, enlargement, policy and allegiance in the European People's Party. In W. Kaiser & J.-H. Meyer (Eds.), *Societal actors in European integration: Polity-building and policy-making 1958–1992* (pp. 15–37). Palgrave Macmillan.

Kerber, S. J. W. (2013). Wettbewerb und Wirtschaftsordnung in sozialethischer Sicht. *Jahrbuch Für Christliche Sozialwissenschaften*, *11*, 21–43.

Kohl, H. (2012). *Berichte zur Lage 1989–1998: Der Kanzler und Parteivorsitzende im Bundesvorstand der CEDU Deutschlands.* Droste.

Kohl, H. (2015). *Kohl, Helmuth: Wir haben alle Chancen, Die Protokolle des CDU Bundesvorstands 1973–1976.* Droste.

Krarup, T. (2019). 'Ordo' versus 'ordnung': Catholic or Lutheran roots of German ordo-liberal economic theory? *International Review of Economics*, *66*(3), 305–323. https://doi.org/10.1007/s12232-019-00323-y

Laar, M. (2010). *The power of freedom.* Centre for European Studies.

Lipgens, W. (1977). *Die Anfänge der europäischen Einigungspolitik.* Klett.

Manow, P. (2001). Ordoliberalismus als Ökonomische Ordnungstheologie. *Leviathan*, *29* (2), 179–198. https://doi.org/10.1007/s11578-001-0012-z

Martens, W. (2006). *Europe: I struggle I overcome.* Springer.

Masala, C. (2004). Born for government: The Democrazia Cristiana in Italy. In M. Gehler & W. Kaiser (Eds.), *Christian Democracy in Europe since 1945, volume 2* (pp. 101–117). Routledge.

McDonnell, D. (2013). Silvio Berlusconi's personal parties: From Forza Italia to the Popolo Della Libertà. *Political Studies*, *61*(1), 217–233. https://doi.org/10.1111/j.1467-9248.2012.01007.x

Misner, P. (2004). Catholic labor and Catholic action: The Italian context of Quadragesimo Anno. *The Catholic Historical Review*, *90*(4), 650–674. https://doi.org/10.1353/cat.2005.0050

Müller-Armack, A. (1947). Die Wirtschaftsordnung Sozial Gesehen. *ORDO Jahrbuch*, *1*(1), 125–154.

Petersen, T. (2008). Die Sozialethik Emil Brunners Und Ihre Neoliberale Rezeption. *HWWI Research Paper*, *5-6*, 1–27.

Poli, E. (1998). Silvio Berlusconi and the myth of the creative entrepreneur. *Modern Italy*, *3*(2), 271–279. https://doi.org/10.1080/13532949808454809

Scharpf, F. (1991). *Crisis and change in European social democracy*. Cornell University Press.

Schluchter, W. (2014). Einleitung: Asketischer Protestantismus und Kapitalismus. In W. Schluchter (Ed.), *Schriften und Reden 1904-11 Max Weber, Max Weber Gesamtausgabe I/9* (pp. 1–90). Mohr Siebeck.

Semino, E., & Masci, M. (1996). Politics is football: Metaphor in the discourse of Silvio Berlusconi in Italy. *Discourse & Society*, *7*(2), 243–269. https://doi.org/10.1177/0957926596007002005

Sombart, W. (1902). *Der moderne Kapitalismus*. Dunker and Humboldt.

Streeck, W. (2013). *Gekaufte Zeit*. Suhrkamp.

Van Kersbergen, K. (1995). *Social capitalism: A study of Christian Democracy and the welfare state*. Routledge.

Weber, M. (1905). Die Protestantische Ethik und der 'Geist' des Kapitalismus. *Archiv fur Sozialwissenschaft und Sozialpolitik*, *20*(1), 1–54.

Weber, M. (1920/1988). *Gesammelte Aufsätze Zur Religionssoziologie I, Photomechanischer Nachdruck Der Erstauflage von 1920*. Mohr Siebeck. (Original work published 1920)

Europe as ideological resource: the case of the Rassemblement National

Marta Lorimer ⓘ

ABSTRACT

Ever since they first entered the European Parliament in 1979, the EU has proven to be a strong legitimising tool for far right parties, providing them with funding, visibility and a higher degree of credibility and respectability. While recent literature has explored some of these dynamics, the role of the far right's ideological positioning on Europe as a source of public legitimacy has been neglected. This paper argues that as a relatively new and contentious political issue, Europe can function as a powerful ideological resource for far right parties by allowing them to convey a more acceptable political message. This argument is illustrated through a case study of two key aspects of the Rassemblement National's ideological approach to the European Union: the party's claim to be pro-European but anti-EU and its opposition to EU integration on grounds of sovereignty.

The construction of legitimacy has been a crux for far right parties.[1] Widely defined as radical, extreme, racist, xenophobic, and anti-Semitic, they have struggled to establish themselves as legitimate actors whose 'access to, and exercise of, power is rightful' (Beetham, 2012, p. 120). In spite of their electoral successes, their fitness to rule has been frequently questioned in virtue of their dubious commitment to the existing (democratic) order or because of their xenophobic political programmes. In several countries, other political parties have refused to create alliances with them, putting in place a 'cordon sanitarie' to keep them out of power (Downs, 2012, pp. 35–38; for exceptions, see Albertazzi & McDonnell, 2016; Fallend, 2012; Zaslove, 2012). Especially in their early years, their successes provoked strong negative reactions, as was the case in Austria after the Freedom Party first entered into a coalition government, or in France when Jean-Marie Le Pen made it to the run-off in the 2002 presidential election. Such reactions, while no longer as strong, still remain present when far right parties achieve positive results (suffice it to think of definitions of the 2014 EU Parliament elections as an 'earthquake').

To counteract such narratives, far right parties have sought to project an image of themselves as legitimate political actors. Some have famously rejected the label of extreme right, claiming to be at best 'extremists of common sense' (Salvini, 2019). Others, such as the Rassemblement National, have undergone reviews of their language and practices in attempts to appear more moderate (Shields, 2013; Stockemer & Barisone, 2017). Their quest for legitimacy has had some success. Whereas the average vote for far right parties in Western Europe was 1.1% in the 1980s, it reached 7.5% in the EU-28 in the 2010s (Mudde, 2019, p. 19). Far right parties have joined in coalition governments in countries such as Italy and Austria and acted as parliamentary support to the centre-right in Denmark and the Netherlands among others (Akkerman & de Lange, 2012; de Lange, 2012). Furthermore, their positions have become more accepted and have even been incorporated in the platforms of mainstream parties seeking to win back voters from the far right (Gruber & Bale, 2014; Herman & Muldoon, 2019; Pytlas & Kossack, 2015).

The European Union (EU) has been one of their unwitting supporters in this process of legitimation. Electorally, the proportional system of representation employed in EU elections along with their 'second-order' nature (Reif & Schmitt, 1980) made it easier for far right parties to gain representation (Hainsworth, 2008, p. 83). This has also come with a gain in resources which could be used to consolidate their results and improve their standing in domestic elections (Reungoat, 2014, pp. 133–136; Schulte-Cloos, 2018). Far from being mere passive beneficiaries of the process of European integration, far right parties have also sought to take advantage of the opportunities offered by it, for example by employing alliances in the European Parliament to enhance legitimacy at home (McDonnell & Werner, 2019; Startin, 2010, p. 439). Paradoxically, while far right parties have staunchly opposed the EU, and opposition to European integration is frequently painted as a marker of marginalisation for political parties (Ivaldi, 2018, p. 286; Taggart, 1998; Vasilopoulou, 2018a), the EU has also been the provider of symbolic and material resources that have helped them become established actors (Fieschi, 2000, p. 521).

Research so far has focused on how the far right's behaviour has provided them with resources for legitimation, however, less attention has been paid to considering whether their views on the European Union may have served similar purposes (for a partial exception, see Startin, 2018). In other words, if one accepts that the EU has provided far right parties with a number of practical and symbolic resources that have enhanced their legitimacy, how did their positions on Europe contribute to this legitimation?

In this paper I argue that Europe can function as a powerful ideological resource for far right parties by allowing them to convey a more acceptable political message. This contention is grounded in the understanding that as a relatively new and contentious political issue to which there is no clear 'ideological' answer (Gaffney, 1996, p. 19), Europe leaves parties leeway to determine their positions and present them in a more acceptable fashion. This argument is illustrated through a case study of key aspects of the Rassemblement National's (RN) ideological approach to the EU. The RN's historical influence on other far right parties (Rydgren, 2007; Van Hauwaert, 2014), its growing focus on issues of European integration (Vasilopoulou, 2018b) and its marked concern with making an appropriate use of language (Camus, 2015, pp. 108–110) make it a compelling example for the article's core argument. Drawing on an in-depth interpretive analysis of party documents produced between 1978 and 2018, the article shows how two of the party's claims helped it address key criticisms moved against it: first, its assertion to be European and defend Europe from the EU; second, its appropriation of positively valued concepts such as sovereignty, autonomy and self-rule to oppose the EU. These claims, it is argued, helped the party present its best face to the world and construct a more legitimate image for itself.

The paper's contribution is two-fold. First, in line with the special issue's interest in studying the ideological dimension of European integration, it shows how Europe may function as an ideological resource available to parties looking for legitimation. Second, it offers an alternative view of the implications of far right parties adopting Eurosceptic positions. Instead of viewing them as markers of marginalisation, it suggests that opposition to the EU, if well packaged, may serve to legitimize far right actors.

At a time where far right parties have become a regular presence in the political make up of most European countries and even governmental forces in some of them, it is important to reflect on the causes of their success. Focusing on how the EU may have helped them achieve public legitimacy, this paper contributes to a wider debate on how they went from illegitimate fringe to legitimate contenders for public office.

Europe as an ideological resource

Far right parties, the opening section has noted, often struggle to establish themselves as legitimate actors. Their inexperience with government is used as an argument to suggest that they lack the competencies to become credible political actors (for an example of this argument, see Ebner, 2019). The nature of their beliefs, on the other hand, raises questions about whether if entrusted with power, they would uphold core values such as equality, solidarity, and non-discrimination. Being deemed unfit to govern, they are frequently presented as insufficiently 'coalitionable' and where possible, kept out of power.

Faced with such issues, there are two options available to far right parties in quest for legitimation. A first option available is to stick to their guns and hope that society adjusts to their presence. Such a process of 'normalisation' might be helped by social changes and by the actions of other actors such as mainstream parties. There is some evidence to suggest that this is what has been happening in recent years: while far right parties have maintained a consistent policy profile, other parties appear to be shifting to the right (Wagner & Meyer, 2017). Given mainstream parties' tendency to co-opt elements of the far right agenda and mainstream their ideas (Herman & Muldoon, 2019, pp. 3–7; Mondon, 2014), the strategy sounds reasonably sound and might eventually pay off. However, it takes time and rests on the hope that others will collaborate. In the meanwhile, parties may also wish to do something to facilitate the normalisation process.

The second option available to far right actors is to alter elements of their behaviour and beliefs to fit in with what is considered as legitimate in a given society. They might behave in such a way that suggests respect for existing institutions, or work within the boundaries of legality. Changes in behaviour, however, require being given the opportunity to exercise power, raising a chicken and egg issue: the far right's limited legitimacy keeps it out of power, but they need that power to construct credibility.[2]

As an alternative, parties can seek to alter their message and tweak their ideology as to project a more acceptable image, as Marine Le Pen did with her previously cited process of *dédiabolisation*. This tweaking may take different forms: it may be of a rhetorical nature and build on less inflammatory language and the eschewal of certain topics; or, it may be of a substantive nature and entail the abandonment of controversial policy commitments and ideas. This appears as a promising avenue because it is less resource intensive, reasonably visible for voters and does not require one to already have power but merely to be competing for it.

Ideological change, however, can entail different costs. If the party is understood as a 'community of principle' (White & Ypi, 2016, p. 14), changing these ideas creates a problem of internal credibility. Activists and voters may view the party as as betraying its long-standing commitments. This poses a conundrum for the party: on one hand, it needs to maintain its core of supporters and hence, demonstrate an attachment to the ideological commitments that keep them together. On the other hand, if it is to reach power and enact its programme, it needs to appeal to a larger constituency. In short, it needs to find a way to 'serve two masters' (Katz, 2014). In this case, how can the party signal continuity with past principle but also get more people on board?

Europe offers an answer to this dilemma. As literature on Europeanization has stressed, Europe opens up a series of opportunities for political actors and offers them a number of strategic and ideological resources that they may 'use' to advance their agendas (Woll & Jacquot, 2010). This is particularly helpful in the context of ideological change because it allows the parties to expand and alter their ideology at a relatively low cost and in a potentially positive fashion, thus balancing the imperatives of internal consistency and external validation.

First, the relatively new character and (until recently) low salience of the European issue means that parties are not wed to pre-existing commitments and hence have some leeway in terms of the position they adopt.[3] While positions will usually be informed by existing beliefs (Hooghe et al., 2002; Szczerbiak & Taggart, 2008, pp. 13–14) and might need to be presented as consistent with the parties' other commitments, it also leaves more space for interpretation. In this process, the nature of European integration as an issue that has no clear ideological answer (Flood, 2002, pp. 7–11; Gaffney, 1996, p. 16) also provides parties with additional space to select their positions. Because it sits uncomfortably on the Left/Right divide (Hooghe et al., 2002; Pirro & Taggart, 2018) and can be interpreted in different ways depending on which aspect of the EU one is looking at (Szczerbiak & Taggart, 2008, p. 238), the EU issue leaves parties enough space to frame it in a manner that is convenient for them. Thus, talking about the EU gives them an opportunity to introduce a new topic and a new approach in their ideological positioning, all the while entailing relatively low costs in terms of ideological consistency.

Second, far right parties can benefit from the political divisiveness of European integration. European integration, in fact, has divided political parties and electorates alike (suffice it to think of the close results of referendums on European integration in the 1990s and 2000s). Opposition to the EU is also a common feature in countries across the European Union, making it a relatively uncontroversial position to hold (Eurobarometer, 2019). This makes European integration a topic on which disagreement is acceptable and where it may be easier to build a legitimate image, as opposed to an issue such as migration which will always leave parties open to criticism on grounds of extremism (see also Startin, 2018, p. 76).

Europe may, in this sense, be conceived of as an ideological resource which allows far right parties to reorient their ideology in a more acceptable fashion and both speak to their traditional electorate and attract new supporters.[4] Its newness ensures that they can adapt their positions without appearing to give up on existing ideological commitments, thus preventing them from losing the support of their own voters. At the same time, its divisiveness helps their position appear as more normal and potentially appealing to a larger constituency.

The remainder of this paper provides an empirical illustration of this argument by showing how key aspects of the RN's positioning on Europe allowed it to address criticisms moved against its ideology. Given the RN's central place in the far right party family, its historical influence on other members of the far right (Rydgren, 2007; Van Hauwaert, 2014) and its growing focus on issues of European integration (Vasilopoulou, 2018b), it was considered to be a particularly relevant case to study. In addition, because the RN is a party that has placed an important weight on using acceptable language in the political battle (Camus, 2015, pp. 108–110), and whose members have acknowledged that the EU helped it construct legitimacy (Reungoat, 2014, p. 130, 134), it is the most likely to have deliberately taken advantage of Europe as an ideological resource. Drawing on an in-depth interpretive analysis based on close textual reading of 65 documents (complete list in online appendix) including manifestoes, opinion articles, interviews, and speeches[5] produced between the party's 1978 attempt to participate in European elections and its latest presidential campaign in 2017, and dealing either specifically, or in some depth, with European issues, the following sections consider two sets of positions developed by the RN: its claim to be pro-European but anti-EU, and its appropriation of positively valued concepts such as sovereignty, autonomy and self-rule to oppose the EU. These arguments, frequently present in the entire corpus, are here illustrated by referring to a small number of quotes which summarise most clearly the discourses brought forward by the party.

Pro-European, anti-EU: rejecting accusations of closed nationalism by claiming a European identity

Legitimacy has been an issue for far right parties because they have been viewed as pushing forward unacceptable ideas concerning, for example, the relationship with minorities and the functioning of the institutions of liberal democracy. The reason for the former is frequently ascribed to their 'closed' exclusionary nationalism or nativist ideology which views Others as inherently dangerous and in need to be kept at bay (Minkenberg, 2000, p. 180; Mudde, 2007, p. 19). In diverse societies, this is viewed as particularly critical because it hinders the integration of new citizens, but also poses problems in terms of broader commitments to values such as equality and the protection of human rights. Less prominently, there is also a concern that this kind of closed nationalism could lead to aggressive foreign policies and destabilisation. At the heart of this concern is the view of far right parties as some twenty-first century reincarnation of the interwar fascists movements responsible for World War Two (a concern which is open to debate: for opposing positions see Copsey, 2018; Mammone, 2009, p. 177; Taguieff, 2014). While in recent years far right parties in Europe in general and the RN in particular have not been too keen to start wars with other countries, this worry still lingers on.

The integration of Europe in the RN's ideology has given the party ammunition to reject such claims by providing it with an opportunity to claim 'Europeanness' against the EU (see also Brown, 2019; Glencross, 2020). Within a context in which advocating for a closed and exclusionary nation accompanied by the proposition of highly restrictive policy measures is frowned upon, this attachment to Europe may contribute to projecting an image of 'openness', clearing a path to acceptability through (moderate) transnationalism.

At the heart of the RN's claim of Europeanness is the party's recognition of a European civilisation, distinct from others and bearer of a proud heritage. The features of this civilisation are already discussed in Jean-Marie Le Pen's programmatic book '*Les français d'abord*', in which he defines Europe as

> A historic, geographic, cultural, economic and social ensemble. It is an entity des-tined for action. Europe is currently divided […] but it guards the possibilities for rebirth, should she rediscover a spiritual, intellectual and political unity and all that has been its spirit: that is, a will to act for civilisation, to refuse to be sub-merged and vanquished. (Le Pen, 1984, p. 154)

Europeans, in a similar fashion, are defined as those who 'Defied the universe, attempted to conquer it, and brought modern economic and technologic pro-gress to the world […] Europeans must be proud of themselves and of their contribution to the world' (Le Pen, 1985, pp. 189–190). Beyond recognising this 'European civilisation', early RN documents also stress the party's belong-ing to this civilisation (e.g., Le Pen, 1984, p. 164), flanking its national identity with a European one.

From the middle of the 1980s, following the Single European Act, the RN started pitting this European civilisation against the EU, and increasingly pre-sented itself as the defender of the former against the latter. This division between Europe and the EU (a distinction popular on the far right, but not exclusive to it: e.g., Freiheitliche Partei Österreichs, 2011; Vlaams Belang, 2014; but also Johnson, 2016) emerged as a result of the intellectual influence of the *Nouvelle Droite* and the *Club de l'Horloge* (Bar-On, 2008; Zúquete, 2018, p. 229ff), and is particularly evident in the following passage from a 1991 party guide, where it is noted that

> The debate on Europe is completely distorted, because there are in fact two radi-cally different conceptions of Europe.
>
> One is founded on the idea that the world is destined to homogenise and unite, and that Europe in this perspective is nothing but a stage. […]
>
> The other is founded on the idea that European nations are menaced in their survival and they have to unite to preserve their identity and retrieve their power. […]
>
> The first conception is that of a cosmopolitan or globalist Europe, the second is that of a Europe understood as a community of civilisation.
>
> The first one destroys the nations, the second one ensures their survival. The first one is an accelerator of decline, the second an instrument of renaissance. The

first is the conception of the Brussels technocrats and of establishment politicians, the second is our conception. (Front National, 1991, p. 115)[6]

Further reinforced by the Maastricht Treaty, this distinction between 'Europe'
and 'the EU' recurs in party documents throughout the nineties and nough-
ties, and in spite of the 2011 leadership change in the RN, survives in the
party to this day. The RN's 2009 European election programme, for
example, stressed that they were not 'against Europe' but 'resolutely
against the fraud that consists […] to build a super state […] without even
building a truly European ensemble but a euro-globalist space' (FN, 2009).
As recently as 2017, Marine Le Pen claimed that 'even though we are resolutely opposed to the European Union, we are resolutely European, I'd go
as far as saying that it is because we are European that we are opposed to
the European Union' (Le Pen, 2017b; see also Le Pen, 2019). Pronounced
shortly after the presidential debacle of 2017, when many accused Le Pen
of holding extreme views of Europe as she campaigned to leave the euro,
this passage may be seen both as a direct response to such critiques of extremism, but also, as a traditional party discourse stressing continuity with the
party's past.

Claiming to be 'European' helps the RN dispel some doubts concerning the
nature of its beliefs because it presents it as more 'open' than commonly
thought. The appeal to a shared European heritage can put to rest concerns
about its likelihood of starting a new European conflict because it suggests
that if in power, it would be unlikely to attack its good neighbours. More
importantly, it also counters the view that its nationalism is limited to the
national space because appealing to a 'European' identity suggests an affiliation that goes beyond the nation state. In this sense, Le Pen's claim to be 'resolutely European' or the RN's idea of defending a true vision of Europe
moderates the party's image because it creates an alternative definition of
the party in which exclusion is underplayed and a certain measure of openness is stressed.

Stressing openness does not entail that all boundaries disappear, but
rather, that they are moved to a different level. Mirroring the fact that Europeanism lends itself to the defence of identity projects of various types,
including nationalist ones (Delanty, 1995, pp. 130–131; Gosewinkel, 2018),
the RN's appeal to Europe still keeps a strict boundary between 'Us' and
'Them' alive. While this border is brought to a higher level, it remains
present, ensuring that the party remains internally credible with those who
support it because of its 'closed' nationalism. In this sense, it may be
thought of as a form of 'constructive ambiguity' which while altering and
nuancing the core message of the party in an acceptable way for outsiders,
also maintains a level of continuity that helps preserve internal credibility.
Thus, by adding an element of transnationalism to their ideology, the RN

can appear as more 'open' to other peoples and cultures, albeit (and importantly) within clear boundaries.

Normalisation through appropriation: reclaiming sovereignty, autonomy, and independence from the EU

If far right parties have suffered from a legitimacy deficit, it is not only because of the content of their ideology, but also because of the way in which it has been presented as a set of beliefs borne out of crisis and falling outside the scope of 'normal politics'. This assumption has been defined by Mudde (2010) as the 'normal pathology' hypothesis, which posits that far right parties hold values that are alien to Western democracies. The assumption made is that far right parties are fundamentally different compared to other parties, which could make them appear as illegitimate or holding unacceptable positions because they are not aligned with the values of their own societies.

Against this backdrop, the inclusion of European issues in the RN's ideology has given the party an opportunity to refocus it on issues of sovereignty, autonomy and independence and present itself as respectful of key aspects of the national polity. Countering the narrative of the far right as an 'extreme' actor living on the edge of society, it helped the RN fashion itself as the defender of values and ideas commonly considered as unquestionably good. Importantly, their critique of the EU on these grounds carries the 'ring of truth' because it targets aspects of the construction which are considered as problematic even by mainstream actors.

Early RN documents made virtually no mention of the issue of national sovereignty in connection with Europe. In the context of the Cold War, what did come up was a discussion of the need for Europe to be autonomous, powerful and independent ('imperial', in Le Pen's 1989 expression; see also Mégret, 1989). The ratification of the Maastricht treaty brought sovereignty front and centre in the RN's understanding of Europe. Transforming the EU from an economic project to an unmistakably political union, Maastricht opened the space for a critique of European integration based on appealing to a nation's ability to make its own choices.

Starting from the early 1990s, one of the central lines of criticism adopted by the RN against the EU is that the EU diminishes a nation's power to make its own laws by shifting the centres of decision-making away from it and empowering obscure 'unelected technocrats.' In a 2007 speech, for example, Jean-Marie Le Pen argued that decision-making power had 'quit the Elysée and Matignon to install itself in the European quarter of Brussels', while a 1999 article in the party magazine *Français d'abord* accused the EU of pushing for the ultimate demise of national democracy, with popular sovereignty being replaced by 'expert' decision making (FN, 1999). The party's 2004 EU election manifesto offers a helpful summary of the accusations the RN moved against the EU throughout the years when it claims that

> A nation's sovereignty is its ability to take decisions freely and for itself. It refers then to the notions of independence and exercise of political power by a legitimate government.

> The entire history of the European construction consists of depriving States of their sovereignty. Firstly, because Europe has seen its areas of intervention becoming larger, to the point that today they cover the whole of the economic, social, and political spheres. Then, because the organization and functioning of the European institutions, as well as their decision-making, tend more and more to lead the notion of Nation-State itself to disappear and to entrust power to technocrats in Brussels. (Front National, 2004)

What is notable about this passage is that in constructing its critique of the EU, the RN redeploys a number of concepts ('sovereignty', 'self-rule', 'independence', 'legitimate government') which are consistent with the party's nationalist ideological core (e.g., Davies, 1999), but which would also be normally considered as essential within a modern democratic state. Marine Le Pen adopted a similar approach in the first point of her 2017 programme when she claimed the need to 'Retrieve our liberty and the control of our destiny by returning its sovereignty to the French people' and reform the EU to reach 'a European project respectful of the independence of France, of national sovereignties and of the interests of the peoples' (Le Pen, 2017a). As with the 2004 programme, she appropriated these central and broadly accepted notions of 'liberty', 'independence' and 'interest of the people' to oppose the EU, all the while maintaining an ideologically consistent message.

What is important about this choice of words is that it helps normalise the RN by allowing it to present itself as broadly aligned with important values in the national polity. When the party appeals to a concept such as sovereignty, for example, it is appealing to a concept that while remaining contested in several empirical and theoretical terms (Bellamy & Castiglione, 1997), remains a central concept in constitutional law and discourse, and is thus heavily embedded as a core part of politics (Troper, 2012, p. 351). Within the French context specifically, the relevance of the principle of sovereignty, as well as its nature as an attribute of the Nation and not merely of the State, can be inferred by its presence in the opening sections of the Constitution, with the French Constitution proclaiming an attachment to the principle of national sovereignty in the preamble and dedicating its second constitutional article to it.

Appropriating widely shared values of the state system in the context of opposition to the EU helps the RN present itself as more aligned with what is considered 'moral and proper' and hence, legitimate. While remaining consistent with its existing beliefs, it allows it to claim that it is committed to certain elements of politics that are not exceptional, but rather, shared across the party spectrum. Thus, like its attachment to Europe, it maintains continuity with the past for existing supporters, but also presents a more acceptable face to outsiders. Additionally, even if their positions could still be perceived as radical, they will no longer appear as outside the realm of normal politics, but rather, as radical expressions of it.

The fact that the RN's positions may be able to resonate with such foundational narratives should also not come as a surprise but should rather be seen as the result of the persistence of elements of nationalism in contemporary polities. In fact, while nationalism is often given a bad name, leading some far right politicians to reject the label 'nationalist' in favour of the more positive sounding 'patriot' (Lorimer, 2019), it is also deeply embedded in European societies, particularly through its relationship with the nation-state as a space built on and consolidated by nationalism. In day-to-day life, nationalism is at the heart of many societies in both 'banal' and 'everyday' forms (Billig, 1995; Skey & Antonsich, 2017) and many of the assumptions of how the nation state works are derived from the nationalist premises injected at the time of foundation and reproduced in laws, understandings, and daily practices. In this sense, the RN may benefit from this 'constant reproduction of a sense of national belonging' (Calhoun, 2017, pp. 20–21) because it makes its message sound coherent with the underpinnings of society.

The party's ability to appropriate widely shared values is not limited to its positions on Europe but may be viewed as an expression of their role as 'pathological normalcies' which are unexceptional from an attitudinal or an ideological point of view (Mudde, 2010). However, what they say about sovereignty with respect to the EU might be particularly helpful to the construction of legitimacy because the way in which the EU is commonly seen as affecting these concepts might give it the 'ring of truth.' The EU, in fact, unlike 'regular' international organisations, challenges these key assumptions of politics both through its institutional structures and through the way it functions. By creating a 'pan-European' assembly, it questions the nation as the natural space of politics. In its executive politics, binding legislation and the need to balance the interests of all member states challenge ideas of national self-rule because laws are not made exclusively by the nationals and are unlikely to ever correspond to the 'ideal' of any individual state (e.g., Scharpf, 2006). In legal terms, the principles of direct effect and the supremacy of EU law indicate that in certain areas, the nation is unable to rule itself as it would conflict with EU law (Alter, 2003). These issues are not raised exclusively by parties such as the RN, but form part of a broader set of critical approaches to the status of democracy and sovereignty in the EU. Debates on the EU's 'democratic deficit' and its complex relationship with popular sovereignty (Brack et al., 2019; Follesdal & Hix, 2006; Mair, 2013), and more recently, critical assessments of the EU's actions in times of crisis (Fromage & van den Brink,

2018; White, 2019) are features of academic and political analyses of the EU beyond the far right. Within the French context, they also chime with strong levels of party-based and popular Euroscepticism (e.g., Eurobarometer, 2019; Goodliffe, 2015). Criticism of the EU on these grounds, then, might be particularly strong because it suggests that the RN is not only holding positions that are acceptable, but also saying things that sound credible and consistent with the analyses of other actors around them.

Conclusion

This article started with the observation that while far right parties have been among the staunchest opponents of the European project, the EU has provided them with a number of resources to enhance their legitimacy. Focusing specifically on how the inclusion of Europe in their ideology may have served similar purposes, the article argued that Europe has been an ideological resource allowing far right parties to convey a more acceptable political message. This argument was illustrated through a case study of the RN's approach to the EU which focused on its claims to be 'pro-European but anti-EU' and its appropriation of positively valued concepts such as sovereignty, autonomy and self-rule to criticise the EU. In doing so, it has contributed to existing literature on political ideologies and the European Union by showing how Europe can function as an ideological resource. Contributing to recent literature on the role of Euroscepticism in the rise of the far right (Pirro & Taggart, 2018), it also suggests that far right Euroscepticism, when correctly phrased, can actually help the parties establish themselves as legitimate political actors rather than entrench their position of opponents to the system.

A note of caution is needed here: while Europe may help the parties, it is unlikely to legitimize them by itself. First, their positions on Europe may still raise some doubts. For example, the claim to be 'European' does not manage to dispel the doubt that the RN may think of 'Europe' as a racial construct. While this may be framed in terms of cultural affinity and 'civilisation-ism' (Brubaker, 2017), it does not fully dissipate doubts about how that cultural affinity is operationalised in practice. Second, legitimisation will in any case require some buy-in and support from other actors. What Europe allows the parties to do is present their best face, but whether others believe them is beyond their control. This can help explain why in spite of strong continuities in the discourses of Jean-Marie Le Pen's Front National and Marine Le Pen's RN observed in this paper (but also by others, e.g., Alduy & Wahnich, 2015), the latter has been significantly more successful than the former. Marine Le Pen has not changed the party's message significantly; rather, she has been acting in a radically different political environment where Europe has become more salient and others have helped her message resonate.

In addition to requiring some caution, it is also important to point towards some of the limitations of this study. Most obviously, the fact that the paper has focused more on individuating mechanisms in a single case study than on testing them means that it leaves questions about generalizability and effectiveness unanswered. In other words, while it has suggested that Europe may function as an ideological resource, it has not attempted to study whether this was indeed the case across countries and whether it was effective. Future confirmatory research may wish to explore this question with reference not only to the RN, but also, to far right parties more broadly. There are some good reasons to expect similar parties to adopt similar positions on Europe: as was mentioned earlier, the claim to be 'European' but 'anti-EU' is not an exclusive feature of the RN but is present in other parties as well. In a similar vein, other parties in the family appeal to concepts such as liberty, democracy, autonomy, sovereignty and self-rule (suffice it to think, for example, of the presence of these terms in the names of parties such as the Party for Freedom and Forum for Democracy in the Netherlands, or the Party for Freedom and Direct Democracy in the Czech Republic). This final note should also serve as a reminder of the nature of these concepts as essentially contested (Gallie, 1956): while many actors may appeal to them, how they interpret them will differ across lines and across time. It may be worth spending more time understanding how these parties specifically understand such concepts, in which ways they significantly differ from other groups' usages, and indeed, if the uses they adopt are compatible with those of others.

Notes

1. The term far right is used as an umbrella term to encompass parties of the extreme and radical right (see also Halikiopoulou & Vlandas, 2019; Vasilopoulou, 2018a, p. 6).
2. Empirically, it is also unclear that such changes in behaviour are what far right parties go for when in power (e.g., Akkerman et al., 2016; Albertazzi & Mueller, 2013), or that there is an appetite amongst their supporters for such moderation (Heinisch, 2003, pp. 101–102).
3. While the process itself is not new, its politicisation is a relatively new matter which started mainly from the late 1980s and early 1990s (Hooghe & Marks, 2009).
4. This may be done deliberately by the parties, for example as part of a strategic choice to alter their language, but may also be the unintended consequence of processes of ideological adjustment engendered by the introduction of a new issue.
5. The use of a variety of sources was meant to limit the extent to which one was capturing purely externally directed material (see Mudde, 2000 for a more extensive discussion of this) and/or exclusively electoral statements.
6. The Front National changed name to Rassemblement National in 2018. Documents produced by the party before 2018 are cited following the original nomenclature.

Acknowledgements

I would like to thank the editors of this special issue and the anonymous reviewers for their constructive comments, and Daphnée Papiasse for the editorial support.

Disclosure statement

No potential conflict of interest was reported by the author(s).

ORCID

Marta Lorimer ⓘ http://orcid.org/0000-0002-9214-3898

References

Akkerman, T., & de Lange, S. L. (2012). Radical right parties in office: Incumbency Records and the electoral cost of governing. *Government and Opposition*, *47*(4), 574–596. https://doi.org/10.1111/j.1477-7053.2012.01375.x

Akkerman, T., de Lange, S. L., & Rooduijn, M. (2016). *Radical right-wing populist parties in Western Europe: Into the mainstream?* Routledge.

Albertazzi, D., & McDonnell, D. (2016). *Populists in power*. Routledge.

Albertazzi, D., & Mueller, S. (2013). Populism and liberal democracy: Populists in government in Austria, Italy, Poland and Switzerland. *Government and Opposition*, *48*(3), 343–371. https://doi.org/10.1017/gov.2013.12

Alduy, C., & Wahnich, S. (2015). *Marine Le Pen Prise Aux Mots: Decryptage du nouveau discours frontiste*. Seuil.

Alter, K. J. (2003). *Establishing the supremacy of European law the making of an international rule of law in Europe*. Oxford University Press.

Bar-On, T. (2008). Fascism to the Nouvelle Droite: The dream of Pan-European empire. *Journal of Contemporary European Studies*, *16*(3), 327–345. https://doi.org/10.1080/14782800802500981

Beetham, D. (2012). Political legitimacy. In E. Amenta, N. Kate, & A. Scott (Eds.), *The Wiley-Blackwell companion to political sociology* (pp. 120–129). John Wiley & Sons.

Bellamy, R., & Castiglione, D. (1997). Building the Union: The nature of sovereignty in the political architecture of Europe. *Law and Philosophy*, *16*(4), 421–445.

Billig, M. (1995). *Banal nationalism*. Sage.

Brack, N., Coman, R., & Crespy, A. (2019). Unpacking old and new conflicts of sovereignty in the European polity. *Journal of European Integration*, *41*(7), 817–832. https://doi.org/10.1080/07036337.2019.1665657

Brown, K. (2019). When Eurosceptics become Europhiles: Far-right opposition to Turkish involvement in the European Union. *Identities*, 1–22. https://doi.org/10.1080/1070289X.2019.1617530

Brubaker, R. (2017). Between nationalism and civilizationism: The European populist moment in comparative perspective. *Ethnic and Racial Studies*, *40*(8), 1191–1226. https://doi.org/10.1080/01419870.2017.1294700

Calhoun, C. J. (2017). The rhetoric of nationalism. In M. Skey & M. Antonsich (Eds.), *Everyday nationhood: Theorising culture, identity and belonging after Banal nationalism* (pp. 17–30). Palgrave Macmillan.

Camus, J.-Y. (2015). Le Front National et la Nouvelle Droite. In S. Crépon, A. Dézé, & N. Mayer (Eds.), *Les faux-semblants du Front National* (pp. 97–120). Presses de Sciences Po.

Copsey, N. (2018). The radical right and fascism. In J. Rydgren (Ed.), *The Oxford Handbook of the radical right* (pp. 105–121). Oxford University Press.

Davies, P. (1999). *The National Front and France: Ideology, discourse, and power*. Routledge.

de Lange, S. L. (2012). New alliances: Why mainstream parties govern with radical right-wing populist parties. *Political Studies*, *60*(4), 899–918. https://doi.org/10.1111/j.1467-9248.2012.00947.x

Delanty, G. (1995). *Inventing Europe: Idea, identity, reality*. Macmillan.

Downs, W. M. (2012). *Political extremism in democracies combating intolerance*. Palgrave Macmillan.

Ebner, J. (2019, May 19). Austria's crisis is a lesson for Europe: far-right parties are unfit to govern. *The Guardian*. https://www.theguardian.com/commentisfree/2019/may/23/austria-crisis-europe-far-right-freedom-ibiza-scandal

Eurobarometer. (2019). Public Opinion in the European Union. Standard Eurobarometer 92 Autumn 2019, Brussels: European Commission. https://ec.europa.eu/commfrontoffice/publicopinion/index.cfm/General/index

Fallend, F. (2012). Populism in government. In C. Mudde & C. Rovira Kaltwasser (Eds.), *Populism in Europe and the Americas: Threat or corrective for democracy?* (pp. 113–135). Cambridge University Press.

Fieschi, C. (2000). European institutions: The far-right and illiberal politics in a liberal context. *Parliamentary Affairs*, *53*(3), 517–531. https://doi.org/10.1093/pa/53.3.517

Flood, C. (2002). Euroscepticism: A problematic concept (illustrated with particular reference to France). Paper presented at the UACES 32nd Annual Conference, Belfast.

Follesdal, A., & Hix, S. (2006). Why there is a democratic deficit in the EU: A response to Majone and Moravcsik. *Journal of Common Market Studies*, *44*(3), 533–562. https://doi.org/10.1111/j.1468-5965.2006.00650.x

Freiheitliche Partei Österreichs. (2011). Party Programme of the Freedom Party of Austria. https://www.fpoe.at/themen/parteiprogramm/parteiprogramm-englisch/

Fromage, D., & van den Brink, T. (2018). Democratic legitimation of EU economic governance: Challenges and opportunities for European Legislatures. *Journal of European Integration*, *40*(3), 235–248. https://doi.org/10.1080/07036337.2018.1450407

Front National. (1991). *Militer Au Front*. Editions Nationales.

Front National. (1999). Le Front National pour restaurer notre identité nationale face à l'Europe fédérale. *Français d'Abord*, November (first half): 10–13, 28–29.

Front National. (2004). Programme pour les elections europeennes de 2004.

Front National. (2009). Programme 'Europe' du Front National: leur Europe n'est pas la notre! Voilà l'Europe que nous voulons.

Gaffney, J. (1996). *Political parties and the European union*. Routledge.

Gallie, W. B. (1956). Essentially contested concepts. *Proceedings of the Aristotelian Society*, *56*(1), 167–198. https://doi.org/10.1093/aristotelian/56.1.167

Glencross, A. (2020). "Love Europe, hate the EU": A genealogical inquiry into populists' spatio-cultural critique of the European Union and its consequences. *European*

Journal of International Relations, 26(1), 116–136. https://doi.org/10.1177/1354066119850242.

Goodliffe, G. (2015). Europe's salience and 'owning' Euroscepticism: Explaining the Front National's victory in the 2014 European elections in France. *French Politics, 13*(4), 324–345. https://doi.org/10.1057/fp.2015.19

Gosewinkel, D. (2018). Europe antilibérale ou Anti-Europe? Les conceptions européennes de l'extrême droite française entre 1940 et 1990. *Politique Européenne, 62*(4), 152–179. https://doi.org/10.3917/poeu.062.0152

Gruber, O., & Bale, T. (2014). And it's good night Vienna. How (not) to deal with the populist radical right: The conservatives, UKIP and some lessons from the heartland. *British Politics, 9*(3), 237–254. https://doi.org/10.1057/bp.2014.7

Hainsworth, P. (2008). *The extreme right in Western Europe*. Routledge.

Halikiopoulou, D., & Vlandas, T. (2019). What is new and what is nationalist about Europe's new nationalism? Explaining the rise of the far right in Europe. *Nations and Nationalism, 25*(2), 409–434. https://doi.org/10.1111/nana.12515

Heinisch, R. (2003). Success in opposition – failure in government: Explaining the performance of right-wing populist parties in public office. *West European Politics, 26*(3), 91–130. https://doi.org/10.1080/01402380312331280608

Herman, L. E., & Muldoon, J. B. (2019). *Trumping the mainstream: The conquest of mainstream democratic politics by the populist radical right*. Routledge.

Hooghe, L., & Marks, G. (2009). A postfunctionalist theory of European integration: From permissive consensus to constraining dissensus. *British Journal of Political Science, 39* (1), 1–23. https://doi.org/10.1017/S0007123408000409

Hooghe, L., Marks, G., & Wilson, C. J. (2002). Does left/right structure party positions on European integration? *Comparative Political Studies, 35*(8), 965–989. https://doi.org/10.1177/001041402236310

Ivaldi, G. (2018). Contesting the EU in times of crisis: The Front National and politics of Euroscepticism in France. *Politics, 38*(3), 278–294. https://doi.org/10.1177/0263395718766787

Johnson, B. (2016, October 13). Boris Johnson: "We are leaving the EU, not Europe. *BBC News*. https://www.bbc.co.uk/news/av/uk-politics-37641405/boris-johnson-we-are-leaving-the-eu-not-europe

Katz, R. S. (2014). No man can serve two masters: Party politicians, party members, citizens and principal–agent models of democracy. *Party Politics, 20*(2), 183–193. https://doi.org/10.1177/1354068813519967

Le Pen, J.-M. (1984). *Les Français d'abord*. Carrère Michel Lafon.

Le Pen, J.-M. (1985). *Pour la France: Programme du Front National*. Albatros.

Le Pen, J.-M. (1989). *Europe: Discours et interventions, 1984-1989*. Groupe des Droites européennes.

Le Pen, M. (2017a). 144 engagements présidentiels. https://rassemblementnational.fr/le-projet-de-marine-le-pen/

Le Pen, M. (2017b). Discours de Marine Le Pen à la journée des élus FN au Futuroscope de Poitiers. https://www.youtube.com/watch?v=fyty5HSaAx0

Le Pen, M. (2019). Discours de Marine Le Pen à la Mutualité pour les Européennes. https://www.bfmtv.com/mediaplayer/video/l-integralite-du-discours-de-lancement-de-campagne-de-marine-le-pen-pour-les-europeennes-1131658.html

Lorimer, M. (2019). "Ni droite, ni gauche, francais!" Far right populism and the future of left/right politics. In L. E. Herman & J. B. Muldoon (Eds.), *Trumping the mainstream: The conquest of mainstream democratic politics by the populist radical right* (pp. 145–162). Routledge.

Mair, P. (2013). *Ruling the void: The hollowing of Western democracy*. Verso.

Mammone, A. (2009). The eternal return? Faux populism and contemporarization of neo-fascism across Britain, France and Italy. *Journal of Contemporary European Studies, 17*(2), 171–192. https://doi.org/10.1080/14782800903108635

McDonnell, D., & Werner, A. (2019). *International populism: The radical right in the European Parliament*. Hurst.

Mégret, B. (1989, May). Les principes fondateurs de notre Europe. *La Lettre de Jean-Marie Le Pen*, (second half): 3.

Minkenberg, M. (2000). The renewal of the radical right: Between modernity and anti-modernity. *Government and Opposition, 35*(2), 170–188. https://doi.org/10.1111/1477-7053.00022

Mondon, A. (2014). The Front National in the twenty-first century: From pariah to republican democratic contender? *Modern & Contemporary France, 22*(3), 301–320. https://doi.org/10.1080/09639489.2013.872093

Mudde, C. (2000). *The ideology of the extreme right*. Manchester University Press.

Mudde, C. (2007). *Populist radical right parties in Europe*. Cambridge University Press.

Mudde, C. (2010). The populist radical right: A pathological normalcy. *West European Politics, 33*(6), 1167–1186. https://doi.org/10.1080/01402382.2010.508901

Mudde, C. (2019). *The far tight today*. Polity.

Pirro, A. L. P., & Taggart, P. A. (2018). The populist politics of Euroscepticism in times of crisis: A framework for analysis. *Politics, 38*(3), 253–262. https://doi.org/10.1177/0263395718770579

Pytlas, B., & Kossack, O. (2015). Lighting the fuse: The impact of radical right parties on party competition in Central and Eastern Europe. In M. Minkenberg (Ed.), *Transforming the transformation? The East European tadical right in the political process* (pp. 105–136). Routledge.

Reif, K., & Schmitt, H. (1980). Nine second-order national elections - A conceptual framework for the analysis of European election results. *European Journal of Political Research, 8*(1), 3–44. https://doi.org/10.1111/j.1475-6765.1980.tb00737.x

Reungoat, E. (2014). Mobiliser l'Europe dans la compétition nationale. La fabrique de l'européanisation du Front national. *Politique Européenne, 43*(1), 120–162. https://doi.org/10.3917/poeu.043.0120

Rydgren, J. (2007). The sociology of the radical right. *Annual Review of Sociology, 33*(1), 241–262. https://doi.org/10.1146/annurev.soc.33.040406.131752

Salvini, M. (2019). Per Di Maio è piazza degli ultrà? Siamo estremisti del buonsenso. https://video.corriere.it/salvini-per-maio-piazza-ultra-siamo-estremisti-buonsenso/2a392f88-79a8-11e9-84cc-19261c23ea92?refresh_ce-cp

Scharpf, F. W. (2006). The joint-decision trap revisited. *Journal of Common Market Studies, 44*(4), 845–864. https://doi.org/10.1111/j.1468-5965.2006.00665.x

Schulte-Cloos, J. (2018). Do European Parliament elections foster challenger parties' success on the national level? *European Union Politics, 19*(3), 408–426. https://doi.org/10.1177/1465116518773486

Shields, J. (2013). Marine Le Pen and the 'new' FN: A change of style or of substance? *Parliamentary Affairs, 66*(1), 179–196. https://doi.org/10.1093/pa/gss076

Skey, M., & Antonsich, M. (2017). *Everyday nationhood: Theorising culture, identity and belonging after Banal nationalism*. Palgrave Macmillan.

Startin, N. (2010). Where to for the radical right in the European Parliament? The rise and fall of transnational political cooperation. *Perspectives on European Politics and Society, 11*(4), 429–449. https://doi.org/10.1080/15705854.2010.524402

Startin, N. (2018). "Euromondialisme" and the growth of the radical right. In B. Leruth, N. Startin, & S. M. Usherwood (Eds.), *Routledge Handbook of Euroscepticism* (pp. 75–85). Routledge.

Stockemer, D., & Barisione, M. (2017). The "new" discourse of the Front National under Marine Le Pen: A slight change with a big impact. *European Journal of Communication, 32*(2), 100–115. https://doi.org/10.1177/0267323116680132

Szczerbiak, A., & Taggart, P. A. (2008). *Opposing Europe? The comparative party politics of Euroscepticism.* Oxford University Press.

Taggart, P. (1998). A touchstone of dissent: Euroscepticism in contemporary Western European party systems. *European Journal of Political Research, 33*(3), 363–388. https://doi.org/10.1111/1475-6765.00387.

Taguieff, P.-A. (2014). *Du Diable En Politique: Réflexions sur l'antilepénisme ordinaire.* CNRS Éditions.

Troper, M. (2012). Sovereignty. In M. Rosenfeld & A. S. Sajó (Eds.), *The Oxford Handbook of comparative constitutional law* (pp. 354–370). Oxford University Press.

Van Hauwaert, S. M. (2014). Trans-national diffusion patterns and the future of far right party research: Independence vs. interdependence. *European Journal of Futures Research, 2*(1), 54. https://doi.org/10.1007/s40309-014-0054-5

Vasilopoulou, S. (2018a). *Far right parties and Euroscepticism: Patterns of opposition.* Rowman & Littlefield International.

Vasilopoulou, S. (2018b). The radical right and Euroskepticism. In J. Rydgren (Ed.), *The Oxford Handbook of the radical right* (pp. 122–141). Oxford University Press.

Vlaams Belang. (2014). Uw Stock Achter de Deur, Verkiezingsprogramma. https://www.vlaamsbelang.org/wp-content/uploads/2016/08/20140318ProgrammaVerkiezingen2014.pdf

Wagner, M., & Meyer, T. M. (2017). The radical right as Niche parties? The ideological landscape of party systems in Western Europe, 1980–2014. *Political Studies, 65*(1_suppl), 84–107. https://doi.org/10.1177/0032321716639065

White, J. (2019). *Politics of last resort: Governing by emergency in the European Union.* Oxford University Press.

White, J., & Ypi, L. (2016). *The meaning of partisanship.* Oxford University Press.

Woll, C., & Jacquot, S. (2010). Using Europe: Strategic action in multi-level politics. *Comparative European Politics, 8*(1), 110–126. https://doi.org/10.1057/cep.2010.7

Zaslove, A. (2012). The populist radical right in government: The structure and agency of success and failure. *Comparative European Politics, 10*(4), 421–448. https://doi.org/10.1057/cep.2011.19

Zúquete, J. P. (2018). *The identitarians: The movement against globalism and Islam in Europe.* University of Notre Dame Press.

"Everything is now in order" – Groupthink, ideology and practical-critical activity in the European financial crisis and beyond

Hauke Brunkhorst

ABSTRACT
The present blockade of political action in the EU can be explained by a fatal combination of elite groupthink on the one hand and the constitutionalization of an ideology centred on the spontaneous evolution of market forces on the other. The different reactions on each side of the Atlantic to the crisis of 2008 revealed the truth that evolutionary theory cannot relieve us from 'living forward', taking political action that either emancipates us from socially-embodied ideology or fails to.

Ideology's naturalization of societal relations began in the eighteenth century with the synthesis of political economy and natural law. It returned in the twentieth century with the synthesis of neoliberal economy and genetic evolutionary theory. The great turn in economic policies from progressive to regressive reformism followed this course from the 1980s onwards. It found expression in the EU's emergence as a cornerstone of neoliberal globalization, as examined in Section 1 below.

Then came the crisis of September 15, 2008. The crisis requires us to draw a critical distinction within this process of evolution between revolutionary praxis and contingent variation (Section 2). Confronted with existential problems, political leaders had to *decide* either to keep to their market-radical ideology and wait for evolutionary market forces to put matters right, or to take a critical stance and emancipate themselves from ideological habits. This seemed easier for born-neoliberals such as the Americans than for later converts such as the Europeans.

The differences can be explained by genealogy, mentality and groupthink on the one side, and constitutional design on the other (Section 3). The question is, what are the chances of practical-critical activity after the deconstruction of European ideology? (Section 4).

Don't mess with evolution!

There exists a *European ideology*, as there once was a German ideology. It is based on a kind of groupthink: that all would be well with a currency union that lacked any common pool of funds to finance fiscal transfers. It is based on the idea of the spontaneous evolution of market-forces.

Everything is evolution, and evolution never stops. But evolutionary theory can only explain retrospectively what has already happened: 'Human anatomy contains a key to the anatomy of the ape. The intimations of higher development among the subordinate animal species, however, can be understood only after the higher development is already known' (Marx, 1973a, p. 46). Therefore, evolutionary theory cannot foresee and prescribe what actors and agencies will and should do prospectively. If evolutionary theory is used to do that, it becomes ideological. Ideology consists in the *naturalization of societal and historical relations* (Engels, 1972, p. 515).

When Margaret Thatcher came to power in 1979, Hal Ashby's movie *Being There* came to the cinemas.[1] In the movie, Peter Sellers acts as Chance, a Rousseauian gardener, unspoiled by education and cultural Marxism. Chance grows up as a kind of slave to an American billionaire, whom he calls the master. For his entire life he resides in a garden shed in the grounds of his master's huge mansion in Washington DC. He never leaves the garden, and his only access to the outside world is a TV-set with a remote-control. He remains unaware that TV performances are connected in some way with a real world beyond the mansion and beyond TV. Ashby's movie begins with his master's death. When the heirs' lawyers appear to check the billionaire's estate, Chance lacks any kind of document proving his legal existence in society. Thus, the lawyers expel him from his shed and from the estate. Leaving the mansion and the state of nature, Chance is soon confronted by a gang of youths who immediately adopt a menacing attitude. When the gang's leader reaches for his knife, Chance reaches for his remote control to switch to another channel. It does not work, and Chance must realize that he has arrived in the state of society.

After some further accidents and misunderstandings, Chance makes friends with Ben, another billionaire who lives in his mansion in Washington. Ben is a conscious member of his class who owes his life to the creativity and inventive spirit of free markets for medical services, a system that enabled him to build a private hospital in his mansion, free of any bureaucratic chicanery. Ben suggests that Chance, who knows the law of nature, should become an advisor to the American President, who still believes with Richard Nixon that 'we are all Keynesians now.' Society remains at that time oriented to *progressive reformism* that endows capitalism with *ever more socialist characteristics* – it had been in crisis however since the end of the Bretton Woods agreement.[2]

Progressive reformism shaped the epoch from the 1940s to the 1980s. On the one hand, it results from a successful class struggle from below that was, up to a point, also in the general interest of the capitalist class. It ensured the long-term exploitability of longer-living, healthier, ever-more-consuming and ever-better-educated, disciplined, individualized, globalized and normalized labour-power, hence stabilizing capitalist society (Offe, 1972, p. 40.ff.). If the basic contradiction of modern capitalism, as Marx has argued, consists in 'the violent destruction of capital *not by relations external to it, but rather as a condition of its self-preservation,*' then Marx was also right to interpret this as 'the most striking form in which advice is given' to modern capitalism 'to be gone and to give room to a higher state of social production' (Marx, 1973a, p. 676, my emphasis).[3] People like the billionaire Ben did follow such advice only reluctantly, and never completely. The working class did not warrant the revolutionary expectations of their intellectual interpreters, but it was strong enough to put the capitalist state under pressure to enforce progressive reformism.

On the other hand, the further the socialist characteristics of late-capitalism progressed, the more living conditions, living quarters and life as a whole were *de-commodified* and released from exploitation imperatives (Esping-Andersen, 1990, p. 21ff.). De-commodification transcends the horizon of modern capitalism: the more it progressed, the more it challenged the existence of capitalism and exceeded the capacities of the capitalist state that, *as* a capitalist state, was bound to an economic system compatible with progressive reformism *only insofar as private exploitation was guaranteed* (Offe, 2006, p. 192).

As long as modern capitalism exists, the 'Herrschaftsrecht' (*right to rule*) of private ownership, especially of 'dead labour' (capital, money, real estate) over 'living labour' (working hours), had to remain untouchable.[4] Until the 1960s, this basic capitalist structure survived even the total regulation of private property, and with it the dark sides of the 'externalizing society' of late capitalism – the dumping of toxic waste off the coast of Africa, in the Sahara region and in Indian rivers, the outsourcing of cheap labour, neo-colonialism, land-grabbing, the consumerist re-commodification of leisure time and public communication, the simultaneity of welfare- and warfare-state, the transformation of democracy into technocracy, cold war anti-communism, and the accompanying structural prejudices of racism, misogyny and homophobia (Lessenich, 2016; Marcuse, 1967).

Classical social-democratic progressive reformism was challenged by the global cultural revolution of the 1960s, which was critical of anti-communism and imperialism, racism and misogyny, and finally achieved the inclusion of formerly excluded nationalities and races, genders and sexual orientations into the project of progressive reformism. For a short historic moment, it looked as if the wildest dreams of the Left were coming true, uniting the 'social critique' of inequality with the 'artist's critique' of alienation (Boltanski & Chiapello, 2007, p. 419ff) in a realistic project of revolutionary or radical reformism (Brunkhorst, 2018). It became realistic to ask for the impossible.[5]

The cultural *choc* was the final trigger for General de Gaulle to put French forces on alert, and for Ben and his fellow capitalists to reach for the emergency break and call for government by the Mont Pèllerin Society, Chance the Gardener, General Pinochet, Margaret Thatcher and Ronald Reagan. The cultural revolution subverted the achievement principle. The capitalist basic institution of free labour markets had been put in jeopardy. The private labour contract, the 'very Eden of the innate rights of man' that was strictly limited to the sphere of circulation, threatened to colonize the separate sphere of production that was bound to the private right to dominate and exploit living labour (Marx, 1973b, p. 123).

Ben arranges the first meeting between Chance the Gardener, the American President and himself. This follows his earlier rejection of the President's suggestion of a further recovery package for the flagging economy. The dissatisfied President turns to Chance: 'Mr. Gardener, do you think that we can stimulate growth through temporary incentives?' The reply comes slowly: 'In the garden, growth has its season. First comes spring and summer, but then we have fall and winter. And then we get spring and summer again.' The President is puzzled, but Ben immediately gets the point, resoundingly in favour of his own class-interests: 'I think, what our insightful young friend is saying is that we welcome the inevitable seasons of nature, but we are upset by the seasons of our economy.' Chance delightedly agrees: 'Yes, there will be growth in the spring.' All applaud. The next day, progressive is replaced by regressive reformism – capitalism *with ever less socialist characteristics*.

Societal relations would now be naturalized once more, as in the liberal political economy of the eighteenth century: The 'entire history of production relations thus appears [...] as a malicious forgery perpetrated by governments' (Marx, 1973a, p. 27). Following Hayek, Chicago-School monetarism, and the teachings of Chance the Gardener, all political intervention to change the *seasons of our economy* was henceforth banned. Engineers and gardeners were now to save the spontaneous ('*kósmic*') evolution of markets from democratically-created positive law and replace it with the politically-neutralized law of nature ('*Nomos*') (von Hayek, 2003, p. 37ff, pp. 97ff, pp. 418ff). Hayek's old dream of 'embedding' the state in the 'comprehensive spontaneous order like a maintenance crew in a factory' was coming true (von Hayek, 2003, p. 49). No evolution without gardener and engineer.

As with the former Soviet planning authorities, the ordo- and neoliberal crew replaced political praxis with technology (Habermas, 1968, pp. 120–145). Moreover, state-interventionism to establish and maintain the market economy turned out to be as high if not higher than that needed to keep a planned economy running (Offe, 1992, pp. 29–49; Offe, 2016). But the liberals had the better technology: 'The wealth of those societies in which the capitalist mode of production prevails, presents itself as an immense accumulation of commodities' (Marx, 1973b, p. 27). The shelves of the shops where Soviet planning authorities ruled were empty, – not those where the (Keynesian) Chinese planning authorities were in charge. It all depends. Only the 'true wealth of modern society, the *free, disposable time*', was not yet realized anywhere (Marx, 1953, p. 589, p. 593). But everywhere the *Kantian mindset* of democracy was colonized by the *managerial mindset* (Koskenniemi, 2006). A red line now ran through the factory, where the words of the German finance minister were engraved in golden letters: 'Elections cannot be allowed to change economic policies' (Tooze, 2018, p. 525).

This line would translate the ideology of naturalizing society into the constitutional design of the EU, leaving to the people the meaningless choice between microeconomic strategies to implement presumably 'self-evident' macroeconomic 'laws of nature' (Marx, 1973b, p. 523). The isolation of the macro-economic basic structure from substantial public debate, decision-making and legislation is today constitutive for the functioning of the EU as a transnational organization.[6] Neither at the EU level nor at that of the member states is it possible any longer to make the macroeconomic naturalization of social relations subject to democratic, bottom-up will-formation, 'elections and other votes' (Art. 20 GBL). The macro-economic 'choices are taken in an institutional setting that provides near-perfect protection against the interference of input-oriented political processes and of democratic accountability in the constituencies affected' (Scharpf, 2015, p. 23).

No one in Europe or beyond tries to mess with evolution any longer. Luhmann banned the subject from theory: 'The subject is no object, what good is it in theory!' (Luhmann, 1973, p. 21, my translation). Francois Furet and Francis Fukuyama declared the end of revolution, history and critical theory. The Amsterdam Rijksmuseum presented Rembrandt as a successful businessman, and a high-ranked functionary of *Labour* admitted in summer 2002: 'We are all Thatcherites now.'[7] Three years later, Tony Blair blocked the debate on globalization with the wisdom of Chance the Gardener: 'I hear people say we have to stop and debate globalization. You might as well debate whether autumn should follow summer.'[8]

Europe was well prepared for the turn. Already in the *Treaty of Rome*, the German-Austrian *Ordoliberalismus* was backed informally by the conservative government of the United States, and finally prevailed over French economic dirigisme in 1957 (Rödl, 2010; Wegmann, 2010). At that time, Germany was still 'politically quarantined' but already 'economically dominant' (Mody, 2018, p. 25). The radical market ideology of Adenauer's minister of economic affairs, Ludwig Erhard, who was a right-wing ordoliberal, and Hayek's great influence in the UK and the Federal Republic of Germany, as well as at the leading economic schools of London, Freiburg and Chicago, ensured a close link between German-Austrian ordoliberalism and American neoliberalism (Fuhrmann, 2017).

Moreover, the special kind of *groupthink* that developed amongst the small group of European leaders, especially from the first debates on a single currency in the late 1960s, could easily be adjusted to the neoliberal episteme, even if none of the participants was a born neoliberal. After the failure of the political and military union in the 1950s and the nationalist blockade of any further European integration by General de Gaulle in the 1960s, the French president Pompidou took the initiative for the single currency in 1969. It was, as Ashoka Mody writes, 'a bad idea at a bad time' (Mody, 2018, p. 5) – and no way to make a dialectical negation of negation out of it that takes us forward to *a higher state of social production*. This Hegelian turn to progress still is blocked by the deeply ironic tacit consent of European leaders' groupthink, supposing that there should be a common currency but without any 'common pool of funds to finance fiscal transfers.'[9] This problem was postponed, and already the Werner-Committee of the EEC completed its report in October 1970 with a reference anticipating Chance the Gardener's idea of natural *growth* 'into a more complete monetary union' that will follow in *spring* after implanting a common currency without any kind of common tax- and financial regime in the previous *fall*: 'This "falling forward" thesis became the European single currency's guiding philosophy' (Mody, 2018, p. 6).

However, the natural law of falling forward in a common currency area with a central bank without a state, governing 19 states without a central bank, was that 'some nations would benefit more than others' (Mody, 2018, p. 7; Offe, 2016, p. 7). A political regime 'originally conceived as a community, even a brotherhood' that 'brings Europeans together', has now become a monetary Union with 'a hegemonic governance structure' that 'tears them apart.' The warnings bypassed any relevant public opinion because of the total lack of a European public sphere. They were heard and well known to the small group of European leaders, but repressed by the 'unwavering collective belief' of groupthink 'that all would be well' (Mody, 2018, p. 7f).

It is exactly as in Smetana's Opera *The Bartered Bride* (Act 1, Szene III) when Kezal (as later Chancellor Kohl) makes the blind marriage deal:

> Everything is now in order,/ And important is just this:/ Give your word as pledge,/ And the bargain's made./ Yes, for I have reconciled/ All the happiness in Land./ For all success depends alone/ On sense and penetration./ When the pair will meet,/ Why, I may be cursed/ If both don't burn with love,/ And glow with passion!

However, Kathinka is (as later some economists) sceptical that the deal will work: 'But first she must see the wooer.' And for the European bargain she adds in prose: *some nations would benefit more than others.* Immediately, Kezal replies with Helmut Kohl's voice speaking Euro-Group-Think: 'To see him too? Ah, confound you!/ There's nothing there to criticize!/ Everything's in order/ Important is just this:/ Give your word as pledge,/ And the bargain's made.' The northern FANGs (Finland, Austria, Netherlands, Germany) now benefit, but soon, in *spring*, after a last hard *winter* of austerity, the southern PIGS (Portugal, Italy, Greek, Spain) will benefit. The investors will arrive with the first swallow, *burning with love* and *passion*. The big trickledown effect comes in *summer*, 'masterly framed' by convergence criteria and the Stability and Growth Pact, both guaranteeing converging and stable growth, and even results for everybody on an increasingly uneven playing field. But there is a caveat: 'So when in case of doubt,/ send The Institutions.'[10]

But that came later, in 2015. In 2007, a year before the climate-catastrophe of Thatcherism, despite some signs of the 'gathering storm', everything seemed to be well in the neoliberal world economy of Europe and America, and the signs were repressed. After a forty-year deregulatory push, the small risk of political re-regulation seemed a bigger risk than a global economic crash. Larry Summers warned 'that even to discuss risks within the system was to incite dangerous political reactions'. Alan Greenspan stated in the *Zürcher Tages Anzeiger*:

> We are fortunate that, thanks to globalization, policy decisions in the US have been largely replaced by global market forces. National security aside, it hardly makes any difference who will be the next president. The world is governed by market forces.[11]

Of course, Europe applauds. European banks 'were the biggest players in the business'. In 2007, the balance sheet of the Royal Bank of Scotland, Banque Nationale de Paris and Deutsche Bank equalled 17% of global GDP, each of them as big as the GDP of their home country (Tooze, 2018, p. 27ff, 69, 82, 112).

Crisis

On September 15, 2008, 'by the break of day [...] a flash' interrupted the *kósmic seasons of our economy* (Hegel, 2010, p. 15ff.).[12] Lehmann Brothers collapsed. The global South paid the price. In Philadelphia where I lived at that time, the always-full floodlights of the Stadium opposite our apartment went out and stayed dark until I went back to Germany in November. The *Federal Reserve's* president, Ben Bernanke, who is not given to over statement, called what happened 'the worst financial crisis in global history, including the Great Depression' (Tooze, 2018, p. 168ff, cf. pp. 147ff.)

> Never before [...] had such a large and interconnected system come so close to total implosion. [...] In the 1930s there was no moment of such massive

synchronization, no moment in which so many of the world's largest banks threatened to fail simultaneously. The speed and force of the avalanche was unprecedented. As Bernanke later admitted [...], 'It was overwhelming, even paralyzing, to think too much about the high stakes involved, so I focused as much as I could on the specific task at hand [... .] As events unfolded I repressed my fears and focused on solving problems' [...] Looking back, it was like being in a car wreck. 'You're mostly involved in trying to avoid going off the bridge; and then later on you say, oh my god!' (Tooze, 2018, p. 168)

The crisis was the Kierkegaardian moment of politics. The evolutionary theories of Chance the Gardener, Friedrich August von Hayek and Niklas Luhmann failed, just in the same way as Hegel's Philosophy failed in spring 1843, during the existential crisis of Sören Kierkegaard's life. Theory, Kierkegaard argues, is 'true with regard to the past that we must *explain and understand life backward* – but it was forgotten that *we must live forward*' (Kierkegaard, 1941, p. 162; my translation, my emphasis). Living forward gives us 'no moment of rest to take the stance: backward' (Kierkegaard, 1941, p. 162; see Kierkegaard, 2013, p. 465f.). Backward, everything is fixed; forward, 'free action might change everything' (Kierkegaard, 2013, p. 346). Marx said the same concurrently: 'revolutionary', 'practical-critical activity' can 'change the world' (Marx, 1973c, p. 5).

The ideological performance of naturalizing society *gave room* (Marx) to another performance, the performance of *autonomy* – but not everywhere. On September 15, the subject was back to politics. Ironically, the neoliberal American leaders Ben Bernanke, Hank Paulson and George Bush made a U-Turn at full speed.

Paulson confronted his staff with the prospect of an 'economic 9/11.' On the morning of September 20, the US Treasury secretary alerted Congress to the fact that unless they acted fast, $5.5 trillion in wealth would disappear by 2pm. They might be facing the collapse of the world economy 'within 24 h.' [...] Bernanke warned that unless they authorized immediate action, 'we may not have an economy on Monday' (Tooze, 2018, p. 165f.)

Without the 'heartbeat of the revolution' (Habermas) that is, as Marx writes, the legislative power that once 'produced the French revolution (and) all great, organic revolutions' (Habermas, 1989, p. 7; Marx, 1976, p. 260); without unprecedented legislative decisions for unlimited bailout and growth programmes; without the flooding of America and Europe with the money of the Federal Reserve (and against the cowardly resistance of Merkel, Steinbrück and Sarkozy, who stuck to the theories of their selfish genes, 'profoundly committed' to the 'supply-side, anti-Keynesian vision of economic policy.'); without these *revolutionary activities*, no spontaneous evolution, no self-organized market, and no neoliberal theory would have saved us from the worst financial crisis in global history (Tooze, 2018, p. 98, pp. 166ff, 189ff, 236, 290f, 332ff).

Ideology, mindset and truth

Crisis reveals the *symptomatic truth* that the same ideology can take different paths in Europe and America (Žižek, 2001, p. 177f.). Ideologies are constellations of ideas, and ideas are not in the head but embodied in social reality. They, as well as their affirmation and critique, exist as social mindsets and practices: 'Language does not transform ideas, so that the peculiarity of ideas is dissolved and their social character runs alongside them as a separate entity, like prices alongside commodities. Ideas do not exist separately from language' (Marx, 1973a, p. 100f.).

The quasi-revolutionary activism of the American neoliberals was certainly not pure voluntarism, as Adam Tooze insinuates in his seminal *Crash*. Only the 'flash of thought' can 'inspire material might to political power.' (Marx, 1976, p. 391, 389). Tooze himself shows how the neoliberal agencies drew Keynesian inferences from neoliberal failure, and besides technical they had normative reasons. From the perspective of the actor, functionalism and neoliberalism are not per se ideologies, and they do not fail in direct confrontation with reality (as correspondence theories of truth assume). The functionalist theories of economic evolution *became* ideologies in praxis, by September 15 at the latest, because social actors and agencies could no longer use them as instruments to cope with a social reality that was their lifeworld.

The agencies who made the U-turn destroyed ideology actively. Even if they were 'not aware of this, nevertheless they did it' (Marx, 1973b, p. 49). Different from Europe's leaders, who had converted late and followed neoliberal doctrines heteronomously, the American leaders had grown up with them, and had learned to justify them autonomously (*Selbstdenken*).[13] To act autonomously, you must want it, and take the risk deliberatively. However, there are social conditions more or less favourable to acting autonomously. Theories – evolutionary political and economic doctrines such as neoliberalism or Marxism – are not only tools like a hammer but constitute the Ego and identity of the actors and agencies who learn to connect the truth (authenticity) of their individual and collective identity with the truth of political, social and economic theories and doctrines. As *paradigms* – clusters of norms, mindsets, interpretative, explanative and justificatory patterns – they constitute scientific and political communities (Kuhn, 1962). During scientific and political-socialization processes, actors do not just learn textbooks but also surrender themselves to the higher authority of these communities. To become free to *reject or acknowledge* a paradigm, one must speak its language fluently.

The German philosopher Schelling calls the process that makes you a fluent speaker the '*Submission unter das Höhere*' – submission to the Superior (Schelling, 1997, p. 364). What Schelling means is that social norms and paradigms, with dramatic intensification during initiate rituals, are 'branded on the body of the initiated person' (Clastres, 1974, p. 159). This kind of heteronomous internalization of the Superior (superior authority) is initially not backed by reason but *may be* rational (*vernünftig*). Therefore, Schelling calls the submission a 'pathetic' (*leidend, sich hingebend*) use of reason (*Vernunft*), and 'pathetic reason' here means a kind of advance payment on reasonability. The active rational use (*aktiven, tätigen Verstand*) of successively internalized paradigms results in the identification of the actor with the respective paradigm (Schelling, 1997, p. 364).[14] Only successful identification enables actors to perform, apply and justify the Superior *autonomously* from a universal point of view, decentering their egocentrism. Relying on Kant, Schelling calls this stage of autonomy the 'touchstone' of 'truth' because she who autonomously submits and justifies the Superior no longer *has to* submit but can also take a rebellious and critical stance against it. Autonomously, we 'subjugate to no law except the law we give to ourselves.'(Kant, 1977a, p. 280f, my translation). Forward-looking, autonomous practical-critical activity 'gains strength to the extent to which it previously identifies with the matter against which it opposes' (Habermas, 1981, p. 450).

Already in November 2002, Bernanke had demonstrated his *autonomous* use of neoliberal doctrines when he had promised at a birthday celebration for Milton Friedman and his co-author Anna Schwartz: 'I would like to say to Milton and Anna: Regarding the Great Depression. You are right, we did it. We're very sorry. But thanks to you, we won't do it again.' Tooze rightly points out that one should not confuse Bernanke's promise with a 'conventional central banker's commitment to price stability' because Bernanke '*was* making a commitment to price stability, but what he was promising to prevent was *deflation*, not inflation.' This makes it plausible to say that the Americans were able to learn 'lessons from history,' and especially that

> Ben Bernanke's placid and undersized persona would soon come to occupy an outsized space in global economic history. He would turn out to be an unusual but highly significant case of the possibility of 'learning lessons from history'. (Tooze, 2018, p. 40)

How does learning lessons from history work?

We can assume with Marx that social agencies such as the working class have 'accepted (*anerkannt*)' the 'spontaneous (*naturwüchsige*) product of a long and painful process of development' by 'education, tradition, habit' (including initiation) and the 'dull compulsion of economic relations' as 'self-evident laws of nature' (Marx, 1973b, p. 52, 523).[15] They submit to the Superior: 'the subjection of the labourer to the capitalist' (Marx, 1973b, p. 52, 523). However, education, tradition and habit in the course of history can also teach us to take a critical stance against the Superior and the naturalization of social relations. Marx's paradigmatic example is the struggle for a normal working day during the nineteenth century. Once the pressure of pain and dull compulsion is reduced by 'the modest Magna Charta of a legally limited working day', the labourer (and the capitalist!) is given time 'for a little culture' to recognize that history (Marx, 1973b, p. 195 and note 166) also maintains the 'counter-memory' (Assmann, 1992, p. 103) of 'progress for the better', embodied in exemplary fashion in the cultural memory of great revolutions which are 'too momentous, too intimately interwoven with the interests of humanity […] *not to be reminded* […] when favourable circumstances present themselves, and to rise up and make renewed attempts of the same kind as before' (Kant, 1977b, p. 357f, 361; Kant, 1970, p. 185 my emphasis). The counter-memory of successful struggles for a normal working day in the nineteenth century makes workers *look forward* to *changing the world*. American and French revolutionaries in the eighteenth century used the stories of the Exodus and Brutus' insurgency as such a counter-memory. The emancipation movement of American blacks in the 1960s used the Exodus: 'When Israel was in Egypt's land/ Let my people go … '

Like all learning, learning from history is problem-solving, and the French, American and Caribbean revolutions solved problems of *egalitarian self-government*, of *overcoming structural social conflicts* by regime-change, of generating power by *constitutional patriotism* – all marks for Kant of the 'righteous zeal' (Kant, 1977a, p. 268) and 'true enthusiasm' of 'revolutionaries' who take 'arms for the *rights* of the people.' Such constitutional enthusiasm proved to be stronger than the armies of Kings and Kaisers who invaded France in 1792 with their 'monetary rewarded' soldiers, and the false 'martial honour' of their noble leaders (Kant, 1970, p. 183). Thus, a cultural counter-memory emerged that gave the 'democratic ideals promoted in the revolutionary period a certain enduring reality' (Thornhill, 2018, p. 41ff.).

Revolutionary learning processes have a long history. Paradigmatic is the internal relation between the biblical stories of *Job* and *Exodus*. Job's dire fate testifies to the fact that human individuals are capable of acting autonomously in accordance with universal moral truth. Job (and in *this* respect not so different from the American neoliberals a couple of thousand years later) submits to the 'Superior' and identifies with its norms and interpretative patterns in an autonomous way, from a universal moral point of view, as we can see from the discussion with his self-righteous friends (who are in *this* respect not so different from European groupthink). However, to get from Job's desperate hope to learning from history needs a real and historical 'tendency' towards progress, and the example of collective agencies who strive for emancipation on the basis of unconditioned morality (Kant, 1977b, p. 357ff.).[16] One can learn from factual and fictive history, written in the spirit of the prophets who invented the Exodus story, that justice must not submit to evolutionary adaptation but adaptation to justice. Therefore, Kant understands the French Revolution as an application of the old saying *fiat justitia, pereat mundus*, as we see immediately from his sophisticated translation:

'Let justice rule on earth, although all the rogues in the world should go to the bottom' (Kant, 1917, p. 179) – and here he means the *monetary rewarded* soldiers and the *martial nobles* of 1792 (the meaning of the Latin 'mundus' then was basically the noble and courtly world).

In fall 2008, Bernanke, Bush, Paulson, the Democratic majority of Congress and Gordon Brown of the Thatcherite Labour Party proved that they had learned the lessons of 1929. They evoked the counter-memory of New-Deal public interventionism – and the rogues in the world should go to the bottom, not least their own Republican Party. To be clear, they did not lead a great revolution – there was no New Deal in 2008 – and they were far from changing the world into an inclusive democracy that controls global capitalism and endows it with ever more socialist characteristics. Nevertheless, the neoliberals of 2008 made a kind of revolutionary U-Turn, and realized the interest of all of us by transforming the Federal Reserve into a global central bank (Tooze, 2018, p. 9, see 218ff.).

This is not just 'rather minimalistic Hobbesian' but also somewhat Kantian unconditionality.[17] The US Federal Reserve

> engaged in a truly spectacular innovation. It established itself as liquidity provider of last resort to the global banking system. It provided dollars to all comers in New York, whether banks were American or not. Through so-called liquidity swap lines, the Fed licensed a hand-picked group of core central banks to issue dollar credits on demand. In a huge burst of transatlantic activity, with the European Central Bank (ECB) in the lead, they pumped trillions of dollars into the European banking system. (Tooze, 2018, p. 9)

To be sure, as long as the dollar is the global reserve currency, the central bank that prints the dollar must make monetary policy dictated by the interest of maintaining the system of global capitalism.[18] However, the American government acted not just as a globalized Hayckian *maintenance crew in the global factory* (von Hayek, 2003, p. 49). What was new was not just the *scale* on which the Fed was ready to intervene (though that too was revolutionary). The scale came not with quantitative easing but with the structurally and functionally new instrument of *swap lines* 'with which the Fed pumped dollars into the world economy.' It triggered Draghi's 2012 'Whatever it takes' speech that factually violated European constitutional law, hence was 'revolutionary' in legal terms. Further, it enabled an even higher scale of intervention during the coronavirus crisis of 2020 by both the Fed and the ECB, when Christine Lagarde did everything to save Italy and Spain as the Germans and Dutch brutally told Italians and Spanish to 'deal with it.'[19]

To save the world from a financial meltdown in 2008, the Fed had to do something immoral that 'provoked long-running and bitter recrimination and for good reasons.' The Fed put in play 'hundreds of billions of taxpayer funds' to rescue the twenty to thirty 'greedy banks' that 'matter at a global level.' Ben Bernanke's "historic policy' of global liquidity support' involved handing 'trillions of dollars in loans to that coterie of banks, their shareholders and their outrageously remunerated senior staff', and 'half of the liquidity support it provided went to banks not headquartered in the United States, but located overwhelmingly in Europe.' (Tooze, 2018, p. 12f). No wonder the 'America First' Republican Party and their conservative social media activists urged their followers to tweet immediately: 'Bernanke has blood on his hands.'[20]

Perspectives for practical-critical activity?

The pathbreaking insight of Tooze's grand narrative is the 'stark truth about Ben Bernanke's "historic" policy' that it destroyed 'the familiar twentieth-century island model of international economic interaction' once and for all. If there ever were, there are no longer any 'basic units' of national economies, trading with one another, running 'trade surpluses and deficits', accumulating 'national claims and liabilities.' Political agencies use this model whenever they appear in public, and it is the familiar TV-world of the economy. It is mere fiction. In this world, VW sells well when its 10 German factories with 100,000 employees sell well, but VW has nearly 700,000 employees in 124 factories in 20 European countries and 11 countries of the Americas, Asia and Africa. The financial system that keeps this system of production running does not consist of 'national monetary flows.' Nor is it 'made up of a mass of tiny, anonymous, microscopic firms – the "ideal of perfect competition" and the economic analogue to the individual citizen' (Tooze, 2018, p. 12).

In 2008 the Fed destroyed this old and new, classical and neo-liberal bourgeois analogy that connects the possessive individualism of natural market relations between isolated individual citizens (nicely represented on the frontispiece of Hobbes' *Leviathan* by the lonely figures at the market-place) with the relations of individualized national states existing in an international state of nature (on the frontispiece represented by the big individual, the Leviathan made of administrative, industrial and military armies of legally-coordinated human individuals). The destruction of this ideology explains much of the rage of the Republicans. The Fed's policy revealed that we inhabit no longer this Hobbesian *and* Rousseau-Kantian world of (potentially) democratic nation-states but 'a world dominated by business oligopolies [...], and its implications for the priorities of government stood nakedly exposed. It is an unpalatable and explosive truth that democratic politics on both sides of the Atlantic has choked on' (Tooze, 2018, p. 13).

In Roosevelt's world of 1933, a national and democratically-legitimated political economy was still possible. Since 2008 at the latest, *national* economy (as scientific discipline *and* as a social system) and *nation-bound* democratic politics have been things of the past. The Fed replaced them in 2008 with post-democratic, technocratic policies that consisted in swap lines of unprecedented scale, performed in close coordination with the ECB, the Bank of England, and strongly supported by the People's Bank of China.

However, unlike the European leading actors and agencies, the Fed was at least backed and supported – if only at the national level – by democratically-legitimated legislative and executive bodies. The EU, equipped with monetary fire-power of a similar size to the US, has no comparable institution, and a central bank without even the American minimum of democratic legitimization. Also due to this fact, the Americans were able *and* decided to do it, whereas the Europeans were trapped by constitutional under-democratization, groupthink and the non-universalizable categorical imperative that *no common pool of funds to finance fiscal transfers should be allowed.*[21]

When Europe faced a 'monetary Stalingrad' in 2008, Steinbrück appealed to national self-interest: 'Not our problem.' 'No talk of joint bailouts' (Tooze, 2018, p. 236,190). Merkel added a line from one of Goethe's poems: 'Ein jeder kehre vor seiner Tür, und rein ist jedes Stadtquartier' (*Everyone should sweep in front of his door and every city quarter will be clean*).[22] Jean-Claude Junker appeased his fellow citizens: 'I see no reason why we should mount a US-style programme in Europe' (Tooze, 2018, p. 191). Merkel promised, as if Queen of Europe: 'There will be no collectivization of debt in the European Union for *as long as I live*' (Tooze, 2018, p. 439, my emphasis). Self-righteously, Steinbrück explained the crisis by reference to 'America's laissez-faire ideology,' and predicted 'the end of Anglo-American [!] capitalism'. Even in 2009, Sarkozy and Steinbrück dreamed of the Euro as the new reserve currency (Tooze, 2018, p. 96, 196, 221). 'It is hard to see how either Steinbrück or Sarkozy could have been more out of touch with reality' (Tooze, 2018, p. 223). Steinbrück's self-righteousness was trumped only by Barroso, who snapped back at a Canadian journalist critical of European austerity:

> Frankly, we are not here to receive lessons in terms of democracy or in terms of how to handle the economy [...]. This crisis [...] originated in North-America, and much of our financial sector was contaminated by [...] unorthodox practices, from some sectors of the financial markets.

He added pompously: 'Europe is a community of democracies.' He had, by this point, already pocketed a contract with a leading American investment bank (Tooze, 2018, p. 437).

During the critical situation of the Euro in 2011–2012 (the 'PIGS crisis'), the constitutional basic standard of *competitiveness* and the categorical imperative that *no common pool of funds is allowed to finance fiscal transfers* triggered the 'self-evidence' of the Eurozone's 'law of nature' (Marx) that *some nations* (FANGs) *would benefit more than others* (PIGS). The law of nature's trajectory led directly to fatal disaster. Only the ECB could save the Euro ('whatever it takes') by breaking the law of nature (and constitutional law), and this was so because it is the only European institution that has the formal legislative power to blackmail Angela Merkel to give her informal agreement, bypassing the entire democratic order of people (Greek referendum), parliaments and courts. The ideology is saved, and *everything is now in order*.

The same happened with the next crisis of 2015. Confronted with the expected victory of the Left in Greece in January, Jean-Claude Junker frankly admitted, 'if the radical left wins the elections, the effects on the mon-etary union are immeasurable. The solidarity of the Eurozone is in greatest peril.' Elections cannot be allowed to change economic policies. The ideology is saved, and *everything is now in order*.

Then comes the pandemic and another world economic crisis. The Germans again say No and praise themselves. The Dutch finance minister Wopke Hoekstra does the dirty job and explains to the European South, with unconcealed racism, that before we transfer anything, we 'first should look at the accounts of the southerners to check if they have saved enough during recent years.'[23] Italy, France and Spain coordinate their practical-critical activity to override the self-evident law of nature that some benefit more than others. Italy, France and Spain now confront Europe with the alternative 'Euro-bonds! European taxes! Democratic government! – or die.' Groupthink is over, ideology is lost, and *nothing is in order*.

Conclusion

September 15, 2008 was the first day of the end of national economic politics. European ideology is as dead as national economy. The credo of the Third Way, 'Good economic policy is what is good for GDP growth', is now fake news. Since this day, questions of distribution – the politics of 'who, whom?' – no longer 'can be weighted up against the general interest in "growing the size of the cake"' (Tooze, 2018, p. 12). Accordingly, Hilary Clin-ton's presidential campaign failed already in the primaries of 2016, and the independent, movement-based Bernie Sanders, who asked 'who, whom?' and announced in all frankness democratic socialism, became with this 'Un-American Activity' (McCarthy) Clinton's strongest competitor and one of the favourites in the 2020 elections. He pushed the Democrats far to the left. With the slogan 'Europe first!', the independent, movement-based Emmanuel Macron killed French Jaurès-style social democracy, marginalized the far right, and won the French presidential elections in 2017. There are more in the pipe-line, some more successful than others, emerging in Greece, Spain, the UK and Italy, and the good news is that it might be an open list.

In 2008 the world was saved by technocratic central banks, and we will need their fire-power to cope with the pandemic economic crisis and climate change.[24] However, since 2008, democratic politics is also back, from below and in the sphere of culture. Occupy Wall Street some months later replied to Merkel's poetic line from Goethe with a more prosaic one: 'None are more hopelessly enslaved than those who falsely believe they are free.'[25] Culture and cultural opportunism has no fire-power, but much more predictive power than political opportunism and empiricist social research. The reading lists and the theatre stages are suddenly full of revolution. The marginal Democratic Socialists of America are replaced by Sanders' quickly-growing *Our Revolution*. The Amsterdam Rijksmuseum last year dropped the businessman, and presented Rembrandt proudly as 'rebel.'[26]

Notes

1. Being There, USA 1979, Director Hal Ashby, https://www.youtube.com/watch?v=TYeVQzTVyLk (15.02.2019).
2. On the distinction progressive vs. regressive reformism: Offe (2016, p. 29).
3. Following this line of argument, Offe shows in his seminal studies on the welfare state that the 'self-negating tendencies' of capitalism are 'unavoidable' within the still existing 'private process of production' (Offe, 1972, p. 11).
4. Marx distinguishes 'dead labour" (*tote Arbeit*) from 'living labour force' (*lebendige Arbeit*) because in his theory of money assets are the reified 'dead' product of the exploitation of living labour during working hours.
5. 'Soyez réalistes, demandez l'impossible' was a surrealist slogan of the Paris May 1968.
6. See von Achenbach (2018, pp. 1025–1035).
7. Kia Vahland, *Der Menschenfreund – In seiner Kunst zeigt Renbrandt sein ganzes Leben*, SZ 1.3.2019, 11; Peter Mandelson according to The Guardian 10.6.2002.
8. Tony Blair, *Conference Speech*, in: The Guardian 27.09.2005.
9. Military union failed in French parliament because parliamentarians feared losing autonomy of taxation.
10. Tom Lehrer, *Send the Marines* (slightly altered), https://www.songtexte.com/songtext/tom-lehrer/send-the-marines-3c72df3.html (21.04.2020).
11. Alan Greenspan, *Ich bin im falschen Jahrhundert geboren*, in: Zürcher Tages-Anzeiger, 9.9.2007.
12. The 'flash' means the French Revolution.
13. Habermas argues that we 'regain and regenerate our self only' dialectically 'through self-surrender (*Selbstpreigabe*)' (Habermas, 2012, p. 85).
14. On the combination of Durkheim and Schelling: (Habermas, 2018, p. 268ff).
15. The critical meaning of the German (Marxian) word '*naturwüchsig*' is missed by the more neutral English term 'spontaneous'. It means that something made by human agency is treated as if it is not socio-cultural but natural.
16. On the important distinction between individual and collective action in Kant and Marx: (Ypi, 2017, p. 673ff; Ypi, 2014, p. 9, 16).
17. Objection of a blind reviewer.
18. Objection of a blind reviewer.
19. Emmanuel Macron, *FT-Interview* 16.4.20 (https://www.ft.com/content/3ea8d790-7fd1-11ea-8fdb-7ec06edeef84 – 26.4.20); see Tooze (2018, p. 11); Mody, *Italy: the crisis that could go viral. Coronavirus threatens to turn Italy's economic and financial crisis into a global one*, BNE March 3, 2020, https://braveneweurope.com/spiked-ashoka-mody-italy-the-crisis-that-could-go-viral (27.4.20).

20. *'Blood on Bernanke's Hands'*, in: Mish's Global Economic Trend Analysis, January 27, 2011, quoted from (Tooze, 2018, p. 376).
21. Angela Merkel, *Speech at the CDU Convention*, Stuttgart Dec. 1, 2008.
22. So she represented it to the press; according to a British official she said: 'Chacun sa merde!' (*To each his own shit!*), Tooze (2018, p. 289ff).
23. *Süddeutsche Zeitung*, April 2, 2020, p. 3 (my translation).
24. Tooze, *Why Central Banks Need to Step UP on Global Warming*, FP July 20, 2019, https://foreignpolicy.com/2019/07/20/why-central-banks-need-to-step-up-on-global-warming/ (27.4.20).
25. See https://de.wikipedia.org/wiki/Occupy_Wall_Street#/media/Datei:Day_12_Occupy_Wall_Street_September_28_2011_Shankbone_33.JPG (12.06.2019). The quote is from Goethe's *Wilhelm Meister*.
26. Vahland, *Der Menschenfreund*.

Disclosure statement

No potential conflict of interest was reported by the author(s).

References

Assmann, J. (1992). *Politische Theologie zwischen Ägypten und Israel*. Siemens-Stiftung.

Boltanski, L., & Chiapello, E. (2007). *The New Spirit of Capitalism*. Verso.

Brunkhorst, H. (2018). Radical reformism. In R. K. Brunkhorst & C. Lafont (Eds.), *Habermas Handbook* (pp. 610–613). Columbia UP.

Clastres, P. (1974). *La société contra l'état*. Zone Books.

Engels, F. (1972). *Umrisse zu einer Kritik der Nationalökonomie (1844), MEW 1* (pp. 499–524). Dietz.

Esping-Andersen, G. (1990). *The Three Worlds of Welfare Capitalism*. Polity.

Fuhrmann, U. (2017). *Die Entstehung der "Sozialen Marktwirtschaft" 1948/49*. UVK.

Habermas, J. (1968). Verwissenschaftlichte Politik und öffentliche Meinung. In Habermas (Ed.), *Habermas: Technik und Wissenschaft als "Ideologie"* (pp. 120–145). Suhrkamp.

Habermas, J. (1981). *Von der Schwierigkeit, Nein zu sagen, in Philosophisch-Politische Profile* (pp. 445–452). Suhrkamp.

Habermas, J. (1989). Ist der Herzschlag der Revolution zum Stillstand gekommen? In D. von Ideen (Ed.), *Forum für Philosophie* (pp. 7–36). Suhrkamp.

Habermas, J. (2012). Eine Hypothese zum gattungsgeschichtlichen Sinn des Ritus. In Habermas (Ed.), *Nachmetaphysisches Denken, II* (pp. 77–95). Suhrkamp.

Habermas, J. (2018). *Auch eine Geschichte der Philosophie*. Suhrkamp.

Hegel, G. W. F. (2010). *Phänomenologie des Geistes*. Meiner, English translation Terry Pinkard.

Kant, I. (1917). *Perpetual Peace*. Allen.

Kant, I. (1970). *Kant's Political Writings* (H. Reiss, Ed.). CUP.

Kant, I. (1977a). *Was heißt: sich im Denken orientieren?* (pp. 265–283). Werke V.

Kant, I. (1977b). *Streit der Fakultäten, Werke XI* (pp. 263–393). Suhrkamp.

Kierkegaard, S. (1941). *Die Tagebücher 1834–1855*. Hegner.

Kierkegaard, S. (2013). *Entweder/ Oder – Ein Lebensfragment, herausgegeben von Victor Eremita*. Holzinger.

Koskenniemi, M. (2006). Constitutionalism as Mindset: Reflections on Kantian Themes about International Law and Globalization. *Theoretical Inquiries in Law, 8*(9), 9–36.

Kuhn, T. S. (1962). *The structure of scientific revolutions*. UCP.

Lessenich, S. (2016). *Neben uns die Sintflut. Die Externalisierungsgesellschaft und ihr Preis*. Hanser.

Luhmann, N. (1973). Selbstthematisierung des Gesellschaftssystems. *Zeitschrift für Soziologie, 1*, 21–46.

Marcuse, H. (1967). *One-Dimensional Man*. Bacon.

Marx, K. (1953). *Grundrisse der Kritik der politischen Ökonomie*. Dietz.

Marx, K. (1973a). *Grundrisse. Outlines of the Critique of Political Economy*. Penguin. 1939-40 ; Retrieved July 28, 2019, from http://www.marxists.org/archive/marx/works/1857/grundrisse/index.html.

Marx, K. (1973b). *Capital I – A critique of political economy, Transl. moore/ aveling*. Penguin.

Marx, K. (1973c). Thesen über Feuerbach (1, 11). In K Marx & F Engels (Eds.), *MEW 3* (pp. 5–7). Dietz.

Marx, K. (1976). *Kritik des Hegelschen Staatsrechts §§ 261–313, MEW 1*. Dietz.

Mody, A. (2018). *Euro Tragedy – A Drama in Nine Acts*. OUP.

Offe, C. (1972). *Strukturprobleme des kapitalistischen Staats*. Suhrkamp.

Offe, C. (1992). Capitalism by democratic design? Democratic theory facing the triple transition in East Central Europe. In Offe (Ed.), *Offe, Varieties of Transition* (pp. 29–49). Polity 1996.

Offe, C. (2006). Erneute Lektüre. Die "Strukturprobleme" nach 33 Jahren. In Offe (Ed.), *Offe, Strukturprobleme des kapitalistischen Staats. Aufsätze zur Politischen Soziologie* (pp. 181–196). Campus.

Offe, C. (2016). *Europe Entrapped*. Polity.

Rödl, F. (2010). Arbeitsverfassung. In . von Bogdandy & J Bast (Eds.), *Europäisches Verfassungsrecht* (pp. 855–904). Springer.

Scharpf, F. (2015). Political legitimacy in a non-optimal currency area. In O. Cramme & S. Hobolt (Eds.), *Democratic politics in a European union Under stress* (pp. 19–47). OUP.

Schelling, F. W. J. (1997). Stuttgarter Privatvorlesung [1810]. In *Schelling, Werke IV*. Beck.

Thornhill, C. (2018). *Sociology of law and global transformation of democracy*. CUP.

Tooze, A. (2018). *Crashed: How a decade of financial crises changed the world*. Viking.

von Achenbach, J. (2018). Transparenz statt Öffentlichkeit und demokratischer Repräsentation. Aktuelle Entwicklung des Verhandelns in Trilogen im EU-Gesetzgebungsverfahren. *Die öffentliche Verwaltung, 24*, 1025–1035.

von Hayek, F. A. (2003). *Recht, Gesetz und Freiheit*. Mohr.

Wegmann, M. (2010). European competition law: Catalyst of integration and convergence. In K. Tuori, & S. Sankari (Eds.), *The many constitutions of Europe* (pp. 91–107). Ashgate.

Ypi, L. (2014). On revolution in Kant and Marx. *Political Theory, 32*(3), 262–287.

Ypi, L. (2017). From revelation to revolution: The critique of religion in Kant and Marx. *Kantian Review, 22*(4), 661–681.

Žižek, S. (2001). *Die Tücke des Subjekts* (E. Gilmer, Trans.). Suhrkamp.

Is the European Union imperialist?

Glyn Morgan

ABSTRACT
A frequent argument of Eurosceptics is that the EU acts as an imperialist power towards its own member states. This argument has recently gained traction both in Hungary, where Prime Minister Orban complains of the EU's moral and political imperialism, and also in the UK, where arguments that the EU intends to reduce post-Brexit UK to a 'vassal state' have motivated Eurosceptics to support a no-deal withdrawal. There remains an important paradox in the charge of European imperialism, however, because the EU is widely thought to lack much international power, at least in comparison to China and the United States. This essay explores the paradox of a political formation that is both vulnerable to the charge of being an imperialist, while no less vulnerable to being itself the victim of imperialism (or 'vassalisation').

A common charge of Eurosceptics is that the project of European Integration constitutes a form of imperialism (Hazony, 2018, pp. 151–154). In recent years, this charge appeared during the Eurozone Crisis, it was reiterated by 'Leavers' – both during and after the Brexit referendum campaign – and it can be heard today in Hungary and Poland in the face of the European Union's (EU) efforts to enforce the rule of law. The charge of imperialism possesses particular potency in the European context. As with the words 'fascism' and 'racism', 'imperialism' is a term of political abuse and severe condemnation. These words are rallying cries, at least in part because they conjour-up episodes from some of the darkest chapters of Europe's history (Müller, 2011). One of the EU's founding myths was that the project of integration would allow Europeans to overcome their dismal past and start afresh (Lacroix & Nicolaides, 2010). If that project actually *is* imperialist, then Europe's efforts of renewal might be judged a failure.

Yet while proponents of European integration are understandably eager to reject the label of 'imperialists', they are no less eager to reject the label of 'imperialised' (i.e., victims of another power's imperialism) or 'vassalised'. Until recently, it would have been quite eccentric to suggest that the EU runs the danger of being the victim of other powers' imperialism. The rise of a so-called 'America-First' agenda in the United States coupled with a more assertive China has changed all that. In a recent book, the current French Finance Minister Bruno Le Maire warned that Europe faced 'vassalisation'. As Le Maire put it:

> Vassalisation is when the US imposes extraterritorial sanctions on the European Union. It's when they impose tariffs on steel and aluminium that will directly affect the lives of workers and the steel plants of northern France. Vassalisation is when China decides to buy entire chunks of strategic infrastructure in Europe. Vassalisation is when self-driving cars will have American navigation systems and Asian batteries. (Mallet, 2019)

Le Maire's usage of the term vassalization is taken from the Brexit debate, where this term and its cognate 'vassal state' have figured very prominently in the political language of proponents of a 'hard Brexit'. Both in the UK and France, the terms 'vassal' and 'vassalisation' have now become weaponized in a political battle to paint one's opponents as unduly willing to sacrifice power and independence to a foreign state. The French President Emmanuel Macron has in this context repeatedly warned that the post-Brexit UK will become 'a vassal state, ... the junior partner of the United States (Macron, 2019)'.

The terms imperialist/vassalized are new and important terms of abuse in current European political debate. From a scholarly point of view, these terms should be approached in much the same way as we approach more established political terms, ideas, and ideologies. Politics is, at least in part, a linguistically constituted sphere of human conflict. We want to understand *why* these terms enjoy current popularity, *who* deploys them, *whether* they possess any normative merit, and *how* they fit together with the fundamental ideas of our public political culture – ideas such as liberty, equality, and democracy (Rawls, 1993). The aim of this paper is threefold. One, it seeks to make normative sense of the pejorative terms 'imperialism' and 'vassalisation'; two, it examines the claim that the EU acts in an imperialist way in its dealings with recalcitrant members like Hungary; and three, it considers both the argument of Brexiters who contend that the EU seeks to reduce the UK to a vassal state, and that of some French politicians who fear that Europe itself might become vassalized.

What's wrong with imperialism?

Unlike the terms 'Empire' and 'Colonialism', neither 'imperialism' nor 'vassalisation' have drawn much attention from political theorists (for an exception, see Morefield, 2014). This is perhaps not surprising in the case of the latter term, which (at least in its present usage) is a new arrival to the language of political debate. But there is an extensive historical and sociological literature on imperialism. A full discussion of this literature would include works by and on Vladimir Lenin, John Hobson, Joseph Schumpeter, and Hannah Arendt. Fortunately, this literature stands at some distance from the more pointed usage of the term in contemporary political debate, where it conveys (to put it crudely and at this stage provisionally) *the unjustified use of power by the Center against the Periphery*.

Before proceeding to further clarify the contemporary usage of the term 'imperialist', it would be helpful to draw attention to recent references, both by scholars and politicians, to the EU as an Empire. The former President of the European Commission, Jose Manuel Barroso, for example, once said: 'Sometimes I like to compare the EU as a creation to the organization of empire … What we have is the first non-imperial empire (Mahony, 2007)'. Unfortunately, Barroso never fully explained the difference between *an imperial Empire* and *a non-imperial Empire*, which left him vulnerable to the Eurosceptic charge that there was no difference at all. A number of prominent political scientists have also employed something like the same distinction that Barroso drew (Marks, 2012; Zielonka, 2007). Gary Marks, for example, compares the EU to earlier empires, but warns that the term empire carries 'considerable normative baggage' and is often associated with coercion, exploitation, and domination. Yet these negative associations, he asserts, 'can be characterised as contingent rather than necessary characteristics in comparative analysis' (Marks, 2012, p. 2). Again, as with Barroso's comment, this is a more problematic move than Marks recognizes, and will do little to persuade the Eurosceptic who thinks that the nation-state is the only legitimate form of political authority, the only acceptable way of reconciling, what Marks refers to as 'scale' and 'community'. For many Eurosceptics, any non-national form of government – regardless of the public goods it secures, regardless of its contribution to liberty, security, and welfare – is *ipso facto* a form of illegitimate domination (Morgan, 2005, Ch. 3).

Marks's acknowledgement that the term 'empire' and *a fortiori* 'imperialist' carry considerable normative baggage provides a useful launching pad. If we are to clarify the meaning of the label 'imperialist', we need to understand its normative baggage. If 'Empire' can be detached from the bad normative baggage of 'imperialism', then 'imperialism' can also be attached to forms of domination that are not obviously Empires. This is simply to recognize that a much wider range of forms domination might be labeled 'imperialist' (see the recent discussions of 'hegemony' and 'primacy' in Anderson, 2017; Reich & Lebow, 2014). Typically, but not always, imperialism will involve some form of political domination, whether exercised directly or indirectly via proxies (as in the case of colonial rule) or diffusely (as in the case of threats, bribes, or undue influence). There are also forms of imperialism that involve economic and cultural domination. At a further distance still from direct political domination, there is the case of so-called 'moral imperialism', which might be defined as the deployment of a universal set of moral values to judge a particular society and its practices. Some critics of the EU's imperialism – Hungary's Prime Minister, Victor Orban, for example – have charged the EU (Germany, in particular) with 'moral imperialism' in its commitment to refugees (Krastev, 2017).

At one level, the charge of 'moral imperialism' is unanswerable in the contemporary European Union. The Founding Treaties of the European Union announce a clear commitment to the following set of so-called 'Article Two' values: 'human dignity, freedom, democracy, equality, the rule of law, and respect for human rights, including the rights of persons belonging to minorities'. If it is wrong, an unwarranted form of moral domination, to appeal to these values as the basis of a political constitution, then the EU is clearly guilty. But that would also mean that the US Constitution is guilty of moral imperialism, and likewise those who appealed to the Constitution to condemn slavery and 'Jim Crow' laws. The more serious worry about the EU is that the project of integration currently proceeds in such a way that it violates its own Article Two values. This is a much more serious charge, for it suggests the possibility that there exists a liberal critique of imperialism that applies to the EU. That is the central worry that motivates this paper.

The most plausible liberal argument against imperialism can build upon Ypi's liberal critique of colonialism, which is to say direct or indirect political rule (Ypi, 2013; for useful discussions see Moore, 2016; and Valentini, 2015). For Ypi, colonialism is wrong, because it 'denies its members equal and reciprocal terms of cooperation' (Ypi, 2013, p. 178). Regardless of any possible benign consequences that colonialism might yield, it involves (i) the unilateral imposition of alien rule – and thus a denial of political autonomy – and (ii) the lack of equality and reciprocity in the ensuing political relationship. Ypi's account actually allows us to distinguish a number of different levels or degrees of imperialism, not all of which we might judge equally harmful. Here it might be useful to draw an analogy with the way that the criminal law recognizes different levels or degrees of murder. Thus murder in the first degree is more serious than murder in the second degree, and so forth. With this analogy in mind, the harm of imperialism – a term that incorporates a broader range of forms of domination than colonialism – might be graded as follows:

Imperialism in the First Degree – a weaker state or territory is unilaterally annexed or falls involuntarily under the direct or indirect control of a more powerful state ('the Center'). The members of the periphery lack the equality and reciprocal associationship enjoyed by members of the Center. This situation describes the standard pattern of nineteenth century British colonialism in Africa and Asia. This situation also describes the treatment of many Native American tribes who were often defrauded out of their territories and confined to reservations of poor and inhospitable land.

Imperialism in the Second Degree – A weaker state or territory (the periphery) voluntarily agrees to join a more powerful state. There is no compulsion or unilateralism involved in the Union. Treaties are freely entered into and signed. Yet once a member of the new Union, the members of the periphery fail to receive the form of equality and reciprocity that defines common citizenship.

Imperialism in the Third Degree – A more powerful state ('the Center') unilaterally seizes a weaker territory or state ('the Periphery') and then applies the same rules to both Center and Periphery, such that the rights of members of the (former) Periphery are no different from the (former) Center. This form of imperialism describes the process of state-building in many Western democracies. Hawaii serves as a good, relatively recent example here. The Kingdom of Hawaii was overthrown with US military support in 1893 and was formally annexed in 1898. Notwithstanding some political and cultural repression in the first half of the twentieth century, Hawaii became a full US state in 1959. Since that date, the citizens of Hawaii have possessed precisely the same rights as those in other US states. It would be wildly implausible to claim that Hawaiians now lack equal and reciprocal membership. Furthermore in 1993 under President Clinton, the US government enacted a law – the so-called Apology Resolution – that formally apologized for the 1893 overthrow of the Hawaiian Kingdom.

Imperialism in the Fourth Degree – A more powerful state (or group of states) offers political membership to a weaker periphery, the members of which vote overwhelmingly in favor of membership. While all members of the periphery find that they enjoy free and equal membership in the sense that their civil and political rights are fully protected, the periphery's financial and economic institutions, including its local banks and supermarkets, are for the most part bought up and replaced by the center's financial and economic institutions. Moreover, the periphery's culture loses appeal. The periphery's youth prefer American rap artists to the local folk singers.

Imperialism in the Fifth Degree – A more powerful state (or group of states) offers political membership to a weaker periphery, the members of which vote overwhelmingly in favor of membership. While all members of the periphery find that they enjoy free and equal membership in the sense that their civil and political rights are fully protected, the Center forces the abolition of all cultural and traditional practices incompatible with freedom and equality as the Center understands those terms. The Periphery finds that it can no longer ban gay marriage, discriminate against local minorities, or refuse to accept refugees.

This five-fold account of different degrees of imperialism clearly reflects a liberal commitment to freedom and equality as fundamental values. From this perspective, imperialism in the first degree is a moral outrage, while imperialism in the fourth and fifth degrees are less so. Indeed, it is unlikely that a liberal committed to freedom and equality would even count *Imperialism in the Fifth Degree* as anything other than a thoroughly desirable form of progress. There remain, however, some hard cases here for liberals. *Imperialism in the Fourth Degree* is especially problematic, both because it is not obvious what counts as voluntary membership in the context of power imbalances and because a foreign state buying up banks and supermarkets might constitute a form of unjust acquisition. Since this form of imperialism is relevant to debates over the impact of European integration on East Europe, it would be helpful to offer a provisional liberal judgement of the harm of this form of imperialism (Krastev, 2017).

The first thing to notice is that liberals use the term 'harm' in a very restricted sense and generally only recognize as harms 'wrongful setbacks to interest' (Feinberg, 1990). The mere fact of unwanted or disadvantageous social and cultural change does not necessarily count as harmful. Indeed, if such change is to count as harmful, it must involve some case of fraud, coercion, or exploitation. This is not to make light of the many undesirable consequences of EU membership for some Eastern and Central European states. Migration has had an especially negative impact on Eastern European states like Bulgaria, which has approximately 2 million of its 7 million population living abroad, and is expected to see a 25 per cent decline in population by 2050 As Krastev asks: 'Is there going to be anyone left to read Bulgarian poetry in one hundred years? (Krastev, 2017, p. 49)'

Some national cultures have disappeared because the people were exterminated or defrauded out of their lands and livelihoods (Native American Indians, for example), but the problems confronting Bulgaria and other Eastern European states cannot be compared to these cases. If an argument is to be made that, say, Bulgarians have been harmed, then it cannot appeal to fraud or coercion. A more plausible line of argument would be to suggest that even though Bulgaria voluntarily joined the EU, they were the victims of exploitation. If this argument goes through, then we can say that Bulgarians have endured *fourth degree imperialism*. The difficulty here, however, is that an exploitative relationship generally requires the following two elements to be present: (i) one party gains disproportionately from the relationship or transaction; and (ii) the other party has no reasonable alternative to remaining in this relationship (Wertheimer, 1996). Whether these two elements are present in the Bulgarian case is debateable. It is certainly not obvious that EU member states gained disproportionately with the admission of Bulgaria and Romania. Nor can it be said that Bulgaria had no reasonable alternative to EU membership. Remaining outside of the EU would not itself have solved Bulgaria's migration problems. As a percentage of overall population, Moldava has lost even more of its population to migration than Bulgaria. Taken together these considerations cast doubt on any claim that the accession of Bulgaria and other East European states has involved a form of exploitation. A charge of *fourth degree imperialism* can thus be dismissed.

Hungary: victim of imperialism?

In the wake of Chancellor Merkl's decision in June 2015 to admit Syrian refugees. Victor Orban, Prime Minister of Hungary broke ranks with other EU member states. Rejecting Merkl's – and more generally, the EU's – 'moral imperialism', as he termed it, Orban argued that each European member state had the right to decide for itself whether to admit refugees. 'We are Hungary. We do not see the world through German eyes', Orban argued. This was not the first time Orban had accused the EU and other European states of imperialism. In 2012, he complained about the EU 'colonial interference', due to the EU's demand that Hungary reform a number of new laws it had enacted to limit the independence of state institutions, including, most troublingly, the judiciary. Hungarians, so Orban insisted, 'will not give up their independence or their freedom, [which] ... means that we decide about the laws governing our own life' (Traynor, 2012).

In order to assess Orban's claims about EU imperialism – moral imperialism, in the context of the refugee crisis, and political imperialism, in the context of demanding changes in Hungary's judicial reforms – it is necessary to provide some context. Hungary, like the other Central and Eastern Countries, joined the EU under the auspices of the so-called Copenhagen Criteria. According to these Criteria, a new member state had to satisfy: '*political criteria* – stability of institutions guaranteeing democracy, the rule of law, human rights and respect for and protection of minorities; *economic criteria* – a functioning market economy and the capacity to cope with competition and market forces; and possess the administrative and institutional capacity to effectively implement the *acquis* and ability to take on the obligations of membership' (EU Commission, 2018). On the face of it, these criteria make perfect sense. The EU is a political and economic entity committed, both at its federal level and at the member state level, to a form of liberal democratic market capitalism. This commitment is evident in the so-called 'Four Freedoms', which are enforced by a super-ordinate legal authority, the European Court of Justice. A state unable or unwilling to commit to these conditions cannot join the EU.

Now it might be objected that the EU is unduly liberal or insufficiently democratic, that it is too heavily skewed towards market freedoms rather social protection, that it favors capital mobility over worker rights: all these criticisms can and have been made by a growing band of Eurosceptic scholars.

But the liberal democratic, market-oriented features of the EU were, through the Copenhagen Criteria, made clear to the new states. If a sensible criticism of these Criteria can be made, it lies in the way that they have worked in practice (Kochenov, 2008). Three difficulties became clear in the 2004–2014 period. First, it became apparent that while the EU had considerable power over the accession countries in the run-up to accession, once admitted this power dwindled away. Second, the definition of the key terms under the rubric 'political conditions' – including, most importantly, the rule of law – proved vague and contestable. And third, the EU never envisaged a scenario where, once admitted, member states would backslide on their commitment to liberal democratic norms. Yet this is precisely what happened, both in Hungary and in Poland. 'Liberal democracies are being dismantled in plain sight', as Dimitry Kochenov notes, 'Hungary with its new constitution and hundreds of laws mak[es] it impossible for the ruling party to lose elections' (Kochenov, 2014, p. 8).

To the extent that the EU has the power to address Hungarian and Polish backsliding it comes in the form of the so-called 'nuclear option' of Article 7 of the Treaty. Crudely stated, this Article adds an enforcement mechanism to take effect in the case of a 'serious and persistent breach by a member state' of Article Two values. The general consensus of EU legal scholars, however, is that Article 7 is too weak to be effective and doesn't function as a deterrent on democratic backsliding. This consensus has given rise to a variety of different proposals to strengthen EU oversight and, if necessary, punishment mechanisms. Scheppele (2013), for example, has called for changes to allow the EU to bundle infringements and bring a judgement of 'systemic infringement' against backsliders with the possibility of cutting EU funds from those found guilty. Others have even called for democratic 'backsliders' to be kicked-out of the EU.

In the face of this conflict between the EU and Hungary (also Poland to a certain extent), does it make sense to accuse the EU of any of the degrees of imperialism outlined above? The charge of moral imperialism is accurate in the sense that the EU is committed to a set of universal values. But the enforcement of those values on states that have voluntarily joined the EU cannot count as a harm. From a liberal point of view – which, it must be emphasized, is the official European point of view as specifically announced in Article Two of the EU Treaty – *Imperialism in the First Degree* involves some form of unilateral annexation. This never happened to Hungary or any other EU Member State, all of whom voluntarily joined the EU and can leave via the Article 50 procedure whenever they wish. *Imperialism in the Second Degree* involves some failure of equality of respect or the denial of a justified claim of political autonomy. Hungarians as individuals and Hungary as a member state have the same rights and responsibilities as other European citizens and member states. Furthermore, the EU lacks the power to enforce a center and periphery power relationship on a member state. Orban himself proudly boasts of how he does a 'peacock walk' for the EU, by which he pretends to comply with their demands but then doesn't (Müller, 2018). Orban's 'peacock walk' cannot be squared with a genuine imperial relationship, which involves effective power and control.

Orban does not have much to say about the issues of cultural assimilation that arise in the case of *Imperialism in the Third and Fourth Degrees*. He does, however, attack the EU for its stance on minority rights. In effect, Orban attacks the EU for *Imperialism in the Fifth Degree*. No liberal can sympathize with this criticism. If it is imperialistic to protect the rights of disadvantaged minorities, then the EU is guilty as charged. But this point simply underscores the general claim of this paper: imperialism comes in many different forms or degrees, not all of which are from a liberal point of view morally problematic. If Orban is to make a charge of EU imperialism stick, then he would have to situate his critique in a nationalist theory of imperialism that recognizes the nation as a higher value than individual freedom and equality. Any such nationalist theory is fundamentally incompatible with the EU in its present form, whose very point and purpose is to elevate freedom and equality in the scale of values above that of the nation defined in ethnocultural or religious terms. To the extent that Orban wants to find fault with the EU on nationalist grounds, then it is difficult to see how he and his supporters can in good faith remain committed to EU membership. The EU simply cannot accommodate this form of nationalism. Perhaps one of the few salutary consequences of the EU's conflict with Orban is that it has served as a reminder of the EU's liberal character and its inability to accommodate illiberal nationalism.

The UK's and Europe's vassalization

The claim that the EU is an imperialist power has also figured prominently in the UK Brexit debate. Here this criticism is sometimes expressed in the form of a claim about how the EU threatens to reduce (or actually has reduced) the UK to a 'vassal state'. In a sense, imperialism and vassalage are two sides of the same coin. If one political entity (the Center) is an imperialist; the other political entity (the Periphery) is its vassal (or has been vassalized). This criticism has loomed ever larger the nearer the UK has come to actually leaving the EU. One of the great puzzles about post-referendum British politics is the way that the pro-Brexit position hardened between 2016 and 2020. In the run-up to the June 2016 vote, many people in the Leave campaign stated that the most likely outcome of their victory would be a form of 'soft Brexit' or 'Norway option', as it was commonly termed. Thus even a figure like Aaron Banks, who funded the Leave EU campaign headed by Nigel Farage, tweeted in December 2015 – 'Increasingly, the Norway option looks the best for the

UK' (Banks, 2016). In the immediate aftermath of the Leave victory, there was something close to a journalistic and scholarly consensus that 'the Norway option' would be the likely outcome of negotiations. A 'no deal' scenario was scarcely imaginable. Yet by the summer of 2019, the Norway option had all but disappeared from view and 'no deal' became something of a litmus test of a person's commitment to Brexit and a precondition of membership in Prime Minister Boris Johnson's new cabinet. Following Johnson's overwhelming election victory of December 2019, the Government's commitment to 'no deal' only strengthened.

There are a variety of possible explanations for this turn towards a 'no deal', including the failure of key political figures (Theresa May and David Davis, among them) to understand how the EU worked and what compromises were possible. Another possible explanation is that the initial expressions of a desire for 'soft Brexit' were nothing more than cynical obfuscations; a hard Brexit was always the goal. Still another explanation is that as Tory politicians embraced the language vassalage, this language took on a logic of its own. The EU had long been defined by Brexiters as an imperialist power. (Even some former Remainers like Theresa May's Foreign Secretary Jeremy Hunt started referring to the EU in these terms.) Having adopted this language, it then became difficult to accept any subordinate trading relationship with the EU – even a trading relationship that was ostensibly quite favorable to the UK. The logic of ideas led to the inexorable rise of 'no deal' as the only available option, notwithstanding certain economic drawbacks.

There were three more specific consequences of this vassalage-based political discourse. First, it made it difficult for the UK government to agree on a transition period (i.e., a period when the UK would remain in the Single Market and Customs Union but without the full political rights of an EU member state). When Theresa May laid out in detail the nature of this proposed transition period (in her so-called Chequers Plan of July 2018), it was met with the following response from Martin Howe, the European Reform Group's (ERG) legal adviser:

> These proposals lead directly to a worst of all worlds, a Black Hole Brexit where the UK is stuck permanently as a Vassal State in the EU's legal and regulatory tarpit, still has to obey EU Laws and ECJ rulings across vast areas, cannot develop an effective trade policy, or adapt our economy to take advantage of the freedom of Brexit, and has lost its vote and treaty veto rights as an EU member state. (Howe, 2018)

A second consequence of this political discourse is that it complicated the task of reaching agreement on any future trading relationship. As politicians like Jacob Rees-Mogg and Boris Johnson deployed the term 'vassal state' to describe any post-Brexit role for the European Court of Justice, people were forced to realize that as a European member state, the UK possessed certain political rights, which it would lose once it left the EU. If post-Brexit UK were still going to be under EU laws and institutions but without its prior legal rights, it was difficult to conceal the fact that the UK had lost something significant. No one was able to explain successfully why the UK was better off with the Norway option than with full EU membership. On this point, liberal anti-Brexiters and sovereigntist pro-Brexiters converged. If there was no going back to EU membership and the Norway option was ruled out as a form of vassalage, then the harder 'no deal' form of Brexit became the only remaining option.

A third consequence of the vassalage-based political discourse is that it complicated the UK's relationship with the US. This was first seen in the immediate wake of the forced resignation of Sir Kim Darroch, the UK Ambassador. Critics of Boris Johnson's failure to support sufficiently his Ambassador in the face of criticism from President Trump expressed their disapproval in the language of vassalage and vassal state (Kettle, 2019). The UK, they argued, was exchanging, one form of vassalage under the EU for another under the US. Going forward, the UK government will have to ensure that any future trade deal with the US can escape the charge that the UK has, or will, become a US vassal. In this discursive context, trade deals will become difficult because they have already been politicized by a language and set of discursive terms that tends to operate as a binary – vassal or non-vassal.

There are two further chapters to the story of how the terms 'vassalage', 'vassalisation', and 'vassal state' have become part of contemporary European political discourse. Both involve the migration of the term to French political debate. One chapter involves the use of the term by President Macron, who has frequently argued that the UK will face 'vassalisation' at the hands of the US, whose relative power will force the British into a disadvantageous trade deal – a far worse deal than the UK enjoyed as an EU member state. The second chapter involves some pro-EU French politicians and scholars, who use the term 'vassalisation' to warn of the dangers posed by an 'America-First' Trump administration and a neo-imperialist China.

Before providing some conceptual precision and weighing the normative baggage of the term vassalization and its cognates, it would be useful to consider more generally the argument that Europe now confronts a new form of imperialism emanating from the US and China. Jean Pisani-Ferry has advanced a robust version of this argument in an influential essay (Pisani-Ferry, 2019). Ferry notes that the world has passed through a stage when globalization was thought to diminish the concentration of economic power to a new era of 'economic monopolies and geopolitical rivalry'. The EU, which was established to overcome nationalism and imperialism, must confront both. More specifically, the EU must find a way of dealing with US and Chinese tech giants, which can call upon support from their national governments. These tech giants are powerful conveyers of economic power and social values. Europe lacks any equivalents. More specifically, the EU faces three difficult challenges. One, it must reassess its laws on Competition Policy. Does it want to use current laws either to create its own corporate giants or to break up American and Chinese corporate giants? Two, it must address the intermingling of economic and security interests. China, in particular, often uses its nominally private companies to secure national security goals. And third, Europe must find a way to avoid becoming 'an economic hostage of US foreign-policy priorities' (Pisani-Ferry, 2019). If Europe were to fail to meet these challenges, the implication of Pisani-Ferry's argument is that Europe would become a vassal of China and the United States. The French Finance Minister Bruno Le Maire has made similar points while explicitly deploying the term 'vassalisation'.

In order to assess arguments about Europe's current or impending vassalization, we need to conduct a similar exercise to that undertaken earlier with respect to the term imperialism. Although the term vassal (or vassalization or vassalage) seems to suggest a binary – either a state is a vassal or it is not – we need to introduce some distinctions between various degrees of vassalage, some of which are clearly incompatible with the EU's liberal democratic self-understanding (as reflected in its Article Two values), and some of which are less so. It is important to recognize that this exercise takes place against the historical backdrop of fundamental changes in the postwar US economic and political international order – a hegemonic order, as it is often described (Anderson, 2017; Reich & Lebow, 2014). European liberals face the tricky task of formulating a response, both intellectual and political, to a new international order where China is much more powerful and the US much less willing to provide public goods. Vassalage (or vassilisation) is not obviously the best term to use to formulate this response. Nonetheless, since it is the word currently in popular use, it is worth offering a liberal theory of vassalage. The aim here is to identify the boundary between acceptable and unacceptable changes in the international order.

Taking as our point of departure the EU's Article Two values, a liberal international order favorable to Europe will be one which (i) allows Europe (acting as individual states or collectively as a bloc) an equal voice in setting the terms of this international order, and (ii) provides Europe with sufficient autonomy to regulate on its own territory all corporate activity that affect its core values, including privacy and sustainability. A liberal international order is compatible with US hegemony but not with a US Empire; 'a hegemon', as Schroeder (2004, p. 299) has argued, 'is … in principle first among equals. An imperial power rules over subordinates'. Imperial power, however, is not the only way of short-circuiting a relationship of equality. Another way is through the persistent application of preponderant relative power in all diplomatic and trade relations. When people worry about the impact of an 'America-First' policy on US-EU relations, they are less worried in Europe becoming a subordinate to an American Empire than being the persistent loser in a transactional relationship. With these points in mind, it is possible to distinguish the following different degrees of vassalization.

Vassalization in the First Degree. This occurs when a state (or group of states) confronts an international order established and maintained by a foreign state (or states). Three further conditions are, however, necessary for vassalization in the first degree: one, the international order will have significant domestic social and economic implications; two, the rules cannot be shaped or vetoed by anyone other than the foreign state; and three, the international order protects and expresses values that are inimical to those preferred by the vassalized state (or states). This description fits the situation that confronted many of the Eastern European states under the Soviet bloc.

Vassalization in the Second Degree. This occurs when a state (or group of states) confronts an international order established and maintained by a foreign state (or states). While this international order has significant domestic social and economic implications, the foreign state (or states) allow some limited say in the rules even if they cannot be vetoed. The imposition of this form of vassalization is further tempered by the fact that the international order protects and expresses values broadly acceptable to the vassalized state (or states). For some critics, this description fits (at least roughly) the situation of West European states under US hegemony in the post-war era (Anderson, 2017).

Vassalization in the Third Degree. This occurs when a state (or group of states) confronts an international system that lacks any well-established procedures or rules. The state (or group of states) must nonetheless deal with one or more relatively more powerful states, whose economic interests they must accommodate, and whose values are inimical to their own. For some critics, this situation describes one possible outcome facing Europe in a G2 world consisting of an 'America First' Trump Administration and Xi's China.

No liberal could be happy to see Europe suffer from first degree vassalization. Fortunately, that seems a very unlikely outcome in the present era. The two other forms of vassalization seem much closer to home. It is not, however, obvious whether second-degree vassalization is more harmful than third-degree vassalization. Is it worse to be formally recognized as an unequal partner in an international alliance (second degree vassalization) or to be the persistent loser in trade deals and diplomatic negotiations (third degree vassalization)? Answers to this question will depend at least in part on the extent to which the dominant states in the international system (China and the USA, in this example) pursue policies inimical to European interests and values. The fear of people like Bruno Le Maire, the French Finance Minister is that China and the US will favor policies on the environment and privacy that are not consistent with European liberal values. The answer to this problem, so Le Maire and Macron argue, is for Europe to become a much more politically and economically integrated political entity.

The conceptual mapping of vassalization provided here can be extended to make sense of the term 'vassal state' in the Brexit debate. One important difference to note, however, is that in the Brexit debate, the language of vassalage is deployed primarily by sovereigntists like Jacob Rees-Mogg rather than liberals – although they now have come to use the term too. The sovereigntist position might be defined in terms of the following two claims: (i) national sovereignty is a requirement of democratic self-government; and (ii) national sovereignty requires ultimate legal authority rather than power, control, or the capacity for independent action. In other words, sovereigntists care primarily about *de jure* or notional sovereignty rather than the instrumental gains that any sovereign state might achieve. This point assumes crucial significance in the Brexit debate, because it means that any sharing of sovereignty – whether in the form of the current European Treaties or in any post-Brexit concessions to the *European Court of Justice* – counts as vassalization. For the sovereigntist, there can be no nuances here. Sovereignty is all or nothing; you either have it, or you don't. This point explains in part the willingness of some pro-Brexit politicians (Nigel Farage, for example) to concede that Brexit would be worthwhile even if it led to economic damage.

The liberal perspective on sovereignty is, however, very different. For liberals, sovereignty is valuable to the extent that it is necessary for freedom, equality and other important values (security, welfare, environmental sustainability, and so forth). If the sharing of sovereignty is better able to secure these values, then the liberal will have no objection. This normative position allows for a more nuanced understanding of the relative merits of different types of international order, some of which the liberal might view as first, second, or third-degree levels of vassalization. In the post-Brexit debate, the distinction drawn above between *second and third degree vassalization* cuts deep. Post-Brexit UK is likely to face a choice between a European legal and commercial order – access to the full benefits of which will require making concessions to the European Court of Justice – and a US trade deal, which is likely to require giving ground on access to the NHS and adopting more permissive standards on food safety. Depending on the nature of the trade deal struck with the US, the liberal is likely to find this form of third degree vassalization a very unwelcome prospect. Sovereigntists, in contrast, (much like Milton's Satan in *Paradise Lost*) might prefer to be lesser vassals in an economic hell than full vassals in an economic heaven.

Concluding remarks

This essay set out to achieve three aims. One, it has drawn attention to and illustrated the usage of some new terms of current European political discourse. The term 'imperialism' is, of course, anything but new. Most of the major European states have a long history as imperial powers. Some scholars argue that this history still continues, albeit under the cover of the EU. What is new is that the EU is now viewed, if from different quarters, both as an agent of imperialism, a political force that seeks to unjustly dominate member states, and as itself a victim (or potential victim) of the imperialism of China and the US. In recent years, the critique of imperialism has come to be expressed in terms of vassalization. An imperialist power reduces another weaker political state to the status of a subordinate. Political opponents now lob back and forth the charge that this or that trade agreement will lead to vassalage. The term first appeared in the Brexit debate but has now radiated out to broader European debates over the place of the EU in a world of increasing geopolitical rivalry. This paper has argued that it is worth taking stock of this new political terminology, because blunt terms of political abuse ('vassal' etc) are often the way that more complex ideas enter the political arena. If we want to understand the language of contemporary political debate, we will need to come to terms with the way debate is conducted in newspapers, blogs, and on the Twitter.

The second aim of the paper was to provide some conceptual clarity and normative evaluation of the terms 'imperialism' and 'vassalisation'. This effort required distinguishing different forms or degrees of each term, some clearly more serious than others. Judgements about degrees of seriousness will entail judgements about relative harm, which themselves are parasitic upon fundamental values. Liberals, nationalists, and sovereigntists have different ideas about fundamental values. It is not then surprising that they will disagree about the harm of different forms of subordination. In recognizing the contested nature of the terms 'imperialism' and 'vassalage', the paper highlighted the deep disagreements that exist between liberals, on one side of the ideological divide, and sovereigntists and nationalists on the other. But even amongst people who share fundamental political values, there will inevitable be disagreements about the acceptability of certain policies, practices and institutions. At the very least, it should now be clearer how 'imperialism' and 'vassalage' are deployed in current political debate and the extent to which these terms rely both upon fundamental values and some account of what policies and institutions are necessary to secure those values.

The third aim of the paper has been to cast light on the claim that a G2 world of the United States and China pose a threat to the values and interests of Europe. This is an important topic that is only likely to become more salient as Europe loses relative power. While the language of vassalage is a rather crude weapon to deal with the complex choices that confront Europe in this new G2 world, other terms used in the debate – 'Empire', 'hegemony', and 'primacy', for example – are no less problematic (Anderson, 2017). Hopefully, the distinctions drawn here between different degrees of vassalage will prove useful in conceptualizing the harm of international power asymmetries and the relative merit of different ways of managing those asymmetries.

Acknowledgements.

I would like to thank the editors of this special issue and the three anonymous reviewers. Thanks also for comments to Dimitrios Efthymiou. Chris Flinn, Esthar Kollar, Annabelle Lever, Kevin Pham, Astrid Busekist Sadoun, Andrea Sangiovanni, Andreas Schelke, Tom Theun, Juri Viehoff, and Fabio Wolkenstein. I wrote the first draft of this essay while a Visiting Fellow at the Collegio Carlo Alberto, Turin. I presented earlier versions at the ECPR Joint Sessions in Nicosia, Sciences Po, and the EUI.

Disclosure statement

No potential conflict of interest was reported by the author(s).

References

Anderson, P. (2017). *The H-Word: The Peripetaia of hegemony*. Verso.

Banks, A. (2016). https://twitter.com/arron_banks/status/682125949245206528?lang=en.

EU Commission. (2018). Draft of withdrawal agreement. https://ec.europa.eu/commission/sites/beta-political/files/draft_withdrawal_agreement.pdf.

Feinberg, J. (1990). *Harmless wrongdoing: The moral limits of the criminal law*. Oxford University Press.

Hazony, Y. (2018). *The virtue of nationalism*. Basic Books.

Howe, M. (2018). The chequers conclusion: A memorandum. https://briefingsforbrexit.com/the-chequers-conclusion-a-memorandum-by-martin-howe-qc/.

Kettle, M. (2019, July 10). Kim Darroch has resigned: Now Britain risks becoming a vassal of the US. *The Guardian*. https://www.theguardian.com/commentisfree/2019/jul/10/after-kim-darroch-britain-risks-becoming-vassal-to-united-states.

Kochenov, D. (2008). *EU enlargement and the failure of conditionality*. Kluwer Law International.

Kochenov, D. (2014). Overestimating conditionality. https://papers.ssrn.com/sol3/papers.cfm?abstract_id=2374924.

Krastev, I. (2017). *After Europe*. Penn Press.

Lacroix, J., & Nicolaides, K. (Eds.). (2010). *European stories: Intellectual Debates on Europe in national contexts*. Oxford University Press.

Macron, E. (2019, November 7). Macron in his own words. *The Economist*. https://www.economist.com/europe/2019/11/07/emmanuel-macron-in-his-own-words-english.

Mahony, H. (2007, July 11). Barossa says EU is an Empire. *EU Observer*.

Mallet, V. (2019, April 2). La Maire calls for new empire to save EU from rival powers. *Financial Times*. https://www.ft.com/content/af7460f4-5523-11e9-91f9-b6515a54c5b1.

Marks, G. (2012). Europe and its empires: From Rome to the EU. *JCMS, 50*(1), 1–20. https://doi.org/10.1111/j.1468-5965.2011.02218.x.

Moore, M. (2016). Justice and colonialism. *Philosophy Compass*, *11*(8), 447–461. https://doi.org/10.1111/phc3.12337

Morefield, J. (2014). *Empires without imperialism: Anglo-American decline and the politics of deflection*. Oxford University Press.

Morgan, G. (2005). *The idea of a European superstate*. Princeton University Press.

Müller, J. (2011). *Contesting democracy: Political ideas in twentieth century Europe*. Yale University Press.

Müller, J. (2018, April 5). Homo Orbanicus. *New York Review of Books*.

Pisani-Ferry, J. (2019). Europe and the new imperialism. *Project Syndicate*.

Rawls, J. (1993). *Political liberalism*. Columbia University Press.

Reich, S., & Lebow, R. N. (2014). *Goodbye hegemony! power and influence in the international system*. Princeton University Press.

Scheppele, K. (2013). What can the European commission do when member states violate basic principles of the European Union? The case for systematic infringement actions. *Verfassungsblog*. https://verfassungsblog.de/wp-content/uploads/2013/11/scheppele-systemic-infringement-action-brussels-version.pdf.

Schroeder, P. (2004). *Systems, stability, and statecraft: Essays on the international history of modern Europe*. Palgrave.

Traynor, I . (2012). Hungary Prime Minister hits out at EU interference in national day speech. The Guardian. https://www.theguardian.com/world/2012/mar/15/hungary-prime-minister-orban-eu.

Valentini, L. (2015). On the distinctive procedural wrong of colonialism. *Philosophy & Public Affairs*, *43*(4), 312–331. https://doi.org/10.1111/papa.12057

Wertheimer, A. (1996). *Exploitation*. Princeton University Press.

Ypi, L. (2013). What's wrong with colonialism. *Philosophy and Public Affairs*, *41*(2), 158–191. https://doi.org/10.1111/papa.12014

Zielonka, J. (2007). *Europe as empire*. Oxford University Press.

Index